D0468720

Boot Camp

1963

Innocence to Upheaval

Second Edition

By Joseph D. Frizzi

This second edition is an updated and revised version of the original "Boot Camp 1963, Innocence to Upheaval" published in 2018 with some changes and additions.

Self-published by Joseph D. Frizzi

No part of this publication may be reproduced, stored in a retrieval system, or transmitted in any way by any means— without the prior permission of the copyright holder, except as provided by USA copyright law.

The opinions and beliefs expressed in this book are strictly those of the author and do not necessarily reflect the views of organizations or individuals mentioned in this book.

Original copyright © 2018 Joseph D. Frizzi

Second Edition copyright 2021 Joseph D. Frizzi

All rights reserved.

Manufactured by

Kindle Direct Publishing

410 Terry Ave N

Seattle, Washington 98109

ISBN: 9798703481714.

Library of Congress Control Number: 2021902348

Other Books by Joseph D. Frizzi

Saved Then Lost? Saved, But Warned? Never Saved?

Understanding the Warnings in Hebrews

Faith Builder

How Getting a Liver Transplant Increased My Faith

Boot Camp 1963

Innocence to Upheaval

Israel:

Proof of God's Existence & the Truth of the Bible

Once Lost, Now Saved

From Darkness to Light

Cooking

For Those Who Can't Boil Water, or Think They Can't

All books are available on Amazon.com-books

Joseph Frizzi

Appreciate any feedback

Email: jdfrizzi@juno.com

Special Dedication

To those who served in Vietnam and did their duty
honorably and didn't deserve the shameful treatment
upon returning.

Inspiration

To Jesael, a wonderful friend who inspires me

Table of Contents

Chapters

Part One: My Background of Innocence

Part Two: My Upheaval: Training at Fort Ord

Credits

Editor: Joseph Frizzi

Formatting Editor: Penny Harden

Cover Design: Angela Hanlon, Penny Harden, and Joseph Frizzi

Cover Artwork: Angela Hanlon

Book Chronology

Original edition: published June, 2018. Some re-editing and reordering of chapters has been done.

Second Edition: Chapters 12-19 written from August 2020 to February 6, 2021.

Introduction

This first part of this second edition is pretty much the same book as the original one, especially the story of my training at Fort Ord, California. It has a few important extra features, including a new patriotic cover. This second edition also discusses events that have occurred since the original paperback was published in June of 2018, such as the confirmation hearings of Supreme Court justice Judge Brett Kavanaugh and, the 2018 midterm election.

This Second Edition contains some extra chapters which were written in 2020-21 reflecting Covid-19, climate change, the Black Lives Matter Movement, and the presidential election of 2020. It contains some re-editing and different phraseology, and like the original edition, the political chapters deal with America's upheaval beginning with the attack of freedom of religion in our schools, Vietnam, and the rise of the Left.

This writing is much more provocative because I discuss the Left in greater detail, namely the differences between Liberalism/Conservatism and leftism in defining the real culture war in Western society. In the original edition, I didn't want the political part to overwhelm the rest of the book, but now I have no such inhibitions and discuss politics much more with "both barrels firing," especially in Chapters 12-20. The book has nine extra chapters mostly dealing with the important events of 2020.

I also expanded on an important observation to this updated book which deals with the confusing part of the divide between liberalism/conservatism and leftism—that many non-leftists, especially liberals, have views that are leftist (such as socialized medicine and sanctuary cities), but their motivation is different from that of the true leftist.

Also, while I took great pains to point out that liberalism and leftism have nothing in common, I added that this also applies to conservatism and the far-right.

I changed the order of chapters 9-11 in order to make it chronological. Most of the first eight chapters are unchanged. Chapter 19 gives perspective on the 2020 election and the time leading up to inauguration day in January, 2021. Finally, Chapter 20 gives a biblical Christian perspective on our country today.

Prologue

People who were born during World War II or are post-war baby boomers seem to agree that 1963 was really the last year of America's innocence. By the term innocence, I don't mean that everything was great with no major problems in America and the world, but compared to the present time, living in the 1950's and the early 1960's was definitely a less complicated time. But, even though our parents and grand-parents had lived through the Great Depression and World War II, to them the world was getting much more compli-cated, especially with the advent of the Cold War and the possible threat of nuclear annihilation. But for us who were young in the 50's and early 60's, it truly was growing up in a relatively innocent time.

For those of you who are younger and don't have first-hand memories of the early 60's, I especially want to reach you because this is really history that I lived through. You can read books or go on the internet and get some good, but also bad information. That is a major reason why I want-ed to tell this first-hand story of my experience of growing up in this time period.

Compared to today, life was simple in 1963. No political correctness existed; Stanford University's mascot was still the "Indians," instead of the "Cardinal." If someone was of-fended, it did not become national news. The word micro-aggression was never used, assuming it had even existed outside of a psychology textbook! Boys were boys and girls were girls and this current sad effort by the Left to minimize the wonderful differences between men and women was non-existent. College didn't include majors in gender studies in order to somehow redefine the sexes in fulfilling some warped sense of equality. It was OK for little boys to play with toy soldiers and learn to shoot a gun, and for little girls to have dolls and play house.

Women are absolutely amazing and very capable of performing with excellence all kinds of work and are outpacing men in many areas. I think it is wonderful that women have so much more opportunity than they did back in the 60's and before. Besides procreation, God meant women to be a blessing to men and I cannot imagine how terrible the world would be without them. It's truly sad that social engineers are trying to create an adversarial relationship between men and women, because they were really meant to complement each other.

No calculated division was evident that we so often see in the identity politics of today regarding race, class, and gender. The politics of race existed in 1963, but it was mainly a battle over civil rights, particularly regarding ending segregation. Many people today take civil rights for granted, but in the early sixties, legal segregation still existed in the South. Segregation was also prevalent in the North. The Civil Rights Act of 1964 finally outlawed discrimination based on race, class, religion, sex, or national origin.

This book is autobiographical, but it really isn't about me, except as an example of a pretty typical middle-class American teenager in the early 1960's. My attempt here is to tell a story with a historical perspective. At times, I go down some rabbit trails along the way, but they are necessary in order to maintain some historical perspective and to really understand how America was in the early 1960's. In doing so, it demonstrates just how much we have changed. Historical perspective is important because, unfortunately, revisionist history is very often being taught today in many of our schools and universities. This revisionist history makes America the problem in the world and draws moral equivalencies between the U.S.A. and some of the most horrendous totalitarian countries where people, especially women, have no rights. Worse yet, many of these totalitarian countries actually have a vote in the UN.

Many on the left, especially the revisionist historians, want to obliterate our American history and heritage by openly, or at least tacitly, supporting the destroying of statues and taking down crosses. Leftist authors of textbooks have also reduced some of our founding fathers to racist white slave owners and apply the standards of today to the reality of the 18th and 19th centuries. If anybody is attending a school that doesn't revise history, they are fortunate. Many good colleges, especially Hillsdale College in Michigan, teach accurate history and have excellent classes on the Constitution. This book is controversial and I go out on a limb to passionately give my viewpoint, at times lacking political correctness which I despise!

The book was originally going to be a simple story about my experience of going through basic training in the Old Army, but because of the important time in our history when I was training in Fort Ord, California, I'm convinced that this has to be more than just a story. The period of my experience in the Army covered in this writing, from June 12 through November 30, 1963, is a significant snapshot into our history. Learning about this time gives a perspective on America at a very critical point in her history. Dark storm clouds were forming on the horizon of our nation's future and the winds of change would shortly begin to reach hurricane force. Before 1963 came to a close, America began to go through a fundamental change, the effects of which are still felt today.

The United States was in the early stages of preparing to enter the Vietnam War which had tragic consequences, not only for the country, but also for those who were killed and wounded in the war and for their loved ones. I was fortunate that I never had to go to Vietnam and I definitely had it much easier than some of my contemporaries, including a few high school classmates who never came home!

The war in Vietnam tore our country apart and helped facilitate the rise of the radical left which is exemplified by the militant protestors who called our troops "baby killers" and spit on them upon their return. This leftist movement of the 60's also began the divisive emphasis of race, class, and gender. It represented the antithesis of faith, family, and patriotism in favor of sex, drugs, and civil unrest. The anti-war protests, with the burning of draft cards and the American flag, were only part of the beginning of upheaval in America—which also included the 1964 Free Speech Movement at UC Berkeley led by Mario Savio, and the racial unrest resulting in riots in the cities. Some of those who were burning the flag and/or violently demonstrating or sympathizing with those who did are now university professors, judges, political commentators, and politicians. In the 1960's, the seeds were sown for today's unrest; America would never be the same. The 1960's was a truly destructive decade which began the loss of America's innocence into upheaval. I will cover this in more detail later in this book.

But the event which truly defined the beginning of the end of America's innocence also happened during this brief period of history in 1963. This sad event was the assassination of President John Fitzgerald Kennedy. President Kennedy's assassination in Dallas on November 22, 1963 shocked the nation into a new reality and few were really prepared for the changes to come.

I hope this book will be a compelling look at that time in history and that it never loses sight of the significance of that era. This second edition continues into more modern history into the 21st century.

Part One

My Background of Innocence

Chapter One

Innocence and Graduation

On June 12, 1963, I graduated from Willow Glen High School in San Jose, California. The ceremony was held at the Santa Clara County Fairgrounds exposition hall in San Jose. My graduation dress uniform consisted of a long red robe with a matching flat-top red hat and a gold tassel. The colors were appropriate since red and gold are Willow Glen's colors. But I have always thought that those flat top hats looked kind of ridiculous and would have been just as happy showing up in shorts and a T-shirt; especially since it was a very hot day! My main concern during the ceremony was that I could possibly trip and fall on the way up the stairs to receive my diploma, or that some smart aleck would act up and make me laugh. I was definitely not into the spirit of the event!

High school was something that I just wanted to get through and graduate from. At the time of my graduation I really had no desire to go on to college and was pretty tired of school. I knew it was important to have a high school diploma, especially in the early 1960's. Of course, now having a BA is about the same value as a high school diploma was back then, maybe even less.

I actually did enjoy a couple of courses in high school and they are about as far apart as one can imagine: English

Boot Camp 1963: Innocence to Upheaval

Lit and Auto Shop! I liked cars and a guy who knew a lot about cars was one of the indicators that he was cool, so I wanted to learn as much as I could because I definitely fell way short in the "cool" department. English literature was something I thought I wouldn't like at all, but it actually turned out that I loved it. I especially liked short stories such as "The Death of Red Peril" by Walter Edmonds, "The Lost Phoebe" by Theodore Dreiser, and anything written by O. Henry, especially "The Gift of the Magi." I liked novels by Charles Dickens, John Steinbeck, and Jack London. As far as any other classes in high school were concerned, I enjoyed Geography and also loved U.S. History, which was my minor in college.

I was a reasonably good student as far as getting a good grade was concerned, but I had a bad attitude towards school and was a pretty lazy student who did the minimum amount of work necessary in order to earn a decent grade. My parents would be disappointed if I didn't receive a good grade, which thankfully wasn't often. They would tell me the same phrase that a lot of kids probably hear: "You are capable of so much better." They never pushed me to get straight A's, but they wanted me to do my best which, unfortunately, I sometimes fell short. My parents valued education and were public school teachers. They both graduated from San Jose State University and my dad later got his Master's degree from Stanford. With that kind of educational background, I am sure that they would have preferred I had gone to college right out of high school. To their credit, they never pushed me into going to college. I think they saw that I wasn't really "into school" at that time, plus I wasn't very worldly or mature and still had a lot of growing up to do. You might charitably say that I turned out to be a late bloomer.

I was a very shy kid and not popular in high school. I never went to any of the Prom dances and had pretty limited social skills. Any situation where dancing was involved was one of the main things that always brought out my shyness because I was afraid to get up and dance. When I went to parties, usually tagging along with my older brother Dave, I would sit there like a bump on a log and felt very self-conscious. It's funny, but some things in your past never quite go away. Dancing situations still bother me to this day and take me back to my high school shyness and insecurities.

I didn't get ridiculed or bullied at school, but I was just kind of a nonentity and was never involved in student government or the other various activities frequented by the popular kids. My only appearance in the high school yearbook is my class picture. The guys who sometimes got bullied were the smart kids, or "brains," who would show up with a briefcase and plastic pen holders in their shirt pocket, which would have a minimum of five pens. Today, they would be called nerds. Plenty of the really smart kids didn't fit the nerd stereotype, but those who did would sometimes pay the price. Effeminate guys who were perceived to be gay were also harassed. Snitches, who would tattle on others for breaking the even smallest rule, were particularly unpopular. Of course, my friends at school were not popular either, but at least we didn't get bullied. I'm truly thankful that the internet wasn't around when I was in high school because of the ease of being able to anonymously and cowardly attack someone on the web.

The only bullying incident I witnessed in high school involved a big fat kid who got bullied by a much smaller, but wiry and tough kid. The smaller kid was known as a "hard guy," which was the term given to anyone having a reputation as a good fighter. The bully punched the fat guy in the stomach, knocking the wind out of him. He made a sound like a baby crying for about a half second as the punch hit him. The bully then quickly landed numerous punches to the face, which made a dull slapping sound, drew a lot of blood, and completed the total humiliation of the poor guy. Bullies are basically cowards and pick on those whom they know can't really fight back. The bully knew that the poor fat kid was no match for him.

It was something that bothered me and that I never forgot. I have often wondered why people (mainly guys) are so drawn to witness a fight. I have come to the conclusion that seeing a fight is similar to driving by a really bad traffic accident. You are drawn to be a rubbernecker and look, but there is a part of you that doesn't really want to see because it will probably bother you for some time. I think the reason why people are bothered is because they can imagine themselves in the same situation.

The activities that my friends and I got involved in were always outside of school. The only events related to high school that we had any interest in were the varsity football games. Willow Glen never lost a game during my four years in high school. They had a California state record winning streak of 42 straight wins, so even those who were not active in any high school activities were very enthusiastic about the football team always showing up at the games. Everybody loves a winner!

I had no idea what I wanted to do in life, except that I knew I was definitely through with school, at least for the foreseeable future. I had always liked custom cars and thought I wanted to be an auto mechanic. When I look at the complexity of today's cars, I realize that might have been a bad choice. I used to love hot rods and custom cars which was my main interest when I was in high school. I would dream about building a Deuce (32 Ford) roadster powered by a Corvette engine and running gear. My usual Saturday night summertime activity consisted of going to the races at the San Jose Speedway and watching the super-modified cars racing on a banked asphalt track. The cars whizzing by at high speeds and the smell of the exhaust and the roar of the engines was exhilarating. I can remember the smell of the Linguica (Portuguese sausage) wafting up into the stands from the concession area.

Going to the Burger Bar with my friends on a Friday night and getting ten burgers for two dollars (plus greasy fries) was really living it up! Bowling and shooting pool at Alma Bowl (which is now a high-rise luxury condo building) was great fun.

Dragging the main was a blast. Cars would slowly make a loop around downtown San Jose and play tunes at the highest volume possible. Blasting Chuck Berry records was especially great! This was the only time that it was actually fun to be bumper to bumper in a traffic jam. Dragging the main was also a great activity in Santa Cruz during Easter Week on Beach Street, which is next to the Boardwalk and amusement park. Hollywood actually did a good job re-enacting how it was during the time I was in high school. The 1973 George Lucas film, directed by Francis Ford Coppola and entitled "American Graffiti," pretty much captures dragging the main and the car culture of the early 1960's. Back then, the worst thing that could happen was possibly getting into a fight with someone in another car, but that was rare. Unlike today, one didn't have to worry about getting stabbed or shot, at least not in San Jose. Drugs were practically unheard of then and the main vices among the "wilder" kids were smoking, drinking, and sometimes fighting.

International events were difficult and dangerous because, in the early 60's, we were still in the midst of the Cold War between the United States and the Soviet Union led by Nikita Khrushchev, but none of that really registered much during my high school years. Kids were too busy having fun and living their own lives locally, much the same way as people now. But the Cuban Missile Crisis, in late October of 1962, was actually an extremely serious event:

In October 1962, the Kennedy Administration faced its most serious foreign policy crisis. Soviet Premier Nikita Khrushchev saw an opportunity to strengthen the relationship between the Soviet Union and Fidel Castro's Cuba and make good its promise to defend Cuba from the United States. It happened when the Soviet Union (USSR) began building missile sites in Cuba in 1962. Together with the earlier Berlin Blockade, this crisis is seen as one of the most important confrontations of the Cold War. It may have been the moment when the Cold War came closest to a nuclear war. The Cuban Missile crisis comes to a close as Soviet leader Nikita Khrushchev agrees to remove Russian missiles from Cuba in exchange for a promise from the United States to respect Cuba's territorial sovereignty. Speaking many years later, Khrushchev claimed that he had won the Cuban missile crisis. He had achieved both his aims - America never bothered Cuba again (which is still a Communist country) and the US missile sites in Turkey were dismantled in November 1962.[1]

In later years, I really appreciated the significance of the Cuban Missile Crisis. But in high school, I had some thoughts of the possible danger of nuclear war, yet in those days people had confidence in America's military strength and somehow knew that the Soviet Union would not dare start a war with us. My parents took it more seriously because they had been adults during World War II and the war in Korea. But for me, in spite of the serious Cuban Missile Crisis or any other turmoil in the world, this was a personal time of innocence and security. I never had to deal with hunger or living in a dysfunctional home. I grew up in a "Leave it to Beaver" type home of which I am grateful. So even though the Cuban Missile Crisis stand-off was a dire situation, my recollections of that time were mainly what songs were popular on the radio and the classes that I was taking in the fall of my senior year. The three songs I remember the most at that time were "The Monster Mash" by Bobby "Boris" Pickett; "Telstar" by the Tornadoes, and "That's Tough, That's Life" by Gabriel and the Angels. Old timers or younger collectors of vinyl would be familiar with these songs. I listened incessantly to top 40 Radio and remember all the songs and when they were popular.

One of my great loves is music and associating music with a particular time in my life helps me to remember what was going on in a certain year. The time that I graduated from high school was also the peak of Southern California surfing music. The most popular song at that time, at least the one played the most often on Bay Area top 40 radio stations, was "Surf City" by Jan and Dean. Another very popular tune in June of 1963 was a non-surfing song called "Ring of Fire" by Johnny Cash, which still is played quite often today.

San Jose was a great place to grow up in the 50's and 60's, long before it became "Silicon Valley." In the early 60's, the Santa Clara Valley was starting to become more urbanized; individual cities were growing into each other until their boundaries became virtually impossible to define. The valley was melding into the rest of the San Francisco Bay Area, but it was spread out and there still was a lot of open space on the Santa Clara Valley floor. There were still orchards and vine yards so picking fruit and "cutting cots" (slicing and pitting apricots) was a pretty good part-time summer job for a high schooler. Both the Almaden and Paul Masson wineries were still located in the San Jose Area and had local vineyards close to their wineries. I can remember as a little kid in the early 1950's when we would drive from San Jose to my grandparent's house in Los Gatos. As we passed by the Almaden vineyards in South San Jose, I would always say: "look at the little orchards." Today, San Jose is pretty unrecognizable in comparison to what it was in the 50's and 60's.

In spite of the usual insecurities associated with being a teenager, I had a happy upbringing and little trials in life compared to others. It was truly a time of innocence. In a similar and parallel to the times way, this period was also a time of America's innocence, but both would shortly be shattered.

The day I graduated from high school was also the day of a significant news event: Medgar Evers, a civil rights activist in Mississippi who worked to end segregation at the University of Mississippi and enact social justice and voting rights, was killed in front of his home in Jackson, Mississippi by a sniper who was a white supremacist Klansman. This would not be the last of such murders in the South. The peaceful protests against racial inequality led by Dr. Martin Luther King would soon turn into violent riots in the cities. The difficult struggle of the Civil Rights movement was about to take a dramatic turn.

Endnotes

[1] https://history.state.gov/milestones/1961-1968/cuban-missile-crisis

Chapter Two

Recruitment and Leaving Home

Almost immediately after graduating from high school, I was at the downtown San Jose Greyhound bus depot and noticed that directly across the street was a U.S. Army recruiting center. I thought of possibly going into the service, especially since I had no other career plans. Whenever I would mention that I was thinking about joining the Army, Kent Prickett, the local butcher's son, would always say "you'll be sorry." He described the horrors of basic training and that it was not what I thought it would be. I had envisioned sort of an adventure with camping and firing rifles. I was naively looking through rose-colored glasses. Kent laughed and said "you have no idea what you are getting into." Against his advice, I finally came to the decision that I wanted to join the U.S. Army. So a few days later, I walked into that recruiting center across the street from the bus depot and was met by Sergeant First Class Vaughan and Staff Sergeant Putty. They were both very nice and personable and explained to me the virtues of the Army; serving the country along with the travel and adventure. It sounded so great and exciting since

Boot Camp 1963: Innocence to Upheaval

I had never even been out of the state of California. I signed a preliminary letter of intent and later officially signed up with my parent's approval since I was only seventeen. I was scheduled to report later to the Army Induction Center in Oakland to take a physical, IQ test, and begin my preliminary processing into the Army. I went to Oakland and passed my IQ test and physical. I was told to report back one month later on July 29th for my final processing and official induction into the Army. I would then take the bus from Oakland to Fort Ord to begin my basic training.

I remember during the IQ tests, guys that seemed pretty smart were lamenting that they had flunked the test. I didn't realize until later that some guys (usually draftees) would think of tricks to disqualify them from service. Another trick was to supposedly put a certain kind of soap in your armpits. This was believed to raise the blood pressure in an effort to be physically disqualified. Some of them even told me of their intentions to get disqualified and they all had similar reasons: "I don't want to go into the Army man, I got a girlfriend, a job, and plans," they would declare, or "I want to go back to school." It came as a shock to me because, frankly, I was a pretty naive kid and never thought that anyone would try to avoid serving their country. Some of those, if they were really paying close attention to the world situation and connecting the dots, may have been thinking about the possibility of going to Vietnam. Once the "official" Vietnam War began in 1965, the number of draftees increased considerably.

The month that followed was my last time of fun and living in a relatively innocent time. My cousin Jerry came to San Jose for his yearly visit. We were like best friends and always had such a good time. We were both really into custom cars and would get great joy out of someone peeling out in their car and burning rubber. It cracked us up, especially since it really irritated my dad. It's funny how one eventually grows up because, like my dad, I don't like it now either.

Shortly before the 29th came around, I was starting to feel the enormity of what was going to happen. I still didn't know much about what the Army would be like, except what Kent had told me, and I started to feel uneasy. Just the thought of leaving home was starting to weigh me down because I had always been susceptible to homesickness and can remember my first day of school on September 11, 1950. I was beginning Kindergarten at Lincoln Glen Elementary School in San Jose. It was on an overcast morning and I was walking to school which was only a half a mile away. I kept on saying to my big sister: "will I be back?" I had no idea what to expect, but in my little boy's mind, I wasn't sure if I would come back home.

It wasn't much better when I went away to YMCA camp in June of 1957. At first, I was pretty homesick although I eventually adjusted and started liking and participating in the softball games, swimming competition, campfires, and skits. The YMCA camp experience also introduced young men to some important things: rank and authority. Each counselor and assistant counselor wore a scarf called a rag around their neck which, according to its color, indicated their rank. At YMCA, we learned teamwork and submitting to authority. It was actually good training for what I would encounter six years later when I joined the Army.

The one thing that didn't rub off on me was the C in YMCA: "Christian." We sang lots of old hymns but they didn't really mean very much to me. At that time, going to church was an obligation and I really had no interest. A lack of a spiritual base was the one big void in my life, except that I didn't know it at the time. I was a nominal Roman Catholic and went to church every Sunday, but had no idea about being "born again" and what that meant. I thought that to "earn" favor with God you had to do good works and "be good enough." In 1991, I received the truth of the Gospel and was born again through faith alone in Jesus Christ and not through any works, so now I have the joy and security of a relationship with God through Jesus Christ.

But the worst time of homesickness was when I got on a bus heading to Oakland on July 29, 1963. My brother Dave and my cousin Jerry came down to see me off. When I boarded the bus, Jerry, Dave, and I were all in tears. Our vacation time was being cut short and I was now literally saying goodbye to the old life of fun and leaving home for the unknown. The bus ride to Oakland seemed to take forever because it was a local route traveling the back roads of the East Bay Area with multiple stops.

I spent all day in Oakland with final processing, which was a pretty boring experience. A common expression in the Army is "hurry up and wait." That was certainly true during my final processing. Eventually they gave us a meal voucher and I received my first meal paid for by Uncle Sam: a hamburger, fries, and a milkshake from Mel's Restaurant in downtown Oakland.

We finally left Oakland at about 7:30 p.m. heading south for an approximately 105 mile bus ride to Fort Ord, CA. It was a typically warm evening at that time of the year and we stopped in Gilroy for a bathroom break. I can still smell the scent of garlic and feel the breezy hot night air in the garlic capital of the world. By the time we finally reached the reception station at Fort Ord, it was 10:30 p.m. All the guys on the bus were pretty exhausted from the long boring day and bus ride. We were about to find out what being a new recruit is all about! As soon as we got off the bus, the yelling started. "Get off the grass!" "Put that cigarette butt out!" "Get in line!" We were finding out what the term "harassment" meant and we would be receiving heavy doses of it for the next few weeks. Basic training was eight weeks long, but a week of reception known as "zero week" began the whole process. To me, having never been exposed to anything like this, it was pretty traumatic! We had to pick up bedding, which consisted of a very thin mattress, blankets, sheets, and pillow. We then double timed (jogged) while carrying our bedding supplies to our barracks. Since we were the last bus to arrive at reception, we had to jog to the furthest barracks, which meant a longer run. It was definitely not fun, especially since we were all so tired. A few comments about the Army which I can't repeat were being expressed and those comments would become very commonplace.

The reception routine consisted of in-processing into the system, which included a very short haircut "scalping," getting uniforms issued, and going through numerous work stations. The work stations consisted of someone at a desk filling out different forms. The daytime consisted of endless waiting in lines. The night time would feature surprise inspections and a dressing down if your bed was not properly made or your footlocker items were not in perfect order. It was all part of the harassment and getting a bunch of civilians to live in a structured environment.

Every morning we would report to the street in front of the reception building. The experience in reception was probably the closest feeling I had to being a prisoner of war, except here they weren't going to possibly kill you. Still, it's a little bit disquieting when someone has total control over you. Spec. 4 Cariola was in charge of the assembly in front of the headquarters and would yell out his instructions. He and all the others were a different kind of an authority that I hadn't previously encountered. The authority figures I knew were my parents, teachers, priests and nuns at church, YMCA camp counselors, and older relatives. I saw them as benevolent and concerned about my well-being. But Cariola and the others seemed almost malevolent. The truth is that they were not, but they simply had a job to do and it wasn't making us feel comfortable! Training in the Army or any other branch of the service presupposes the possibility of having to go to war. As difficult as reception was, war would be much worse.

Soldiers who were permanent party (through basic training and assigned to Fort Ord) had a pretty high status as far as we were concerned. Since the majority of the soldiers at Fort Ord were trainees, even somebody who was still a private E-2 without even one stripe, got to wear the 6th Army patch and showed the status of not being just a trainee. Another status symbol was faded clothing. That meant that you had been in the Army a long time compared to us trainees. The clothing is called army fatigues. The fatigues are olive green, made of cotton, and quite soft and comfortable, especially compared to wool! We also wore combat boots, which took some getting used to since I never wore anything but either tennis or regular shoes.

After we completed in-processing, the main activities during the day consisted of going on detail, which meant some kind of work party. We were constantly riding in the back of army trucks to our destination, which usually was a building that had to be swept, mopped, toilets cleaned, and the grounds cleaned up. To this day, the smell of Pine-Sol cleaner immediately takes me back to that time. One work detail that I really enjoyed was cleaning the inside of a church, then watering the lawn and yard. I was by myself the whole day and escaped the reception experience for a nice break. Spending the day at a church was not really a spiritual experience, but it was peaceful and somehow comforting because it reminded me of home.

The performing of guard duty was another kind of work detail. My shift was guarding the motor pool from 8 p.m. to Midnight. It was kind of boring walking around the vehicles, but the solitude was another break. The one thing you had to avoid at all costs was getting caught sleeping on guard duty. That would likely result in a Court-Martial. After all, we were being trained to possibly go into combat. Sleeping on guard duty and not detecting an approaching enemy could get someone killed!

All of us new recruits were finding out that being a trainee in the Army is not very much fun. That being said, one of the nice things about training at Fort Ord, California was the weather. Fort Ord, which closed down years ago, is now California State University-Monterey Bay and is located in the Monterey Bay Area between Marina and Seaside. The summertime weather is usually cool and pleasant although it can get foggy and cold. People sometimes complained of being too cool even in August and September! After arriving at my permanent post overseas, I constantly heard many horror stories from soldiers who had their basic training at Fort Polk, Louisiana, or Fort Campbell, Kentucky, or anyplace east of the Rockies with lots of heat and humidity in the summertime. I was thankful for Fort Ord!

"The area's climate is characterized by warm, dry summers and cool, rainy winters. The Pacific Ocean is the principal influence on the climate at Fort Ord, causing fog and onshore winds which moderate temperature extremes. Daily ambient air temperatures typically range from 40 to 70 degrees Fahrenheit, but temperatures in the low 100s have occurred. Fog is common in the morning throughout the year. Winds are generally from the west.[1] Thankfully at Fort Ord I don't remember days exceeding 100 degrees that summer. We did, however, see some fog. The one big negative to Fort Ord's nice weather was that those who went to Vietnam were in for a rude awakening of terrible weather, which consists of tropical heat, humidity, and monsoon rains.

Boot Camp 1963: Innocence to Upheaval

An outbreak of spinal meningitis was one very scary event that was taking place at Fort Ord in the early 1960's. The following is an excerpt from an account by Jim Carnett, a basic training recruit (February-April, 1964) from Southern California:

In 1962, meningococcal meningitis appeared in pestilential proportions at bucolic Fort Ord on Monterey Bay. I was just getting ready to graduate from Costa Mesa High School. Many young U.S. Army recruits died at Ord over the coming several years. I remember reading alarming news reports about various outbreaks. Those outbreaks continued until basic training was suspended for a period at the fort in November of 1964. The training regimen resumed in 1965 and new outbreaks, tragically, ensued. The height of the season for meningitis, I'm told, is spring. I took my basic training at Ord as a 19-year-old recruit from February through April of 1964.

Even as (25,000 soldiers) at California's Ford Ord were being trained for action against an enemy that might be as distant as Vietnam," wrote Time Magazine in an August 1964 article, "they were already engaged in mortal combat with an insidious and invisible invader right in their midst. Spinal meningitis has struck down 59 trainees this year and killed nine of them."

Those numbers would climb higher by year's end.

A UPI story on Oct. 14, 1964, announced that a 22-year-old Ord recruit died of meningitis two days after the Pentagon ordered strict quarantine procedures at the base to combat the spread of the disease. By then, I'd finished my basic and was posted at Fort Benning, Ga.

In basic, I learned to be alert for symptoms of meningitis: sore throat, headache, stiff neck and high fever. The disease can also include a severe rash and can be transmitted by close proximity, physical touch or inhaling another's breath.

While I was at Ord, our barracks' windows were kept open all night to maximize ventilation. As a consequence, we nearly froze. I sleep with an open window to this day.

February through April is cold in Monterey, and damp. For most of the nine weeks I was there during the winter and spring of '64, I suffered from a raw throat, cough and runny nose. But I never reported for sick call.

To my mind, it was preferable to risk contracting meningitis than be recycled back to a previous week of training due to illness. I was loath to attach extra days to my prescribed Ord stay. So, I stayed away from the medics. The threat of being recycled and spending additional time at Ord scared me more than meningitis.[2]"

During my time at Fort Ord, which was just prior to the worst of the meningitis outbreak, I heard that they were already having a problem with spinal meningitis. I was somewhat concerned, but adjusting to military life and the difficulty of the training period kept my mind occupied with trying to get through basic training. Because of that, I was practically oblivious to the threat of the disease. But it was a time of relative stability so fortunately we didn't have to go through any of the precautions such as sleeping with our windows open at night.

Some of the world events going on during my week of reception:

A July 29, 1963 article in Newsweek Magazine, which was the day I arrived from Oakland to the Fort Ord reception station, reported that in Brussels while privately talking to the Belgian Foreign Minister, Paul-Henri Spaak, Soviet Premier Nikita Khrushchev considered Berlin to be a weapon in the cold war. Khrushchev put it this way: "Berlin is Kennedy's sore toe which I can step on now and then." Tensions between the U.S.A. and the Soviet Union existed over the Berlin Wall, Cuba, nuclear proliferation, and many other issues.

There was also an article about President Kennedy trying to get the auto industry on board to support the civil rights bill, which passed in 1964.

Endnotes

[1] www.militarymuseum.org/FtOrd.html

[2] JIM CARNETT, who lives in Costa Mesa, worked for Orange Coast College for 37 years.www.latimes.com/socal/daily-pilot/opinion/tn-dpt-me-carnett-20160621-story.html

Part Two

My Upheaval: Basic Training at Fort Ord

Chapter Three

Over the Hill to Basic

The first week of life in the Army was finally coming to a close and I was about to encounter another very rude awakening, which turned out to be the true beginning of my personal upheaval! While in reception, we all heard horror stories about basic training and how difficult it was getting through the program. But, in spite of what I had heard, I figured that basic training would probably not be that much worse than reception. But, if I thought that leaving home and then going through reception center had been bad, I soon discovered that things would go downhill.

August 5, 1963, a pleasant day weather wise, turned out to be pretty hellish. Each company sized group out of reception was assigned to a basic training company usually consisting of 100 to 200 soldiers. Each group was transported from reception to their appropriate basic training company location in an open trailer pulled by a semi-rig. The trailer held about 70 men including our equipment so we were pretty much crammed in like sardines. The slang used to describe our transportation was "cattle truck." I think many of us felt like cattle heading for slaughter. The trip to our basic training destination was about two miles and it was literally over a hill. Once loaded into the truck trailer, I started to change my mind about basic training not being much worse than reception. The best way I can describe how I felt during that short trip was a sudden feeling that things were about to get worse. It turns out, that I was proven right!

As soon as we arrived in front of our basic training company headquarters, the yelling began. It was more intense and profane than what we had encountered at reception. The SDI (Senior Drill Instructor) and four platoon sergeants were bellowing: "get off that truck on the double." They were yelling some of the same things that we encountered at reception, only much worse: "get off the grass," "stand at attention," "put out that cigarette," "pick up that cigarette butt." We also had our heavy duffel bags containing all our clothing and supplies. They would yell "put down that bag," and then immediately yell "pick up that bag." To make matters worse, right next door, Company D was in their final week of basic and they were having a great time laughing at us. "You guys are really going to get it," they shouted.

Then something happened that I will never forget. It is one of those moments that can really shake you up and I can still see it like it is frozen in time. I experienced a few of those moments during basic training, but this one was the worst. All of a sudden I heard this whimpering. On the grass was one of the recruits lying on the ground in the fetal position and literally shaking and sobbing. He had cracked under the pressure of the very intense harassment we were facing. I felt sorry for the guy, but seeing that made things worse. I don't know what happened to him, but we never saw him again.

We were assigned to Company C, 1st Battalion, 3rd Brigade. A battalion usually consists of 300-800 soldiers, and a brigade consists of 3,000 or more. The Brigades were commanded by Frank Caufield, who was a Brigadier General (one star). The Fort Ord Post Commander was Edwin Carnes, a Major General (two stars).

The 1st battalion barracks were all lined up parallel to each other and looked basically identical. Fort Ord opened in 1917, and these barracks looked about that old, but they were actually built for the World War II era in the early 40's and were considered only temporary, but they still seemed to be pretty well built. We referred to them as "firetraps" because they consisted of very old and dry wood and would probably go up in flames very quickly. After lights out, fire watch was a very important duty during our time in the barracks. Smoking after lights out was a serious offense! The barracks were a beige off-white with green trim including the roof. Each company had their own street which was about a third of a mile long. The street went over a hill and was parallel to the company next door. Next to company C was B on one side and D on the other side. Since the company buildings and streets all looked the same, it would have been pretty easy to mistakenly go to the wrong company if one was not careful. The only difference was the location of the Monterey Cypress trees and the other shrubs. In each company, the mess hall was located close to the top of the hill at about the midpoint of the street's length. Our company was split into four fifty man platoons, each commanded by a platoon sergeant. They were known as the cadre and they were some of the toughest guys I had ever seen, at least through the eyes of a 17 year old. In 1963, it was still the "Old Army" so some of the older leaders were either veterans of World War II or Korea and had most likely been in combat. Each wore that ominous looking shiny black cadre helmet liner. They had total authority over us and we were at their mercy.

Our platoon sergeant was a Staff Sergeant (three stripes with one rocker) named Buenaventura Bajo. Sergeant Bajo was originally from the Philippines. He had a heavy accent and he was one tough hombre. He was not the largest man, but he was definitely in shape. One of his favorite expressions was: "you people move like old ladies." I was on the receiving end of that expression a couple of times when I didn't move fast enough. He would say "Camon Frissi, you move liked an 'ol lady." The Company Commander was a First Lieutenant named Anthony Heyfron. He was pretty young and seemed to be a decent guy. The Senior Drill Instructor (SDI) was Sergeant First Class Renfro. He had a stocky build, a large head, and a beefy face. His helmet almost seemed too small for his head. He had thick curly black hair, piercing pale blue eyes, and a very pale complexion turning red when he was agitated, which seemed to be almost constantly.

The leadership actually had a very tough job molding raw recruits off the street into a precision fighting force. If the higher-ups, the brass as they were called in the military, noticed any sloppy marching or some other deficiency, they would blame the company commander and the SDI since they were in charge. If they did receive a dressing down from the higher-ups, we would hear about it! They would indicate that they got their rear end chewed only they used another word for rear end! The company clerk was PFC Earnshaw who seemed to be a pretty happy go lucky guy. We always envied him because he was permanent party with tailored faded fatigues and we all joked that he probably got to drink coffee and eat donuts all day.

The first thing we were taught was getting into some kind of a formation. Much of early basic training was discipline and the learning of all kinds of marching in formation. We learned the "preparatory command" and the "command of execution." A classic example is the word "forward," the preparatory command, and the word "march," the command of execution. Whenever they gave the command of execution, it always sounded kind of like "haw." A few times during marching in formation someone would screw up with disastrous results. One marching preparatory command is "to the rear" and then followed by the command of execution "march," which simply means that everyone is supposed to pivot completely around and go in the reverse direction. You can imagine what happened when someone was not concentrating and continued going forward. A few collisions occurred, which were then followed by the yelling of "meathead" bellowed by the SDI. It was pretty funny if one wasn't the guilty party, which fortunately, I never made that mistake. But I was involved in one of those situations myself and, although the results were less disastrous than colliding with another soldier, it was still quite mortifying. Everyone was at attention and the preparatory command was given "eyes" and followed by the command of execution "right." This meant that you turned your head to the right as far as it could go. I wasn't paying attention and kept looking forward. Sergeant Renfro slowly swaggered up to me and said "you know something Frizzi, I like you because you always pay attention." Then he proceeded to turn my head with his hand on my cheek, which was like a slow motion slap on the side of my face. He didn't hit me because corporal punishment was not used by the cadre. As he was turning my head he grumbled "get your eyes to the right." When I think of it now, it's pretty hilarious, but it wasn't then!

We also had many dreaded inspections which were regarded as something akin to the "inquisition." The six items inspected were the bunk, foot locker, shoes and boots, belt buckle, brass insignia, and rifle. The bed spread on the bunk had to be tight enough so a quarter would bounce. The footlocker had to have all toiletries on the top shelf located in a precise order. The bottom part of the footlocker had to have all items of underwear, T-shirts, and socks folded neatly and in a precise location. The boots, shoes, insignia, and belt buckle had to be shined. Our rifles had to be spotless. Sloppiness resulted in a verbal chewing out and about 20 push-ups, but it wasn't long before we all started to get somewhat used to the regimentation and, as time passed, everything became a little less overwhelming.

With all the push-ups given for screwing up (and many times not) plus all the physical training we received, we were all getting into fighting shape. Physical training (PT) was a big part of early basic training and usually consisted of calisthenics and fast marching or jogging in formation.

One of the most difficult parts of physical training was the long jogs (double time) at port arms. Port arms consisted of holding your rifle at a 45 degree angle across your chest while running. The M-1 rifle weighs 9.5 pounds so by the end of the double time (usually a mile), your arms were burning and you were out of breath. As everybody got into better shape, it gradually became better, but still not easy. The first few times were brutal.

The calisthenics consisted of jumping jacks, push-ups, sit-ups, pull-ups, running in place, and all kinds of stretching exercises. They were led by Sergeant First Class Allsbrooks, who was the one cadre that everybody liked. He was an African American and very personable and seemed like a genuinely nice guy. I think all of us wished we were in his platoon because Sergeant Bajo was all business, but being all business was Sergeant Bajo's job and he was doing it well.

One question that is always asked is: "how was the food in the Army?" That depends on where you are. At our basic training unit, the food was OK but not that good. The dining hall is called a "mess hall," and I often thought that name pretty well described the food there on some days. After basic training, in my second eight weeks, the food was great. We were fed by students from the cook school and they had to put out good food or else. The first time we went to "chow," as they say in the service, was at breakfast.

They had scrambled eggs, bacon, potatoes, and the most wonderful looking lamb or pork chops. They were nice and brown and looked so good until I took a bite and discovered that it was liver, one of the few foods that I cannot stand! I don't know if it's the taste or the consistency of liver. I think it's probably both!

I started getting used to the routine. It was never fun, but it eventually became more tolerable—even though it was definitely never easy. Our typical schedule was as follows: we would get up at 4:30 A.M., which took some getting used to, wash up and go to breakfast. After breakfast, at about 6 A.M., we would then fall out into formation and receive instructions concerning the uniform of the day. We would then go back to the barracks and put on the specifics of our uniform for that day. The uniform items usually included a pistol belt and canteen for lighter duty, and a backpack with entrenching tool (shovel), and gas mask for a heavier day. Our hat would consist of a block cap for lighter duty, and a steel helmet with a helmet liner for a heavier day. The block caps were referred to as "Castro hats" because they looked like the military hat that Cuban dictator Fidel Castro always wore. In 1964, the block cap was replaced by the baseball cap. All throughout my time in the service, the wearing of a hat outdoors was always required.

As basic training went on, we would either be firing rifles, going on maneuvers (which will be explained later), and of course, still a lot more marching in formation and physical training.

One of the main news events going on at this time in 1963 had to do with the civil rights movement and the non-violent marches led by Dr. Martin Luther King. They were non-violent on the part of the marchers, but opponents of their cause would resort to violence. A lot of overblown and manufactured news exists today concerning the so-called dangerous White Supremacist Movement. Unlike today's media created White Supremacist Movement, in 1963 it was truly a reality with more white supremacists than the small fringe-group minority of extremists today. In 1963, a lot of opposition to the civil rights movement and Dr. King's marches existed, even among mainstream people.

Another news event was the signing of the Partial Nuclear Test Ban Treaty (PTBT) by the United States, the United Kingdom, and by the Soviet Union on August 5, 1963, which was the same horrible day I arrived at basic training. The PTBT banned nuclear weapons testing in the atmosphere, outer space, and underwater, however, it still allowed underground detonations. The impetus for the test ban treaty was provided by rising public anxiety over the large number of nuclear tests and the resulting contamination spread throughout the atmosphere from radioactive nuclear fallout. With more environmental awareness today, it is hard to imagine that nuclear bombs were actually being detonated in the atmosphere and in the Pacific Ocean.

"Negotiations initially focused on a comprehensive ban, but this was abandoned due to technical questions surrounding the detection of underground tests and Soviet concerns over the intrusiveness of proposed verification methods."[1] The verification was to make sure no one was cheating, of which the Russians were famous. Today we have that same problem with the so-called Iran deal. The newest thermonuclear weapons (hydrogen bombs) were being tested and they were much more powerful than the atom bombs dropped on Hiroshima and Nagasaki.

A test ban was also regarded as a means of slowing nuclear proliferation and the nuclear arms race. The PTBT did have some success: though it did not halt nuclear proliferation or the arms race, it did result in a substantial decline of concentrations of radioactive particles in the atmosphere. Final ratification of the PTBT was in October, 1963.

Another world situation in August of 1963 was the imminent threat of all-out war in Vietnam and the extent of America's involvement in their support of the corrupt South Vietnamese dictator Diem. Historically, the U.S. had consistently denied the presence of combat soldiers in Vietnam, but in the following year, 1964, air bases and other installations manned by American Special Forces and advisors were being attacked by the Viet Cong guerillas resulting in American casualties. It was felt that we had to strike back and could not allow ourselves to be driven out of Vietnam.

Officially, the U.S. didn't send combat troops into Vietnam until the escalation in March of 1965, but the reality was different. I remember in the period between 1963 and 1965, the official reports from Washington politicians to the media and general public were pretty optimistic that the "situation" in Vietnam was going well, but behind the scenes there was pessimism. Those in the Department of State and the CIA, military officers, and the media were decidedly less optimistic. Later in this book (Chapter 10), there is more about Vietnam; the history of French Indo-China and the early days of the war.

Endnotes

[1] From Wikipedia, the free encyclopedia

Chapter Four
Barracks Life

An important life experience I learned in the Army resulted from exposure to different kinds of people. The High School I attended was probably about 95% white. Not a lot of racial or cultural diversity existed while growing up in the Willow Glen District of San Jose in the 1950's and early 1960's, so going into the Army was definitely a culture shock. It was my very first experience of being with African Americans, or Negroes, as they were referred to then. I still remember my first African American friend. His name was Andy Woods. He was from Oakland and probably the nicest and sweetest guy in the entire company. Ronnie Bolden was another African American guy whom I liked very much. It made me realize that people are all the same—in a human sense, we all have the desire for acceptance and the capacity to love (and to hate), and there is good and bad in everyone. I have often thought why it had to take meeting someone like Andy Woods or Ronnie Bolden to cause me to fully realize that. Why do some people prejudge others? The reason is: to God, we are imperfect sinners (Romans 3:23), whether saved through the new birth through being born again (John 3:8), or not. This explains why even some good people can still sometimes disappoint and look down upon those who are different.

Our company contained lots of different personalities and we were all confined to a relatively small space. The barracks building was two-stories and we had around twenty-five men to each floor. That was pretty crowded, especially with only one bathroom on each floor. Lack of privacy was something that everybody had to get used to.

Some guys were nice, or at least OK, and a few I really couldn't stand. I won't name the ones I didn't like because I only mention names if it's a positive description or at least absolutely necessary for the purposes of this book. Many of the guys that I could not stand were constantly talking in great detail about their sex lives back home with their "broad," a derogatory term used for women. The way they talked about their wife or girlfriend showed their general attitude as demeaning towards women. That bothered me because I had always thought that women are so awesome, and still do! It is great that women today have so much more opportunity. It is so cool to see women excelling in jobs that, in the past, were more limited to men. It is one of the good results of the very early Feminist-Movement fighting for the vote and equal pay and opportunity before it was corrupted by the left into the circus of burning bras, the attack on the relevance of men in their role as husbands and fathers, abortion on demand, and the redefining of the sexes. So in some ways, women are better off today than in 1963, but are still used as pawns by the left as well as sometimes still suffering marginalization and abuse. Recent revelations of verbal and sexual abused in the workplace are heartbreaking. Women and men were meant by God to be a blessing to each other, not adversaries, slaves, or masters.

For the most part, we all got along well which is extremely important since the purpose of our training was to be team mates and facing the potential of going into combat together. Anybody who was either a snitch or a barracks thief would be subject to the infamous "blanket party," which consisted of the throwing of a blanket over the offending person's head and being punched by multiple guys. It's kind of a cowardly act and platoon sergeant Bajo warned us early on that blanket parties "pissed him off" and would not be tolerated.

Some scuffles and intense arguments happened, but no real fights. If there had been a fight, the code of silence would take over since the entire platoon would be punished because fighting was not allowed. So don't let the platoon sergeant find out! One incident occurred where a small skinny bully, who was a nasty kid, would attack this big guy and kick him in the butt repeatedly. Instead of defending himself, the big guy, who was kind of nerdy, would almost comically hop away while the bully would follow and continue kicking him. I was hoping he would turn around and nail the bully, but he never did. Normally, the code of silence would have kicked in and the cadre would've never found out about the incident. But the bully, besides being nasty, wasn't very bright either and he committed his act in the street right in front of the company headquarters building. He was the only one who got punished, so it was pretty comical seeing him get stuck with every nasty job imaginable.

Those who had some college were considered for being chosen as squad leaders. Squad Leaders wore a dark armband with two stripes (that of a Corporal). Ranked above the squad leaders was someone in each platoon who was designated a Sergeant and wore the armband of a Staff Sergeant. Our designated sergeant's name was Jones and he was in his thirties with a Master's degree. He seemed really old to most of us who were 17 or 18. Our squad leader was Jeffrey Gaynor who was from Oakland. He was a decent, conscientious, serious guy and was a great squad leader. I felt sorry for him because it was not an easy job. He was also Jewish, which in those days, some guys (including some that I could not stand) would quietly use the term

"Jew boy" when referring to Gaynor. That was a common derogatory term used against Jews and probably still is to this day. Unfortunately, even today, anti-Semitism has never gone away and seems to be on the rise, which is one of the indicators that we are indeed in the end times according to the Bible.

Whites and blacks got along OK considering the times, but there was always this subtle unspoken undertone of racism on both sides. Racial slurs were usually not openly directed at African Americans or other minorities, but in private they were pretty common. One fight happened in the field between a white guy and an African American which was racial in nature. It was no surprise because the white guy was considered a "cracker" and had openly made racial slurs in the past. Fortunately, that was the only fight I saw.

But racial tensions were definitely on the rise at that time. The Civil Rights Movement was in full swing under Dr. Martin Luther King and much of the South was reacting in opposition. Even in areas outside the South, opposition existed to the marches. Racism was prevalent in America then and I can remember people calling him a trouble maker and a Communist. The civil rights struggle would soon take an ugly turn in 1964 with the beginning of the "long hot summers" and an even uglier event in April of 1968 when Dr. King was assassinated in Memphis.

A few practical jokers existed in the barracks. The target of their jokes would more than likely be someone who was universally disliked by virtually everyone in the barracks, and we had a few. One prank was called "short sheeting," which consisted of remaking that person's bed, but folding the sheet in such a way that it ended in the middle of the bed. When one would try to get into bed, their feet would only go in about three feet and would hit a dead end. It was comical when, before realizing what had happened, they would continue struggling to get completely under the covers. Another common practical joke was covering someone with shaving cream or putting shaving cream in his boots while he was asleep.

Much of barracks time after dinner and until bedtime consisted of shining and polishing shoes and brass. The belt buckle of our uniform was shiny brass. A compound called "Brasso," was practically a necessity in the Army. The belt buckle and the brass insignia on our dress uniforms had to be shining. Our shoes had to be highly polished and/or spit shined. Spit shining consisted of applying a generous amount of polish to the shoe or boot. Since most everyone smoked, almost everybody had a cigarette lighter. The flame of the "Zippo" cigarette lighter would melt the polish into the boot, but you had to be careful that you didn't burn the surface. Then the shoe or boot would be brushed to work in all the polish to form a base coat. The analogy in painting would be to apply a coat of primer paint first before applying the final coat or coats of color paint. Finally, the arduous process of working in more polish with water (or spit) would occur. A moist rag or cotton ball with polish would be applied by rubbing in circles. As soon as a shine began to show, more polish with spit or water would be applied with more rubbing in circles. Eventually, after about four applications, the shoes would shine like patent leather.

One of the notoriously unpleasant jobs associated with being in the Army is kitchen police, better known as KP. The term "police" or "policing" in the Army simply means to clean. Policing the grounds is picking up paper, cigarette butts, etc. Kitchen policing is varied: washing dishes, cleaning tables, sweeping and mopping the floor. One job that is always associated with KP is peeling potatoes and I did some of that too. The Mess Sergeant was usually a grouch and someone who was still a buck sergeant (three stripes) after twenty-something years of service. That usually meant he had been busted (reduced in rank) a few times. Our mess sergeant probably fit into that category.

One of the really bad things about pulling KP duty was missing an important part of basic training. The part I missed was learning to take your rifle apart and put it back together again. You had to know how to do this in order to properly clean your weapon so it would function under fire and pass inspection. Fortunately, a real nice kid in our barracks named Kuliu, I believe, from Fresno patiently taught me how to tear down and put my rifle together again.

Many times, I have some trouble getting to sleep. Either I am contemplating a problem in my mind, thinking about a song, or just having trouble turning off my thoughts. Sometimes, I am fidgety and just cannot get into a relaxed and comfortable position. I had no such trouble in the Army! The minute my head hit the pillow I was out. Lights out was 9:30 p.m. and we got up at 4:30 a.m. We were training hard and exerted a lot of energy during the day, so by the time it was bedtime, we were all pretty exhausted. I really hated to see the lights go on at 4:30!

In the evening, we actually had some down time and could even relax. We could go down to our nearby PX to buy supplies (usually cigarettes and toiletries) and listen to tunes on the juke box. The song that was mostly played on the Juke box was "Wipe Out," an electric guitar Southern California surfing instrumental by the Surfaris, a group from Glendora, California in eastern Los Angeles County. Although actually released in early 1963, Wipe Out was still a very popular song during the summer. One would seemingly hear it every time the radio was turned on. It had to be the number one instrumental of 1963. "Wipe Out sold millions of records and song downloads worldwide. According to BMI Inc. the song has been played on the radio over 5 million times."[1] The surfing term "Wipe Out" simply meant falling or being knocked off your surfboard and crashing into the ocean while riding a wave. It was played so much (even still today) that I actually got sick of it, although I liked the flip side "Surfer Joe." The last part of Surfer Joe told of his joining the Marines, being stationed at Camp Pendleton, and having all his blonde locks of hair cut off. I am not blonde, but could relate to that and his situation of losing his freedom.

Sunday was our day of rest and down time which usually consisted of watching TV or just sitting around and visiting. We also had the option of going to church, of which I took advantage. I was a nominal Roman Catholic, but not really very devout. I was brought up that you had to go church, so to me, it was an obligation. I would have just as soon slept in on Sunday rather than having to get up and go to church. But while in basic training, I attended the Catholic Mass. The whole experience of going to church seemed peaceful. I really enjoyed being there and I think the reason is that it reminded me of home. I missed home and going to church had always been a part of my home life. It was a feeling of nostalgia.

After the fourth week of basic training, we had an open house and the families were allowed to visit. We were all in our dress uniforms and the company commander would explain what our training was about and its importance. We were allowed to go home for the weekend on pass. That was the shortest weekend I have ever spent in my life! It was strange coming home because I was so used to the rigorous routine and discipline. After I returned, we started our second half of basic training and it didn't get any easier.

49

Endnotes

[1] https://thesurfaris.com

Chapter Five

Train Fire

One of the main functions of basic training is learning how to shoot and maintain your weapon. The rifle is always called the "weapon" and should never be referred to as a "gun," which is most definitely the wrong thing to say, especially in front of the cadre sergeants. I made that mistake once and received a very stern rebuke, as did some others as well. The service rifle is also called the "soldier's best friend." We used the M-1 Garand rifle, which is a .30 caliber semi-automatic rifle that was used during World War II (eventually replacing the Springfield rifle), the Korean War, and also saw limited service in Vietnam. In 1964, the M-14 was introduced and the M-1 was eventually replaced in the 1980's. The M-1's effective firing range is 500 yards. It weighs 9.5 lbs. and is heavy, which we all noticed while lugging it around all day! It has a rate of fire at 40–50 rounds/minute and it uses a .30-06 cartridge. The 30 is the caliber, the 06 represents 1906, the year that it was first introduced, and the bullet diameter is 7.8 mm. This was the standard round for service rifles and 30 caliber machine guns until the 1980's. The M-1 is top loaded with an 8 round clip that snaps into a spring loaded breach. When the last round is fired, the breach opens, the clip ejects, and a new clip needs to be inserted. Before going out to train fire, we had to make sure we had an adequate supply of loaded clips in our ammo pocket. Clips were fairly easy to load and that had to be done in time for being called out to final formation.

The location of our company was really fortunate during the time of train fire because we were the company with one of the closest barracks to California State Highway 1 and the ocean breeze. The shooting range was just on the other side of the highway so we had the shortest march to our destination. Some of the other companies, especially those which were located further east of us in the newer concrete barracks, had to travel an extra mile or more. Of course, when our company had to go east up into the hills, we were much further away and also had to march the extra mile, so it all evened out.

I remember in times long past when I was riding along Highway 1 as a civilian visiting the Monterey Peninsula. As I passed Fort Ord, I'd see soldiers marching in formation and think: "poor suckers, they're out there marching and I am free." In August of 1961, two years before I went into the Army, we stayed a week at a dear friend's house in Monterey. Fran Langshaw had a vending business on post and I would ride in with her and help out. Little did I realize that two years later I would be a recruit sitting in that same snack bar or post-exchange (PX) using those same vending machines. Now that I was the one marching along Highway 1, I thought back to those happier times. Of course, someone driving by and looking at us was probably saying "poor suckers." Being there close to the highway was so close to freedom, yet so far away. I felt a mixture of nostalgia and yearning. To me, in many ways, being in the Army felt like being in prison. Highway 1 represented freedom and was like a magnet drawing me towards many memories of happier nostalgic times, and yet reminding me of the futility of my situation. When I think back on basic training, it really wasn't that bad, but for a young kid who had a lot of growing up to do, it was still sometimes hard.

Much of the Fort Ord Train Fire area consisted of sand and ice plant which seemed to be everywhere, especially by the ocean where the shooting range was located. The sand, ice plant, and the smell of the sea air reminded me of that earlier time in August of 1961 when I played golf at the nearby Pacific Grove Golf Course on the Monterey Peninsula. The front nine had almost no trees, just sand and ice plant on both sides of the fairway. I got used to seeing a lot of it because I was such a lousy golfer that's where my ball usually ended up! These memories were just another reminder of my former life of comparative innocence.

When going to the shooting range, we wore our steel pot (helmet) and marched to the cadence of drummers. It was about a one mile march across (underneath) highway 1 to the train fire area. Train fire consisted of shooting at targets placed at a distance of 100 yards. We were actually shooting out towards Monterey Bay. A huge sand wall kept any stray rounds from going into the ocean, but a few guys would aim high just for "fun." That area was usually kept clear of any boats, but if anyone did wander into that territory, they could end up getting shot. I never heard of that happening, but it was possible. One of the types of guard duty assigned to recruits was the observation post. The purpose was to look for boats that might be getting into the train fire area and call it in to base. I appreciated that particular guard duty because it was an easy way to find solitude in the guard shack way up in the sand dunes overlooking Fort Ord and Monterey Bay.

When shooting at targets, we usually broke up into two man teams: one shooting and the other at the shooter's side monitoring the success rate of hitting the target. I am somewhat hard of hearing today and I am convinced that partnering with another shooter is part of the cause. Every time my partner would fire the rifle, my ears would ring even though they were covered by my helmet. It is said that anything that makes your ears ring is not very good for your hearing. For the three weeks of train fire, my ears would ring about fifty times each day! When I fired the rifle, my ears were fine, but being beside of the rifle causes you to absorb more of the loud sound.

Initially during train fire, targets were stationary, but later they would suddenly appear out of the ground. The targets were only about two feet high, were curved at the top and shaped like a small tombstone. I was a pretty good shot, but I also learned a couple of tricks. If you missed, it was better to miss the target low rather than shooting over it, so if the bullet hit in front of the target, sometimes it would ricochet into the target or at least kick up rocks that would trip a sensor and cause the target to fall. We would use what we learned here later on in basic when we went on maneuvers and had to fire at targets that suddenly appeared. The one thing that basic training couldn't prepare you for is firing at a real person, but the idea of that person trying to kill you would be a good reason to kill him first.

The cadre at train fire wore the same black helmet liner as our company cadre staff except that it had a white ring around it. The train fire cadre all had the rank of Sergeant First Class (three stripes and two rockers). Attending the train fire or any of the other classes during basic meant sitting on bleacher seats, but train fire classes were more like entertainment. The instructors were mostly African American and some of the funniest guys I have ever heard. Their humor was very off color so I really can't mention it in this writing, but at the time, it was hilarious. They could put to shame many of the so-called comedians and comics of today. One thing they would always say: "you have to squeeze the trigger, not pull it."

The other main part of train fire was called TD, or target detection. Someone would wear camouflaged clothing and be out in the bushes. We were supposed to find him. I was pretty bad at TD, but others would find him right away. We were finished with train fire after the end of the fourth week, about the last week of August. My birthday is on the 31st and it was probably the most underwhelming birthday I had ever spent!

The major news event at that time was significant for the civil rights movement. On August 28, 1963, Dr. Martin Luther King gave his "I have a dream speech." I was completely unaware of the speech at the time it was delivered. My main worry was getting through basic training. Because it was such a historic and powerful speech, I am showing the full text:

I have a Dream by Martin Luther King, Jr
August 28, 1963

Delivered on the steps at the Lincoln Memorial in Washington D.C. on August 28, 1963

Five score years ago, a great American, in whose symbolic shadow we stand signed the Emancipation Proclamation. This momentous decree came as a great beacon light of hope to millions of Negro slaves who had been seared in the flames of withering injustice. It came as a joyous daybreak to end the long night of captivity.

But one hundred years later, we must face the tragic fact that the Negro is still not free. One hundred years later, the life of the Negro is still sadly crippled by the manacles of segregation and the chains of discrimination. One hundred years later, the Negro lives on a lonely island of poverty in the midst of a vast ocean of material prosperity. One hundred years later, the Negro is still languishing in the corners of American society and finds himself an exile in his own land. So we have come here today to dramatize an appalling condition.

In a sense we have come to our nation's capital to cash a check. When the architects of our republic wrote the magnificent words of the Constitution and the declaration of Independence, they were signing a promissory note to which every American was to fall heir. This note was a promise that all men would be guaranteed the inalienable rights of life, liberty, and the pursuit of happiness.

It is obvious today that America has defaulted on this promissory note insofar as her citizens of color are concerned. Instead of honoring this sacred obligation, America has given the Negro people a bad check which has come back marked "insufficient funds." But we refuse to believe that the bank of justice is bankrupt. We refuse to believe that there are insufficient funds in the great vaults of opportunity of this nation. So we have come to cash this check -- a check that will give us upon demand the riches of freedom and the security of justice. We have also come to this hallowed spot to remind America of the fierce urgency of now. This is no time to engage in the luxury of cooling off or to take the tranquilizing drug of gradualism. Now is the time to rise from the dark and desolate valley of segregation to the sunlit path of racial justice. Now is the time to open the doors of opportunity to all of God's children. Now *is the time to lift our nation from the quicksand of racial injustice to the solid rock of brotherhood.*

It would be fatal for the nation to overlook the urgency of the moment and to underestimate the determination of the Negro. This sweltering summer of the Negro's legitimate discontent will not pass until there is an invigorating autumn of freedom and equality. Nineteen sixty-three is not an end, but a beginning. Those who hope that the Negro needed to blow off steam and will now be content will have a rude awakening if the nation returns to business as usual. There will be neither rest nor tranquility in America until the Negro is granted his citizenship rights. The whirlwinds of revolt will continue to shake the foundations of our nation until the bright day of justice emerges.

But there is something that I must say to my people who stand on the warm threshold which leads into the palace of justice. In the process of gaining our rightful place we must not be guilty of wrongful deeds. Let us not seek to satisfy our thirst for freedom by drinking from the cup of bitterness and hatred.

We must forever conduct our struggle on the high plane of dignity and discipline. We must not allow our creative protest to degenerate into physical violence. Again and again we must rise to the majestic heights of meeting physical force with soul force. The marvelous new militancy which has engulfed the Negro community must not lead us to distrust of all white people, for many of our white brothers, as evidenced by their presence here today, have come to realize that their destiny is tied up with our destiny and their freedom is inextricably bound to our freedom. We cannot walk alone.

And as we walk, we must make the pledge that we shall march ahead. We cannot turn back. There are those who are asking the devotees of civil rights, "When will you be satisfied?" We can never be satisfied as long as our bodies, heavy with the fatigue of travel, cannot gain lodging in the motels of the highways and the hotels of the cities. We cannot be satisfied as long as the Negro's basic mobility is from a smaller ghetto to a larger one. We can never be satisfied as long as a Negro in Mississippi cannot vote and a Negro in New York believes he has nothing for which to vote. No, no, we are not satisfied, and we will not be satisfied until justice rolls down like waters and righteousness like a mighty stream.

I am not unmindful that some of you have come here out of great trials and tribulations. Some of you have come fresh from narrow cells. Some of you have come from areas where your quest for freedom left you battered by the storms of persecution and staggered by the winds of police brutality. You have been the veterans of creative suffering. Continue to work with the faith that unearned suffering is redemptive.

Go back to Mississippi, go back to Alabama, go back to Georgia, go back to Louisiana, go back to the slums and ghettos of our northern cities, knowing that somehow this situation can and will be changed. Let us not wallow in the valley of despair.

I say to you today, my friends, that in spite of the difficulties and frustrations of the moment, I still have a dream. It is a dream deeply rooted in the American dream.

I have a dream that one day this nation will rise up and live out the true meaning of its creed: "We hold these truths to be self-evident: that all men are created equal."

I have a dream that one day on the red hills of Georgia the sons of former slaves and the sons of former slave owners will be able to sit down together at a table of brotherhood.

I have a dream that one day even the state of Mississippi, a desert state, sweltering with the heat of injustice and oppression, will be transformed into an oasis of freedom and justice.

I have a dream that my four children will one day live in a nation where they will not be judged by the color of their skin but by the content of their character.

I have a dream today.

I have a dream that one day the state of Alabama, whose governor's lips are presently dripping with the words of interposition and nullification, will be transformed into a situation where little black boys and black girls will be able to join hands with little white boys and white girls and walk together as sisters and brothers.

I have a dream today.

I have a dream that one day every valley shall be exalted, every hill and mountain shall be made low, the rough places will be made plain, and the crooked places will be made straight, and the glory of the Lord shall be revealed, and all flesh shall see it together.

This is our hope. This is the faith with which I return to the South. With this faith we will be able to hew out of the mountain of despair a stone of hope. With this faith we will be able to transform the jangling discords of our nation into a beautiful symphony of brotherhood. With this faith we will be able to work together, to pray together, to struggle together, to go to jail together, to stand up for freedom together, knowing that we will be free one day.

This will be the day when all of God's children will be able to sing with a new meaning, "My country, 'tis of thee, sweet land of liberty, of thee I sing. Land where my fathers died, land of the pilgrim's pride, from every mountainside, let freedom ring."

And if America is to be a great nation this must become true. So let freedom ring from the prodigious hilltops of New Hampshire. Let freedom ring from the mighty mountains of New York. Let freedom ring from the heightening Alleghenies of Pennsylvania!

Let freedom ring from the snowcapped Rockies of Colorado!

Let freedom ring from the curvaceous peaks of California!

But not only that; let freedom ring from Stone Mountain of Georgia!

Let freedom ring from Lookout Mountain of Tennessee!

Let freedom ring from every hill and every molehill of Mississippi. From every mountainside, let freedom ring.

When we let freedom ring, when we let it ring from every village and every hamlet, from every state and every city, we will be able to speed up that day when all of God's children, black men and white men, Jews and Gentiles, Protestants and Catholics, will be able to join hands and sing in the words of the old Negro spiritual, "Free at last! free at last! Thank God Almighty, we are free at last!"[1]

That magnificent speech shows how different the country was in the early 1960's compared to today. In the fifty-five years since that speech by Martin Luther King, much progress has been made concerning civil rights, and in particular, regarding race relations. It is interesting to note the terminology that was used back then. The word "Negro" was the term in the early 1960's that was used when referring to African-Americans. Later on in the 60's, that term then became offensive and was replaced by the word "black." For example, in the late sixties, the "Black Panther" party was a very well-known militant group. Now the term black is somewhat falling out of favor and the more acceptable term is African-American.

Back then, police brutality was much greater than the relatively isolated instances we see today. Police brutality and racism still exist in America today, but compared to the 1960's and before, it is now relatively nonexistent. Unfortunately, since the radical left wish to divide the races over the false narratives of systemic racism and police brutality, relations between black and white may actually be getting worse. Black Lives Matter is a sad contrast to the genuine movement towards civil rights and racial equality led by Dr. King. To the radical left, I am about to make a statement which they would consider racist: "All lives matter!" In chapter 14,--"Black Lives Matter," more detail will be given on this movement.

Endnote

[1] The Avalon Project Yale Law School Lillian Goldman Law Library © 2008 Lillian Goldman Law Library 127 Wall Street, New Haven, CT 06511.

Chapter Six

Out in the Field

Fort Ord basic training was geared to the infantry (ground troops). We all had a lot to learn about being outdoors in the field and the various activities that are involved. We often practiced war games and/or maneuvers, which is kind of a generic term for attacking and holding positions. These games usually consisted of advancing on a position and taking cover behind a tree, rocks, or anything that was available while advancing forward. Of course, in real war the hope would be that you wouldn't get shot or blown up while going from tree to tree or rock to rock! Two of the games I remember most were: attacking a hill and the infiltration course.

The attacking the hill course consists of running up a hill that has a 30 degree incline and strategically placed rocks and dirt mounds that one could hide behind. As soon as I reached these sources of cover, I would duck behind the cover and then look and shoot at a pop-up target. Our bayonets were fixed, so when I got to the top of the hill, I would encounter a hanging dummy which I would stab with my bayonet. Going up that hill with all my gear on (a 40 pound backpack) was very taxing, but I was young and the adrenaline kicked in.

The infiltration course was very intimidating. The idea is to stealthily advance upon an armed position. It was about dusk when we went through the infiltration course and, as we were in the bleachers watching the course from the side, we were then given a demonstration of the firepower that would be flying over our heads. All of a sudden, multiple machine guns simultaneously opened fire with all tracer rounds making a solid and shimmering orange flashing sheet appear over the course. To say the least, it was intimidating! Strategically placed M-80 explosives would detonate somewhat close to you, which also may have contributed to my loss of hearing! The course was clearly marked so that no one would really get blown up. Everything was OK as long as one didn't go off course or stand up! I had to crawl about 75 yards on my belly while machine guns were firing these live rounds about five feet over my head. If someone panicked and stood up, they were dead! Fortunately, nobody ever panicked. I ate the dust through the entire course and didn't dare even begin to rise up! Fortunately, it was dusk so I didn't run into a snake or Tarantula!

An important part of our training was the use of the soldier's other main weapon: the Hand Grenade. We each had to throw a hand grenade over a concrete wall. In case the grenade was dropped before it was thrown over the wall, a deep concrete lined pit surrounded the throwing area. The grenade would have to be thrown down the pit otherwise it could kill someone. I have heard of cases where someone would panic and drop the grenade on the ground. The instructor would then throw it into the pit. A lever on the side of the grenade was squeezed and a pin with a round metal loop was pulled out starting the timing fuse once the lever was released. Five seconds later, it would explode, so it needed to be thrown over the wall soon as possible. Fortunately, everyone successfully threw it over the wall.

While out in the field, we had to qualify for proficiency in shooting our weapon. The test basically consisted of firing in the prone position (on your belly) and also firing in the upright position (on one knee). In only about a two minute time period, about 30 pop-up targets on a hill would alternately and suddenly appear in various locations and I had to hit them. I already knew how to shoot the rifle because of the earlier classes in Train Fire. I qualified as a Marksman, which meant that I missed a few targets, but still qualified.

One part of basic training that we all learned to fear was gas. Tear gas (or CS gas) was used for training. Gas could be, and had been used in past wars as a lethal weapon. The slang for CS is "cry sooner." The first thing we had to learn was to get our gas mask out of the pouch and on quickly. If anybody was too slow, they would pay the price. Even afterwards, the cadre would make us take off the mask while residual gas was still in the air to get a taste of it. CS gas burns the lungs, eyes, skin—breathing it is not a pleasant experience. Because of that, I was very motivated to be able to get my mask on quickly. One gross but positive thing about tear gas: it cleared up the "Fort Ord Crud." Because Fort Ord has a cooler damp climate, there were constant cases of sinus colds and congestion. Even breathing a small amount of it would literally clear out your sinuses of any nasal congestion. The closest thing resembling the effects of tear gas on the sinuses is a large helping of really strong horse radish.

The following gives more information on the gas that we were in awe of:

CS gas is a solid–liquid–gas. The compound 2-chlorobenzalmalononitrile (also called o-chlorobenzylidene malononitrile; chemical formula: C10H5ClN2), a cyanocarbon, is the defining component of a tear gas commonly referred to as CS gas, which is used as a riot control agent.

CS gas [2-chlorobenzylidene malonitrile] is the most commonly used 'tear gas' in the world. ... Exposure to the spray causes distressing symptoms including lacrimation, eye pain, blepharospasm, a burning sensation in the throat and nose, increased nasal secretions, chest tightness, sneezing, coughing and retching.

Is CS gas dangerous? CS gas (2-chlorobenzylidene malononitrile) is one of the most commonly used tear gases in the world. Law enforcement agencies have found this agent invaluable when faced with combative suspects, for riot control, and for alleviating hostage and siege situations.

Despite its ubiquity across the globe and in United States, tear gas is a chemical agent banned in warfare per the Chemical Weapons Convention of 1993, which set forth agreements signed by nearly every nation in the world — including the United States. Aug 14, 2014

As with all non-lethal or less-lethal weapons, there is some risk of serious permanent injury or death when tear gas is used. This includes risks from being hit by tear gas cartridges, which include severe bruising, loss of eyesight, skull fracture, and even death.[1]

In addition to being exposed to the gas in the open air, we also had to go through the gas chamber, or "tent," and were required to take off our mask and breathe some gas before exiting. Definitely not fun!

What is the Gas Chamber?

The gas chamber is a room that has a controlled concentration of CS (orto-chlorobenzylidene-malononitrile) gas, more commonly known as tear gas. Tear gas is the active ingredient in Mace™ and used for self-defense and for riot control by the police. Tear gas is an irritant; specifically, it irritates mucous membranes in the eyes, nose, mouth and lungs, causing tearing, sneezing, coughing, etc.

The Process

On or about the second week you will be subjected to the gas chamber. You will follow your daily schedule, so if you are scheduled to go to the gas chamber in the afternoon, I suggest eating a light lunch. Taking a few breaths of tear gas on a full stomach is not a good feeling.

Before entering the gas chamber, you will be trained on how to fit your protective mask and chemical gear. Learning how to clear your mask is important. Some recruits fail to pay attention to these instructions, and regret their lack of attention while in the gas chamber.

A number of different things can occur while you are in the gas chamber. I will explain to you the most common method Drill Sergeants use to move the recruits through the gas chamber.

You will line up in a group (usually 5 to 15 recruits) outside of the gas chamber door. Your group will be asked to file into the gas chamber. Once inside the gas chamber you will be joined by a Drill Sergeant (or several of them). The room will be very foggy. The fog you see is CS gas, and you may smell it slightly through your mask. You will see a Drill Sergeant with a coffee can next to a table. This coffee can will have a flame inside — this is the CS gas burning. A Drill Sergeant will touch your shoulder, and ask you to lift your mask and state your name, rank and social security number. Many recruits get nervous and forget the answers to these simple questions. If you remain calm, you will do fine.

As the Drill Sergeants touch your shoulder take in a deep breath, close your eyes, lift your mask, answer the questions in one breath, put your mask back on, and clear the mask. This part of the gas chamber is not difficult if you stay calm. However, over the years, Drill Sergeants have learned that recruits accomplish this without inhaling any CS gas. The Drill Sergeants want you to inhale the gas, and recognize the importance of chemical gear. Therefore, after your whole group is finished stating their name, rank and social security number, they will ask you to take off your mask and file out in order without closing your eyes.

The Treatment: As you are exiting the gas chamber, your eyes will fill with water, and mucous will fill your lungs and face. The best treatment is air. Immediately upon exiting the gas chamber, you should open your eyes. This will seem like a hard task under the circumstances, but keeping your eyes open in fresh air will allow any discomfort to dissipate very quickly. I cannot emphasize enough to not touch your eyes. You will no doubt feel the urge, but touching and/or rubbing your eyes is the worst thing you can do. Take deep breaths of air with your arms over your head, and you will be surprised how quickly the CS leaves your system. In less than a minute you will be nearly, if not, 100 percent better.

Smile Pretty.

Typically a historian will follow your basic training company for 9 weeks. At the end of basic training, this historian will have a book for sale filled with pictures of all the events you have accomplished. The pictures from the gas chamber are not exactly pictures you want your friends and family to see. You will probably have drool on yourself, and it will look like you just sneezed 47 times in a row without access to tissues. So, as you exit the gas chamber, look for the historian and head in the other direction. Don't forget to put a pack of tissues in your cargo pocket before you enter the gas chamber!

SGT Michael Volkin is the author of "The Ultimate Basic Training Guidebook: Tips, Tricks and Tactics for Surviving Boot Camp."[2] A vital part of our gas training concerned nerve gas. Nerve gas is a neurotoxic gas that shuts down the nervous system's ability to send messages to the muscles and other vital parts of the body.

***Nerve gas,** Is a weapon of chemical warfare that affects the transmission of nerve impulses through the nervous system. The organophosphorus nerve agents Tabun, Sarin, and Soman were developed by Germany during World War II but not used. They and a newer agent, VX, were produced in huge quantities and used in subways by members of AUM Shinrikyo." "Used by the U.S. and Soviet Union during the Cold War; their stockpiling and use during war are now* *banned by the Chemical Weapons Convention of 1993. A single droplet of VX or Sarin, if inhaled or in contact with the skin, can be absorbed into the bloodstream and paralyze the nervous system, leading to respiratory failure and immediate death. Sarin was used in 1995 in a lethal attack in the Tokyo subway attack."*[3]

The only cure at the time of our training was atropine, which is toxic. But in the case of exposure to nerve gas, atropine serves as the anti-dote. We were not exposed to nerve gas while in training, but we did carry in our gas mask bag a single dose of atropine. To use atropine, the cap on the tip of the needle was removed and then one would have to inject the atropine into the body (usually the upper leg) within a few seconds. The effect of nerve gas would be similar to being bitten by the most poisonous snakes in the world, most of which have neurotoxic venom. The fact that such a weapon exists and could be used is very sobering.

Funny how fear can become a real motivator! We spent lots of time marching in the countryside east of Fort Ord, which consisted of Oak studded hills, Coyote Bushes, and Poison Oak. At times we would hear someone yell "gas," and we all got so jumpy that we were going for our gas masks, even if someone moved suddenly. It was probably one of the field sergeants causing us to practice getting our masks on, or some wise guy being "funny."

We had our outdoor classes in bleachers. Since we all got up early and had a pretty grueling day physically, many of us were constantly on the verge of falling asleep. One incident that I will never forget involved a poor guy who made the mistake of falling asleep during the instructor's lecture concerning the gas mask. The instructor quietly told us to put on our gas masks. He then gave the sign for us to be silent by putting his finger to his lips. The offending soldier was on the bottom row of the bleachers and the instructor popped a gas canister and placed it on the ground right below him. A cloud of CS gas enveloped him and he began screaming like he was on fire. Some guys grabbed him and held him down while another put his mask on for him. It was a difficult lesson for that soldier to learn.

Endnotes

[1] https://en.wikipedia.org/wiki/CS_gas

[2] *Military.com | by Sgt. Michael Volkin*

[3] https://www.britannica.com/science/nerve-gas

Chapter Seven

Bivouac

At the beginning of our sixth week of training, we were preparing to camp out for one week. This part of training is commonly known as bivouac, which consists of setting up a temporary camp outdoors—basically a small tent city. The type of training was the same as when we had previously been in the field, except now the field was actually our home for a week! At least we did avoid the long march out to the field and then the return march back to our barracks, but we still did a lot of marching in formation during our one week stay in the wilds. It was kind of like going camping, but nothing like I envisioned before joining the Army; it was much less fun! That one week turned into seven long days! The worst part for me was not being able to take a hot shower. They did have makeshift showers, but they were not the same. At the time, I imagined what it must be like for those who are in combat with numerous days in the field with no shower. But they are going through stuff that is so much worse, I doubt if that is the main thing on their minds during combat!

The bivouac area was a nice countryside setting of rolling hills and oak forest. It was located east of Fort Ord and further away from the cooling influence of the ocean breeze. It was mid-September and the weather was much hotter inland. Naturally, we really appreciated the shade of those oak trees. The dry hills of coastal California are the home of the Pacific Coast Rattlesnake. Those in the very front marched a lot looking down! We were all pretty cautious in any shaded area or place where a rattlesnake would try to escape the hot sun.

Most of the day's activities consisted of marching, war games/maneuvers, and having classes at various locations. We would march along trails that were usually sandy and dusty. The marching would kick up a lot of dust, so the worst thing that could happen was being at the end of the line. With three platoons ahead of you, it would result in breathing a lot of dust. Fortunately, the order was rotated just to make it fair.

Since we were away from our company barracks, the mess hall would truck in deliveries of food for breakfast, lunch (sometimes), and dinner meal. The guy that got assigned KP on bivouac week was really lucky because he didn't have to be out in the field. He could stay back at the company, sleep in a regular bed, and enjoy a hot shower, plus no one was around. Of course, he would still have to put up with the grouchy old mess sergeant, but it was a small price to pay for a hot shower and a relatively comfortable bed each night.

Since we were away from the "tent city" at lunchtime, the mess truck would meet us in various locations. When a regular mess hall meal was sometimes not delivered for lunch, field rations were a common meal while on bivouac. It consisted of a pack of very stale cigarettes, some kind of a dry packaged energy bar, canned fruit, meat and beans. Field rations were OK depending on how hungry one was, which for most of us, was all the time.

Lunchtime hot meals delivered in the field meant being away from the company mess hall dishes which required using mess kits, consisting of metal sectioned bowl/plates, cover, cups, and utensils. After lunch, we would all get in line to wash our mess kit. We would first dip the kit into water to rinse it and then dip it in very hot soapy water to wash it. After a thorough wash in hot water, we would finally rinse the mess kit with a spray hose. You had to hold it a certain way so your hand would not end up getting scalded in the hot water. Unfortunately, a few guys were not so careful and got burned or dropped their kit into the hot water. When that happened, they would get no sympathy from the sergeants, only a lecture on being more careful the next time. It was very important to have the hot water thoroughly clean grease or leftover food so that bacteria would not form. If a kit was not properly cleaned and bacteria free, one could get the "GI's," a slang word for diarrhea, which would be a complicated situation out in the field!

Field sanitation was one of the important subjects of training while on bivouac. It consisted of latrines at camp and digging a hole to cover up anything done outside of camp. The sergeants would describe in the grossest terms possible what would happen if feces were not properly buried. The theme was basically "flies in close proximity to food." The regular bathroom we used at the tent city consisted of a tented outhouse, so for most of us used to indoor plumbing, the outhouse was an adjustment.

I mentioned earlier that some experiences I will never forget. Something happened that was one of those very unforgettable experiences. We were sitting in the bleachers and about to attend a class. The instructor sergeant was holding his microphone and setting up the sound system. All of a sudden, a spark and popping sound came from his microphone and he was apparently being electrocuted.

He was yelling, shaking, and twitching on the ground. One soldier in the front row tried to come to his aid and grabbed a hold of him. It turned out that whole thing was staged and the soldier who touched him actually did the wrong thing and should have unplugged the unit. It was really a very shocking experience, pun intended!

Another unforgettable experience involved observing the penalty suffered when a soldier is careless with his weapon. One guy made the mistake of letting the tip of his rifle barrel hit the sandy dirt. Upon seeing the inexcusable deed, the SDI grabbed the rifle, opened the breach where the clips are loaded, and stuffed sand and dirt into the rifle. He then opened and closed the breach repeatedly in order to really work in the dirt and sand. He then jammed the barrel tip right into the sandy dirt. The offending soldier was then told to have it spotless by lights out!

Something that was a constant irritant throughout our basic training was the cigarette bum. Cigarettes were dirt cheap back in those days and you could buy a carton of cigarettes for less than two dollars. But some soldiers would not buy their own and mooch off of other people. They kind of had an attitude of entitlement (which is a pet peeve of mine) like they were owed free cigarettes. In the early 60's, most everybody smoked so plenty of guys were available for the cigarette bums to hit for a smoke. Cigarette bumming was worse at bivouac because we were not back at post and couldn't replenish our cigarette supply at the PX. The cigarettes we occasionally got in the field rations were pretty stale, but they were all that we had. The cigarette bums would hoard their cigarettes and pretend like they were out, which would really tick people off.

One guy had an ingenious plan to discourage cigarette bumming, or at least get back at them. He had bought a bunch of small pins at the PX and would "rig a pack." He always carried an extra pack of rigged cigarettes with a pin inserted into each cigarette. It was really comical to see the cigarette bum try to flick the ash, which of course remained stuck because of the pin. Finally one last flick in frustration would send the entire cigarette contents (except the filter) smoking to the ground. All of us thought that was pretty funny.

During a break in formation the command would go out: "light 'em if you got 'em." Before we were through, the cigarette would have to be put out because the very short break time was over. One thing we learned is "field stripping" a cigarette. You would knock off the burning head to the ground, making sure it is put out and put the rest of the cigarette in your pocket to smoke later. That would cause your uniform to really reek of stale smoke! The smell was similar to walking outside past a smoky bar with its front door open.

In some ways, being in a tent was actually kind of fun. My tent mate's name was Hopkins. He was from Mohave, California and we got along well. He had a small transistor radio and at night we listened to KMBY 1240 A.M. Monterey. We weren't supposed to be listening to the radio, so we had to keep the volume down to avoid really getting into trouble. The song I always remember listening to in the tent was "Wham," a soul guitar instrumental by Lonnie Mack. We slept in the Army equivalent of a sleeping bag and were basically sleeping on the ground. Although it was not very comfortable, sleeping was never a problem since we were all exhausted at the end of each day. Since I was so young, I never had any back problems from sleeping in an uncomfortable position. I would hate to try it now!

The last day of the week long bivouac consisted of a 20-mile march back to our company. We were probably only three or four miles away, but we took the long circuitous route via the west side of the Salinas Valley. We were still in the oak forest, but getting close to going into the valley and it was a lot hotter on the Salinas side of the hills than on the Monterey Peninsula side. The hills separating Salinas from the Monterey Bay Area are not very high; it is more of a mesa.

The march began very early in the morning and it was just one long march on a hot day with an occasional ten minute break. During the breaks, the first thing I (and many others) would do is to take off my boots and socks, lie on my back, and elevate my feet up the trunk of a tree. While marching, I would constantly crave an ice cold Coke or any soft drink. We were later told that the march was actually almost thirty miles. It seemed like it was never going to end!

During that march, something truly amazing happened. One of the things that got me through the toil and difficulty and sore feet was a song that kept going through my head. As long as I can remember, I have always loved music. I love to take long walks and often there is a tune going through my head. It is like I have all my favorite songs audibly memorized and play them whenever I want. I was definitely "listening" to tunes just to break up the monotony and get through the long march. All of a sudden a tune with actual music and lyrics popped into my head. I then realized that it was a song I had never heard before. Amazingly, until writing this book, I had forgotten all about that song heard in my head 55 years ago. In fact, I was recently taking a long walk in an adjacent neighborhood with narrow roads and oak trees when I remembered that song. Part of writing this book was visualizing the different parts of my basic training in order to jar my memory. As I was trying to remember the march, I had a picture in my head of walking down the trail amid the oak trees and remembering what I was feeling and thinking. It wasn't until that recent walk in the neighborhood among very similar oak trees that I suddenly remembered the song. The instruments consisted of a Hammond B-3 organ and a low frequency floor shaking bass played on foot pedals; a blues guitar, harmonica, and drums. The song is a semi-slow rolling type of blues ballad which I called "All I Ever Wanted" and it appears at the end of this chapter. There have been many songs recorded with the same title, so I researched all these songs to make sure that it wasn't just something I had heard before, but it was totally new. I had sort of written a song! The heat and fatigue of the march made me feel almost delirious at times—maybe that somehow gets the creative juices going.

We didn't get back to post until about 6 p.m. My feet and lower legs felt like they were going to fall off. When we finally arrived back at our company barracks, we were allowed to crash on our bunks. It felt so good to have my boots off and feet up. The actual date of the march was September 18, 1963. Certain days you remember and that march was an unforgettable experience!

The next day, there was a call to give blood. You "volunteered" to give blood or else. The or else was usually KP or some other kind of dirty job. The Army definitely had ways of making one do what they wanted. When I reported to give blood, I was rejected because of low-blood pressure, which no doubt resulted from dehydration and exhaustion after an almost thirty mile march.

Some world events occurring on September 18, 1963:

The USSR ordered 58.5 million barrels of cereal from Australia. Apparently the agricultural system under Communism and central planning, even with a huge area for potential farming, wasn't working out so well. No wonder!

Rioters burned down the British Embassy in protest of the formation of Malaysia.

Boot Camp 1963: Innocence to Upheaval

The first tested flight of the ASSET project (Aero-thermodynamic-elastic-Structural-Systems Environmental Tests), which was a winged space payload vehicle, was carried out. The goal was to develop a manned spacecraft which could return from orbit and land on a runway.[1] Less than six years later, on July 20, 1969, the United States would land a man on the moon.

Endnotes

[1] From Wikipedia, the free encyclopedia

All I Ever Wanted

All I ever wanted was fortune and fame

Where everybody around would know my name

All I ever did was play life's game

All I ever got was sorrow and shame

Now I realize that I was to blame

I sowed a lot of corruption and I reaped the same

Instrumental interlude section w/organ, guitar,

drums, and harmonica.

When I met you, all of my dreams came true

You took my hand and you chased away my blues

Now I realize that all I ever needed was you.

Chapter Eight
The Second Eight Weeks:

The End of Basic Training to Advanced Personnel Training

Throughout basic training we were being threatened, not only with the threat of being shipped to Vietnam, but also getting recycled. Being recycled meant taking all or part of basic training over again which was simply unthinkable. One had to either screw up an aspect of training, have a disciplinary problem, or a medical incident in order to be recycled. There were some guys I went through basic with who were the worst screw ups I have ever seen, yet they still graduated, so probably not a lot of guys got recycled. Since I knew that we were all going to graduate from basic training, I was now enjoying a relatively easy and relaxed post basic training zero-week (which was really most of the actual eighth week). This "easy eighth week" kind of made up for the unpleasant zero-week in reception and consisted of cleaning equipment, turning it in, and cleaning the barracks. I also got to ride around in the back of a truck all day on various work details. It was kind of fun, especially since I knew I was practically through basic training and things would get better. One detail, which required some physical exertion, was loading and carrying around ammunition in a 2½ Ton truck (deuce and a half) out to the advanced infantry training area. We carried various boxes of 30 cal. machine gun rounds, hand grenades, mortar rockets, M-80 explosives, and tear gas bombs. Some of the other work details were considerably less exciting like delivering chairs, tables and filing cabinets, pulling weeds, picking up trash, cleaning toilets & bathroom floors, sweeping and mopping the barracks floors, and other pretty mundane stuff.

We now could have been the ones laughing at the new recruits next door arriving in those infamous cattle trucks. I felt kind of sorry for them but knew that they would get through basic OK. I wondered how many of them (and those in our company) would end up in Vietnam and possibly never return home. Eight weeks ago, we arrived in those same cattle trucks wearing our un-faded darker green fatigues and received derisive laughter from the company next door getting ready to graduate. We also got yelled at unmercifully by the cadre, but now we were ready to graduate and there was a relative peacefulness.

One of the interesting things that happened was the change in personality of the platoon sergeants who had total authority over us. When we were training they were all business, but when training was over, they were just regular guys. We all sat around and shot the breeze with our platoon sergeant, Sergeant Bajo, and we were joking and laughing together. Even our SDI, Sergeant Renfro, turned out to be a really nice guy, but you would never have known that during our training. At that time, he would yell so much that his voice would start to crack. But then, he wasn't supposed to be a nice guy.

I felt sorry for Private Lloyd. He came over the hill with us from reception, but shortly after arriving, he developed infantigo, which is a contagious bacterial disease caused by either bacteria-strep (streptococcus) or a staph infection (staphylococcus). These bacteria can enter the body through openings in the skin from such causes as eczema, rashes, insect bites, burns, or cuts. The results are ugly open sores and rashes. He went to the hospital and couldn't be in a barracks with other guys. He missed the entire basic training period and had to be recycled. After being released from the hospital, he worked in our company supply room. As we were graduating, he was just getting ready to start basic training with the new group who would soon be coming over in a cattle truck from reception. We kind of felt bad for him and nobody teased him about how he could have been all done with basic. We tried to encourage him with "it's really not that bad," which was actually true. It was one of our good and nice moments and showed true camaraderie with a fellow soldier.

We were now getting ready to report to our respective assignment locations for our second eight weeks of training and I was happy to be staying at Fort Ord. I reported to my new advanced training post on the first week of October, 1963. The location was only about one-half mile from where I took basic. I signed up to be a Personnel Specialist and attended eight weeks of school. I knew that I would end up working in a personnel department overseas which turned out to be the second largest Army hospital in Europe at the time, located in West Germany. Of course, back then, personnel was still called personnel rather than human resources. In the 1960's, the Santa Clara County Department of Social Services was called the County Welfare Department.

On the week that I reported to personnel school, a significant natural disaster was occurring: Hurricane Flora (September 26–October 13, 1963) killed, according to later estimates, over 7000 people in the Caribbean, 5000 of those deaths in Haiti. But, except for one death in Miami due to the rough surf caused by Flora, the hurricane largely spared South Florida and the rest of the Eastern Seaboard.

On September 30, Flora reached hurricane status just east of the Caribbean. It then quickly became a Category 2 hurricane as it slammed into Trinidad and Tobago. There, it triggered several deadly landslides before moving on to the island of Grenada. Flora took a terrible toll on the small island, killing 36 people and seriously injuring another 500.

After moving over Grenada, Flora strengthened briefly to a Category 5 storm with 170-mile-per-hour winds. On October 2, the hurricane, now a Category 4, struck Haiti. The island's coastal villages were decimated by the winds. Most damaging, though, was a 12-foot storm surge, which overwhelmed virtually all the homes and other buildings near the ocean. It is estimated that 5,000 people died in the disaster. The survivors were faced not only with rebuilding their devastated nation, but with the loss of nearly the entire coffee crop for the season, a huge economic blow. This huge storm, which also killed large numbers of people in Cuba and wreaked havoc elsewhere in the Caribbean, was one of the most deadly hurricanes in history.

Flora next moved northwest toward Cuba. It slowed and stalled nearby on October 4, battering the island for nearly three days. As much as 20 inches of rain fell in some places, including Oriente and Camaquey, and a levee at the Canto River broke, causing a deadly flood. At least 1,000 people were thought to have died in Cuba and an estimated 175,000 were left homeless by Flora, though the government, under dictator Fidel Castro, was not forthcoming with detailed information. Cuban farmers also lost virtually their entire sugar and coffee crops for the season to the storm.[1]

In my second eight weeks of clerk school, I had the choice of signing up for (BAAC), the Basic Army Administrative Course, or (PASC), the Personnel Administrative Specialist Course. I enrolled in PASC, which is an advanced training course for personnel and was kind of like high school again, except we had ashtrays.

One of the classes was typing, but since I already knew how to type, it was pretty much of a breeze. Back then, I could actually type pretty well, but now it is practically a miracle that I can even write this book! I learned to type on a manual typewriter and you learned to strike the keys. An electric typewriter or a computer keyboard has a totally different touch so striking the keys doesn't work so well. I remember our typing instructor, Sergeant First Class Cawthorne, who was an elderly gentleman. He would always start out by saying "alright men" and then go through the drill: "KKKK space, LLLL space, MMMM space" and so on. It got pretty monotonous!

A lot of the other classes consisted of learning to fill out various forms included in the 201-file, which contained a soldier's entire Army history. When they got promoted, the paperwork would be in the file; if they got busted, same thing. Leaving a post and transferring to a new location, the date and location of departure and arrival would be recorded. This was a part of my job when I went to Germany.

There were no computers back then, so everything was on paper. Carbon paper was still used to make duplicate copies and stencils were used to make multiple copies. Copy machines had already been invented and XEROX Corporation had introduced them in 1959. IBM Electric typewriters had also been in service since the 1950's, but we didn't have the latest equipment so I never saw either during my time at personnel.

Barracks life was more relaxed in our second eight weeks of training, especially compared to the rigors of basic training. We didn't have any weapons, helmets, backpacks, or any of the equipment that we had in basic. We still had to wear our "Castro hats" and make our beds correctly. The possibility of a surprise inspection was a reality. The two dreaded inspections were: The IG (Inspector General) and the CMI (Command Maintenance Inspection). These inspections would usually consist of a full Colonel coming through and glancing around quickly before leaving. It seemed like kind of a joke to us, but you had to be ready just in case they actually conducted a thorough inspection.

In the morning we still fell out into formation in front of our barracks and we marched in formation to each class. We also had to do KP, which I did once. As usual, the mess sergeant was a grouch who would yell at me and the cook school students! Right next to our line of barracks was the cook school, so our mess hall was staffed by students learning to become cooks and the food was pretty good. Another mess hall detail was called Dining Room Orderly (DRO) which consisted of cleaning the tables, the salt and pepper shakers, sweeping and mopping the floor. At the time it wasn't that much fun, but as I look back, it was a great experience for young men because many of us were out of high school and had limited work experience. So while KP and DRO were kind of menial jobs, it was still teaching young men the value of work.

One of the great differences between basic training and clerk school was that the evenings were now considered free time and we could shoot pool, go bowling, or just relax. I always remember going to the pool room where we would shoot pool and listen to music. The one record album that we all loved was "James Brown at the Apollo," which we would listen to over and over while shooting pool. The most popular tune on the radio during my second eight weeks was "Deep Purple" by April Stevens and Nino Tempo, a brother and sister duet from Niagara Falls, New York. They were truly one of the great all time groups and extremely popular during the sixties. Hearing that song immediately brings me back to the fall of 1963.

We also got to go home on pass every weekend, of which I took full advantage. The bus ride from Fort Ord to San Jose was the opposite of when I traveled down from Oakland, both in terms of direction and mood. Instead of being apprehensive about what I would encounter in the Army, I now was through basic training and pretty well settled into army life. I would leave Saturday morning and return Sunday evening and they were still the shortest weekends I have ever spent!

An event occurred, which had a profound effect on me personally and the country; it was the beginning of America's loss of innocence and into upheaval. The day was Friday, November 22, 1963. It was at the end of my 7th week of training at the school, so I was close to graduating. We were in a classroom lab learning how to fill out one of the forms which are commonly found in the 201-file when our instructor came in with the following announcement: "We now have a new Chain of Command. President Kennedy has just been assassinated." You could have heard a pin drop in the room! The President is the Commander in Chief of all the armed forces and now he was gone. It was as if America had just been attacked. The news especially made me feel bad because the instructor announced it in such a matter of fact way, almost as if he really didn't care. Everybody was in a state of shock. I felt emotional grief, yet numbness and a sense that the world would now be changed forever. It was on this seemingly fitting gloomy overcast day that most of the Fort Ord post personnel gathered at the Parade Grounds, which was a huge open field. We stood at Parade Rest as a show of mourning and respect. I can remember seeing the funeral on TV and watching his son John-John with that famous and poignant salute. It was emotionally gut wrenching!

As far as attempting to figure out and comment on any of the conspiracies regarding the number of shooters involved; whether the Russians, Mafia, Johnson or the CIA were behind some kind of a plot; or the motivation of Lee Harvey Oswald himself, I am left with one impression: Lee Harvey Oswald was a very disturbed individual and a misfit who blamed others for his failures in life. He was also described as having no moral sense and a desire to be noticed as someone greater than he actually was in reality. He fit the perfect profile of somebody who would commit such a crime.

During the last week of school, each one of us received our orders as to where we would be assigned. I was assigned to the 2nd General Hospital in Landstuhl, West Germany. Everybody going overseas was required to receive a series of immunization shots, which was never fun. Back then, they used air guns which would inject a needle sized jet of the vaccine directly into the skin under high pressure, so the fluid actually functioned as the needle. The end of the gun barrel made contact with the skin. Sometimes, there would be blood as a result, yet they were in such a hurry they never seemed to always clean the end of the barrel with alcohol or apply it to the skin, so I'm sure the blood could have possibly come in contact with the next person in line. I wonder how many cases of Hepatitis may have been transmitted.

On Friday, November 29, 1963, I graduated from the Personnel Administrative Specialist Course and the next day I would depart from Fort Ord. I had completed my first seventeen weeks in the Army. Some notable events on that day included:

The establishment of the Warren Commission by President Johnson to investigate the assassination of President Kennedy; Trans-Canada Airlines Flight 831; A Douglas DC-8 carrying 118, crashed after taking-off from Dorval Airport near Montreal, Canada. There were no survivors; the Beatles released their first blockbuster single "I want to Hold Your Hand," which really began their enormous popularity and launched the "British Invasion." One year earlier, in the fall of 1962, they had a song out called "Please Please Me," which had moderate success, but it never began their break out in popularity in the U.S. I can remember thinking "The Beatles, what an odd name." After arriving in Germany, in early January of 1964, everybody was playing the record "I Want to Hold Your Hand" and the flip side "I Saw Her Standing There." It was the first time I had ever heard those songs and when I realized that it was the Beatles, I remembered that name from the previous year.

On Saturday morning, November thirtieth, my dad picked me up and I left Fort Ord for a two week leave before shipping out overseas. It was surreal being at home and yet still in the Army. I did a lot of the same things with my friends that I did before joining the Army, but it wasn't the same. I felt like I had lost the carefree feeling I had in high school; I had changed and was no longer the naïve kid who left home and joined the U.S. Army. I had lost my innocence, but there were those who would go to Vietnam and lose much more! America also began losing her innocence and the world would never be the same.

On Friday, December 13, 1963, my two week leave was over and I said goodbye to family and friends. I boarded a United Airlines jet at San Francisco International Airport for a five-hour flight to Idlewild International Airport (now JFK) in Queens, New York City. I took a bus to Fort Dix, New Jersey and arrived during a blizzard, and to me, it was the coldest place on earth! A week later, I departed from Brooklyn, New York for an eight day journey across the North Atlantic to West Germany and my overseas post. Fort Ord would shortly become a distant memory.

Diane and I were recently vacationing in Monterey, California and we decided to visit nearby Fort Ord. Fifty plus years had passed by since I had gone through my training there. Fort Ord is currently being used as a state university campus, national monument—military museum, and also part of the Monterey County Parks System. There are numerous hiking trails which are probably the same ones that I marched on while out in the field and during the 20-mile march. Going back there and hiking up those same trails is definitely on my "bucket list." But it would be another bittersweet experience because, although the long marches were a tortuous experience, it would bring me back to when I was young in a simpler time; a time that I sometimes still miss.

Some of the old army buildings at Fort Ord still remain and are in use, others are dilapidated and they will soon be demolished. The place had changed so much that when we found the location of my basic training company, it was almost unrecognizable. I was nostalgic and also sad at the same time. The whole area was surrounded by a cyclone fence. The barracks, which had been so painted and well maintained, were dilapidated and seemingly ready to fall down under their own weight. The once off-white beige paint with green trim was mostly peeled and exposing old and rotting wood. Tall weeds were growing out of cracks in the asphalt streets and the trees and shrubs were sad looking, some dying from the lack of care. The place was like something forlorn and abandoned that nobody cared about anymore.

Looking at the old barracks was sad because I realized how much time had passed since I was a young man. I had sweet memories of a time when my parents and many other loved ones were still alive. It was also a time when America was closer to God. Even though the experience of going through basic training was tough, I still cared about this place and what it represents—I had spent an important and formative part of my youth at Fort Ord.

Soon the old barracks will be torn down and a shiny new college classroom building or perhaps a dormitory will be built where the barracks once proudly stood. Nobody, except the soldiers who went through basic or served as permanent party, will remember that this place ever existed. It will simply be reduced to a museum experience. Only a few remnants of the old buildings still left will serve as a memory of a once great Army base. The vibrant and strong fighting men, who were our leaders back then, are now either long gone or very elderly. It makes you realize that life is a vapor which quickly evaporates. I was saying goodbye forever. When we departed, my eyes were brimming with tears.

Trails and Dunes

Long ago when I was young and a dollar was a dime

I marched along the trails and dunes in a simpler time

When America was strong and our flag was revered

We knew who we were and God was still feared

I think of the memories of times more benign.

The trails of sand and dirt are still there

With hikers and joggers everywhere

Where once they were trod by boots of men

In a more innocent time was then

But now the times are somehow a snare.

I looked at the highway and I was sad

I did not realize what I had

I wanted to be free from obligation

The discipline of serving the nation

But I was only a lad.

The memories remain of times long past

The years of change have gone by so fast

The innocent times have turned to upheaval

In many ways, they are increasingly evil

The simpler times could never last.

To the changes, nothing is immune

The existence of God, they now impugn

The old buildings have all come down

The trees and plants are turning brown

All that's left are trails and dunes.

The only cure for a world so sad

Is the good news for which I am glad

That God sent His Son to this earth

To give us hope through the new birth

Anything more, I cannot add.

JDF

June, 2018

Endnotes

[1] www.history.com/this-day-in-history/hurricane-devastates-haiti

Part Three

Beginning of America's Upheaval

Chapter Nine

The beginning of the Attack on the Freedom of Religion

America's Departure Away From God and Legislating through the Courts

America's upheaval began when it started moving away from God, specifically regarding the first major attack on the freedom of religion which happened during the 1960's. This event in history involving the schools had such a profound influence that it can scarcely be overstated. It began the long slide down a slippery slope in the direction of a secular-progressive society. Progressivism is the euphemistic term for leftism, but leftism is anything but progressive!

This significant event was the Supreme Court decision of Engel vs. Vitale (1962), which I believe signified the true beginning of America's upheaval. The left can't get its radical agenda passed through the legislature, so it uses the judiciary which was never intended to enact laws. This is why so many lawsuits occur every time the mainstream tries to prevent the left from pushing its agenda. Also, when a conservative candidate for the Supreme Court is offered, the left always oppose him or her, which explains the smear tactics used against Judge Brett Kavanaugh at his confirmation hearing. The left use lies and coercion in order to deny freedom of religion—whether it's a peaceful protest at an abortion clinic or refusing to bake a cake for a gay wedding.

Since this Supreme Court decision involved the schools, I must tell of an amazing aspect of my public school education. When I was in Grammar school in the 1950's, a notable program of public education was called "Religious Training." Many people today find it hard to believe that such a thing ever existed and was actually sanctioned by a public school district, especially in California! But when I was in the sixth grade (1956-1957), every Thursday afternoon a San Jose Unified School District bus would pick up kids to go and attend religious training. I was Roman Catholic so the bus would take the Catholic kids to the local Catholic Church for Catechism; the other kids would go to their respective places of worship; and those not affiliated with any religion would get a break. I wasn't interested in religious training or anything that had to do with church, but it sure was a great way to "get out of school" for an hour. But the existence of sanctioned religious training in public school during the 50's (and before) stands in stark contrast to today where such a sanctioning of religion in a public school (and many private schools) would be unthinkable and subject to a lawsuit!

The case of Engel vs. Vitale involved the recitation of prayer in public school, which had been challenged by a lawsuit and finally ended up in the Supreme Court. The First Amendment Establishment Clause states: "Congress shall make no law respecting an establishment of religion." In Engel vs. Vitale, the Court ruled that for public schools to hold an official recitation of prayers violated the Establishment Clause.

The main objection raised by some of the justices was probably the requirement of prayer in some states. In 1962, school prayer was common and thirteen states required daily prayer or even Bible reading in public schools. This was interpreted as being coercive and placing pressure on students who didn't practice religion. At that time, scripture reading or prayer was heavily biased in favor of Christianity; especially Christianity based on the Bible, which has always been the number one target of the secular left and still is today. This decision applied to any religion, but Christianity was clearly the dominant religion in America at that time. This was one of many other court actions throughout history that has pitted the left against traditional and Christian America—notably concerning gay rights, abortion, and the placing of religious symbols (especially Christian) in public locations. Of course, in my hometown of San Jose in the 1990's, no problem existed in the placing of a hideous bronze sculpture of Quetzalcoatl, an Aztec snake god, in a central downtown public square.

Justice Potter Stewart was the only dissenting vote in Engel vs. Vitale and the only one who got it right and properly discerned the true meaning of "separation of church and state." Justice Stewart's dissent stated that the Establishment Clause should not be used to prevent voluntary prayer at the beginning of the school day. He further said that the Establishment Clause was only meant to prevent the government from establishing a national religion, which was the original intent of the Establishment clause. The following is a word for word interpretation of the Establishment Clause which states that its purpose is to prevent the government from "respecting an establishment of religion." Justice Potter Stewart wrote:

I think the Court has misapplied a great constitutional principle. I cannot see how an "official religion" is established by letting those who want

*to say a prayer say it. On the contrary, I think that
to deny the wish of these school children to join in
reciting this prayer is to deny them the opportunity
of sharing in the spiritual heritage of our Nation.
He continued with excerpts from speeches made by
presidents of the United States from Washington to
Kennedy that made some sort of reference to God or
religion. He also used Jefferson's Second Inaugural
Address. On March 4, 1805, President Thomas
Jefferson said: ". . . I shall need, too, the favor of that
Being in whose hands we are, who led our fathers, as
Israel of old, from their native land and planted them
in a country flowing with all the necessaries and
comforts of life; who has covered our infancy with
His providence and our riper years with His wisdom
and power, and to whose goodness I ask you to join
in supplications with me that He will so enlighten
the minds of your servants, guide their councils, and
prosper their measures that whatsoever they do
shall result in your good, and shall secure to you the
peace, friendship, and approbation of all nations."[1]*

The vote, taken on June 25th, 1962, was six to one with
two abstentions. This decision was very unpopular with
many people across America and reflected the fact that, in
the early sixties, America was still largely a Christian nation or
at least considered religion a positive thing. Those opposed
to the decision argued that by taking away the prayer, the
court was taking away the option for students to practice
freedom of religion—a right stated in the First Amendment.
Over twenty states argued that a voluntary prayer before
school did not violate the Establishment Clause.

Again, the separation of church and state simply means
that a government cannot establish an "approved state
church or religion" like that which is done in the Middle

East, Cuba, China, or many other totalitarian countries. These totalitarian countries then declare all other religions illegal and the practice of other religions as punishable by prison or even death. In the Middle East, non-Muslims, especially Christians and Jews, are persecuted. In Cuba the approved church is the Roman Catholic Church, although the Castro's have tried to persecute Cubans who wish to openly practice their religion. In China, the approved religion for "Christianity" is officially state-sanctioned churches. "The Chinese Government has begun a renewed crackdown on believers attending unregistered churches and Christian parents taking their children with them to church. Chinese law strictly forbids adults to teach children religion and restricts Christian worship to the state-sanctioned Three-Self Church."[2] Chinese over the age of 18 are only permitted to join officially sanctioned government registered Christian groups sanctioned by China Christian Council.

But true Bible-based Conservative Christianity in China, Cuba, and many other countries is persecuted and virtually forced underground. Thus, Bibles are often confiscated and need to be smuggled into many countries. This is the very coercion that the Establishment Clause meant to prevent. Allowing prayer in a public school simply doesn't come close to the establishing of a coercive state religion. Contrast the authoritarian countries mentioned with the situation here in the U.S. with the right to practice any religion of one's choosing, including the right to not practice any religion at all. So to compare sanctioned prayer in school with the coercive policies of evil totalitarian regimes is ridiculous.

Regarding groups that advocate the separation of church and state, it depends on the agenda as to how "separation of church and state" is defined: a traditional mainstream definition is the separation of government from religion, especially from a mandatory state-sponsored religion as previously mentioned in this chapter. That is the correct definition. A progressive leftist position would be the banning of all religion (except possibly Islam) from any government institutions, including the schools.

This Supreme Court decision was a classic example of what we see too often today: a few people get offended so everybody else has to suffer. But amazingly enough, faith based activity including prayer is once again common in schools today and many school related religious activities take place outside of the school. As long as the prayer is not "officially" sanctioned by the school district (like it was during the 1950's and before), it now apparently is OK, although freedom from faith groups are still fighting against any religious activity in the schools (or even by outside student groups). Students of all faiths are allowed to pray, even aloud or in groups, as long as it doesn't disrupt class or school events. Faculty and staff, however, are not allowed to lead or even participate in student prayer. But critics still maintain that by not sanctioning school prayer, the Supreme Court still effectively kicked God out of the schools and succeeded in getting rid of a long-standing tradition of recognition of the importance of God.

It is important to note that school prayer technically was not banned by Engel vs. Vitale, but practically, it resulted with the schools getting rid of all religion because of the fear of reprisal:

"In two landmark decisions – Engel v. Vitale on June 25, 1962, and Abington School District v. Schempp on June 17, 1963 – the Supreme Court declared school-sponsored prayer and Bible readings unconstitutional. The rulings provoked unprecedented controversy, says Melissa Deckman,

affiliated scholar with the Public Religion Research Institute in Washington, D.C. "School boards got so paranoid about dealing with religion that they just said, 'We shouldn't do any of that at all,' "she says. Schools struck religion from curricula, teachers avoided the topic, and children got the message that religion took place off campus. But then, Professor Deckman explains, people began "to say, 'Look, religion is part of who we are and our culture.' "Yes, the rulings restricted public school employees – but what about students? Could they say grace in the cafeteria or meet outside class to study the Bible, Quran, or Torah? Could religious organizations offer after-school programs? While teachers couldn't preach, could they address religion academically? In court case after court case, the answer was a resounding yes"[3]

But addressing religion academically has also created a new controversy—the claim that the schools are teaching Islam (even the practice of it) and other religions, but excluding Christianity. Whether these claims are true or not, one thing is clear: there is a polarization between those who reject all religion, those who only accept Christianity, and those who advocate the acceptance of all religions as good.

Many Christians even make the claim that the turning away from God largely began with the Engel vs. Vitale Supreme Court decision and has resulted in the gradual removal of God's blessing from America. They further claim that removal of God's blessing can explain much of the serious problems that America has dealt with in the last 55 years, both internationally and domestically. The Bible tells us that even God's beloved Israel, "the Apple of God's eye" (Zechariah 2:8) was judged after they fell away from God and turned to their own way.

It's interesting to note that shortly after this decision in 1962, the Vietnam War and racial rioting in the cities began which was America's greatest trial in the 1960's. Another decision, Roe vs. Wade in 1973 legalizing abortion was followed by the oil embargos and trouble in the Middle East, culminating the 1970's with the rise of radicals in Iran and the taking of American hostages.

This subject of God possibly removing His blessing from America will be further discussed in Chapter 20.

Endnotes

[1] https//www.pbs.org/Jefferson/enlight/prayer/htm

[2] Morning Star News-Morningstarnews.org, idem Israel My Glory Magazine, -Jan-Feb 2018, p.8-Friends of Israel Gospel Ministry, Inc., P.O. Box 908, Bellmawr, NJ 08099.

[3] https://www.csmonitor.com/.../School-prayer-50-years-after-the-ban-God-and-faith, June 16, 2013...Melissa Deckman, affiliated scholar with the Public Religion Research Institute in Washington, D.C.

Chapter Ten
Vietnam

The following content of this chapter tells of America's long involvement in Vietnam and why the war was fought. My comments are by no means the complete story, but I believe they give an overview of the world events leading up to the Vietnam War. While we in the armed forces were aware of Vietnam, the civilian population in America was largely unaware of what was happening before the Gulf of Tonkin incident in 1964, and the war's further escalation in 1965. So this chapter is my attempt to make sense of Vietnam in relation to the time period covered in this book; it mostly deals with the history involved and the early years of the war.

During our basic and second eight weeks of training at Fort Ord, those in charge constantly threatened us concerning the possibility of being sent to Vietnam. Any screw-up committed would be followed by the threat: "you're going to Vietnam." The threats continued even after I was through with my sixteen weeks of training and then stationed at my permanent post overseas. At the time period of my Fort Ord training in 1963, we weren't "officially" fighting in Vietnam, but it was understood that we were involved. American military advisors and special-forces were already present there in support of the South Vietnamese government. We all thought it was a foregone conclusion that America would be fully involved fighting in Vietnam, which turned out to be correct. In 1964, the year after my training at Fort Ord, the American involvement in Vietnam and the casualties suffered began to significantly increase. "The Vietnam War was a long, costly armed conflict that pitted the communist regime of North Vietnam and its southern allies, known as the Viet Cong, against South Vietnam and its principal ally, the United States. The North Vietnamese government and the Viet Cong were fighting to reunify Vietnam. They viewed the conflict as a colonial war and a continuation of the First Indochina War against forces from France and later on the United States. ... Beginning in 1950, American military advisors arrived in what was then French Indochina."[1]

The root cause of America's involvement in the Vietnam War, both in a support role and later in a combat fighting role, revolved around the belief that Communism was threatening to expand all over Southeast Asia and beyond. It was called the "Domino Theory" and it was believed that if one domino fell to Communism, such as Vietnam, then the rest of Southeast Asia would fall to Communism. The communist takeover of China in 1949 under Mao-tse-Tung and the bitter war in Korea (1950-1953), which was fought to prevent a communist takeover of Korea, gave a lot of credence to this Domino Theory. President Eisenhower promised American support to Ngo Dinh Diem, who was the new Prime Minister of the Bao Dai government in October of 1954. The purpose of American support of Diem was in order to ensure a non-communist Vietnam. Following through on that commitment, American aid to South Vietnam actually began as early as January, 1955. "In addition to the United States, South Vietnam was backed by anti-communist countries and members of the South East Asia Treaty

Organization (SEATO) which included the United States, South Korea, Australia, the Philippines, New Zealand, Thailand, Khmer Republic (later overthrown by Khmer Rouge), Kingdom of Laos and Republic of China (Taiwan)."[2]

I can remember hearing the term "French Indo China" in the news while growing up in the 1950's. "The Vietnam War was the result of the First Indochina War (1946–1954). France, who had ruled Vietnam for one-hundred years and wanted to continue holding on to Vietnam as their colony, fought the communist Viet Minh forces led by Ho Chi Minh. Ho Chi Minh was the leader of the communist forces of Vietnam. He grew up anti-colonial and anti-French. He died nearly six years before his forces succeeded in reuniting North and South Vietnam under communist rule. Saigon, the capital of South Vietnam, was renamed Ho Chi Minh City after it fell to the Communists in 1975."[3] The French were defeated and forced to leave Vietnam In July, 1954. "Nationalist forces under the direction of General Vo Nguyen Giap trounced the allied French troops at the remote mountain outpost of Dien Bien Phu in the northwest corner of Vietnam. The Battle of Dien Bien Phu was the decisive engagement in the first Indochina War (1946–54). After French forces occupied the Dien Bien Phu valley in late 1953, Viet Minh commander Vo Nguyen Giap amassed troops and placed heavy artillery in caves of the mountains overlooking the French camp. Boosted by Chinese aid, Giap mounted assaults on the opposition's strong points beginning in March 1954, eliminating use of the French airfield. Viet Minh forces overran the base in early May, prompting the French government to seek an end to the fighting with the signing of the Geneva Accords of 1954."[4]

The defeat of the French forces at Dien Bien Phu led to France's withdrawal from Indochina and the separation of Vietnam at the 17th parallel into North and South Vietnam. "However, a second Indochina war would begin in 1956 which would include American forces and would eventually escalate into the Vietnam War."[5]

The Vietnam War was really a "proxy" war in the Cold War. The Soviet Union and the United States could not risk directly going to war because of the threat of nuclear annihilation, but each supported a different side. The Soviets supported North Vietnam. They also supported the Viet Cong—Vietnamese rebels in the South who fought against the South Vietnamese government and the United States. During both the Eisenhower and Kennedy administrations, thousands of U.S. military advisers were sent to South Vietnam to train the Vietnamese military forces. Also, hundreds of millions of dollars in military and economic assistance had already been given to South Vietnam.

Ngo Dinh Diem, president of South Vietnam was Roman Catholic and a staunch anti-communist who refused to ally himself with Ho Chi Minh. Instead, he supported the U.S. backed government and made himself president in 1955. He was a corrupt dictator and it was the classic example of America supporting a dictatorship as the "lesser of the two evils," when compared to Communism.

Tran Le Xuan, known as Madame Nhu, was the First Lady of South Vietnam even though she was not married to Diem, but rather, she was actually the wife of Ngo Dình Nhu, who was the brother and chief-advisor to President Ngo Dinh Diem. But since she and her family lived in the Palace together with Diem, she was considered to be the first lady. Tran Le Xuan was power hungry, arrogant, and was known for her outspoken and incendiary rhetoric, especially when attacking the Buddhist community along with the American presence in the country. She was forced into living in exile in France after her husband and her brother-in-law, Ngo Dinh Diem, were both assassinated in 1963.

President Diem had initiated a brutal crack-down on protests by Buddhists against his government, which was largely Roman Catholic. He imprisoned and murdered hundreds of Buddhists, causing the U.S. to remove its support. Buddhist protests had also included gruesome immolations causing great fear and revulsion in the U.S. Also, the U.S. was concerned that the Diem government was failing. President Diem was overthrown and killed in a coup d'etat taking place on November 2, 1963 in Saigon by a military junta headed by General Duong Van Minh. General Minh then replaced Diem as president. Of course, it is believed that all this was done with the tacit approval, or at least acquiescence of the United States. Three weeks later, President John F. Kennedy was assassinated and Lyndon B. Johnson then became President of the United States. Johnson didn't make any immediate changes to Kennedy's policies, or his team of policy advisers on Vietnam. However, an incident in the Gulf of Tonkin occurred which led to the eventual escalation of the war.

"On 2 August 1964, North Vietnamese patrol torpedo boats attacked the USS Maddox (DD-731) while the destroyer was in international waters in the Gulf of Tonkin. There is no doubting that fact."[6] However, the North Vietnamese claimed that the destroyer was in their territorial waters. On August 4, two more U.S. destroyers reported that they were under attack. In response to this second attack on American warships, President Lyndon B. Johnson authorized retaliatory air attacks against North Vietnam. He also asked Congress to pass the Gulf of Tonkin Resolution. Congress passed the Gulf of Tonkin Resolution on August 7, 1964, authorizing President Johnson to take any measures he believed were necessary to retaliate against North Vietnam and to assist any Southeast Asian country whose government was thought to be jeopardized by communist aggression. It greatly expanded the president's powers for

an eventual major escalation of the war in 1965. "This resolution declared, 'The United States regards as vital to its national interest and to world peace the maintenance of international peace and security in Southeast Asia.' The House
passed the resolution by a unanimous vote; the vote in the
Senate was 98 to 2. Johnson's popularity soared in response
to his "restrained" handling of the crisis. The Johnson administration went on to use the resolution as an excuse to
begin heavy bombing of North Vietnam in early 1965."[7] On
March 8, 1965, the Marines came ashore north of Da- Nang
and represented the first "official" American combat troops
to land in Vietnam. The escalation was now fully underway.
Casualties suffered in Vietnam were huge: One out of every
10 Americans who served in Vietnam was a casualty. 58,148
were killed and 304,000 wounded out of 2.7 million who
served. Although the percent that died is similar to other
wars, amputations or crippling wounds were 300 percent
higher than in World War II. 75,000 Vietnam veterans are
severely disabled.[8]

In 1995, Vietnam released its official estimate of their
war dead: as many as 2 million civilians on both sides and
some 1.1 million North Vietnamese and Viet Cong fighters.
It has also been estimated by U.S. sources that between
200,000 to 250,000 South Vietnamese soldiers died in the
war.

The question is always asked: "who won the war?" In terms
of the final objective of keeping Vietnam from going communist, the U.S. lost. But in terms of who won militarily, the
U.S. clearly won. It was a case of largely winning in battle,
but losing the war. A perfect example is the 1968 Tet Offensive which was a costly, but crushing defeat for the communists:

*"The first phase of the assault began on January 30
and 31, when NLF forces simultaneously attacked a*

114

*number of targets, mostly populated areas and plac-
es with heavy U.S. troop presence. The strikes on the
major cities of Huế and Saigon had a strong psycho-
logical impact, as they showed that the NLF troops
were not as weak as the Johnson Administration
had previously claimed. The NLF even managed to
breach the outer walls of the U.S. Embassy in Saigon.
Although the first phase of the offensive became the
most famous, a second phase also launched simul-
taneous assaults on smaller cities and towns on May
4 and stretched into June. A third phase began in
August and lasted six weeks. In the months that followed, U.S. and South Vietnamese forces retook the
towns that the NLF had secured over the course of
the offensive, but they incurred heavy military and
civilian casualties in the process.*

*At the end of the Tet Offensive, both sides had
endured losses, and both sides claimed victory. The
U.S. and South Vietnamese military response almost
completely eliminated the NLF forces and regained
all of the lost territory. At the same time, the Tet Offensive weakened domestic support for the Johnson
Administration as the vivid reporting on the Tet Offensive by the U.S. media made clear to the American public that an overall victory in Vietnam was not
imminent.*

*The aftermath of Tet brought public discussions
about de-escalation, but not before U.S. generals
asked for additional troops for a wide-scale "accelerated pacification program." Believing that the U.S.
was in a position to defeat the North, these military
leaders sought to press for a U.S.-South Vietnam offensive. Johnson and others, however, read the situation differently. Johnson announced that the bombing of North Vietnam would cease above the 20th*

parallel and placed a limit on U.S. troops in South Vietnam. Johnson also attempted to set parameters for peace talks, but it would be several more years before these came to fruition. Within the United States, protests against continued involvement in Vietnam intensified. On March 31, 1968, Johnson announced that he would not seek a second term as president. The job of finding a way out of Vietnam was left to the next U.S. president, Richard Nixon.[9]

It is interesting how the economy of Vietnam has fared under Communism. Although they initially tried to stay true to the economic principles of Lenin and Marx, Vietnam soon discovered that the Communist-Socialist economic principles simply didn't work and had to adopt some capitalistic principles in order to survive like other communist countries including Red China. A change in economic policy was finally instituted in 1986 when the Vietnamese government introduced a series of economic and political reforms known as "Doi Moi" (Renovation). Doi Moi was an attempt to revive the economy that had been held back by three decades of war and another decade of a post-war economic crisis. Doi Moi policies shifted the planned centralized economy into the so-called "socialist-oriented market economy," which is a multi-sectoral market economy. Private enterprise, the lessening of control, and foreign investment were now encouraged. Vietnam, since implementing these free-market reforms in the mid-1980s, has become one of the world's fastest growing economies with the goal of becoming a modern and industrialized nation by 2020.

What we can take away from the Vietnam War is that it was micromanaged by the so-called "brain trust" in Washington instead of letting our armed forces fully fight—including beyond the borders of North and South Vietnam into enemy sanctuaries in Laos and Cambodia, although escalation beyond Vietnam later occurred under Richard Nixon. As the war dragged on, it became more and more unpopular with the American public. Much of the violence taking place on college campuses in the 1960's and into the early 1970's was because of the war. We may have been able to militarily defeat North Vietnam and end the war much sooner, but our leaders no longer had the will to continue the fighting. "Basically the Vietnamese wanted to win more than the Americans did. There were a couple of reasons for this. First, the Americans were an invading force, and the Vietnamese were fighting on their own soil. Second, the Americans were not willing to make an all-out commitment to win."[10] We were also worried about retaliation by the Soviets or Chinese and possibly starting World War III.

It was also an impossible situation because there was not a clear definition of victory short of the complete annihilation of North Vietnam. Lack of a clear definition of victory is a similar problem regarding our wars in the Middle East. We were fighting an enemy on their own turf under conditions favorable to them. In spite of that, our troops fought bravely and militarily won the war but lost the "political war" and, when all is said and done, we could not prevent Vietnam from turning Communist.

A black marble Vietnam monument plaque in Downtown San Jose, similar to the one located in Washington, D.C., lists the names of 242 soldiers from San Jose killed in the Vietnam War. The name of the monument is "Sons of San Jose." I remember three who were high school classmates that are on that memorial: Rudy Melendez (who lived one street over from me); Bill Palenske, and Larry Williams. I also remember Jimmy Curry, who was a real nice kid whom I knew from elementary school.

Endnotes

[1]   https://www.archives.gov/research/military/vietnam-war/ca-sualty-statistics.html

[2] www.historynet.com/vietnam-war

[3] www.historylearningsite.co.uk/vietnam-war/ho-chi-minh/

[4] www.history.com/topics/battle-of-dien-bien-phu

[5] Ibid.

[6] https://www.usni.org/magazines/navalhistory/2008-02/truth-about-tonkin

[7] This Day in History, August 7, 1964

[8] The Vietnam Conflict Extract Data File of the Defense Casualty Analysis System (DCAS)

[9] The Tet Offensive, 1968 - Office of the Historianhttps://history.state.gov/milestones/1961-1968/tet

[10] www.slate.com/blogs/quora/2014/11/.../why_did_america_lose_the_vietnm_war.htm...Tony Morse Managing Partner of the Spatial Analysis Group

Part Four

America's Current Upheaval: The Left

Chapter Eleven

The Left: An Overview

Five years ago, if I had read much of the contents covered in the next ten chapters I would have probably dismissed it as conspiracy theory. But the last four years of the Trump presidency and the left's efforts to unseat him convinced me that we have entered an era of a stepped-up internal attack against our country. The left decided that Trump had to go at all costs because his policies of America First are anathema to the left who basically want fundamental change and the destruction of America as we know it today. These are strong words, but the left's desire for fundamental change basically boils down to freedom vs. totalitarianism. Loss of all our fundamental freedom is the direction our country is heading and the current targets are the freedom of speech, religion, assembly, and the right to bear arms.

The left are the single most insidious force in America and throughout the world and behind the tumult and division which began in the 1960's. Prior to the 1960's, the Left have mostly been associated with the Communist attempt to infiltrate America. The left of today are still breeding discord in the streets, but have also entered the courts, the media, pop culture, wall Street, high-tech and other industry, schools and universities, and politics at a greater rate than ever. The left are much more dangerous today.

This chapter introduces the core beliefs of Leftism, but it's important to make a distinction between a true radical leftist mentality, leftist leaning, and a liberal: a true or radical leftist mentality loves power, hates freedom, hates America, and will do anything possible to fundamentally change America into an authoritarian ruled nation; a leftist leaning person, while believing the core beliefs of Leftism that America needs to be fundamentally changed, does stop short of advocating the overthrowing of the existing government establishing authoritarian rule—even though fundamentally changing America in a leftist direction will achieve that; a liberal misguidedly believes a lot of the core beliefs of leftism, but believes in change through convincing people rather than coercing, loves the country, and believes in its institutions. Liberals today are now more often defined as "moderates" while Leftists are now mistakenly defined as "Liberals." I believe that leftism has become a more common view than it was fifty years ago largely because of indoctrination from the media and academia.

Apolitical people are also influenced by the media and academia so if one is apolitical but reads the typical newspaper, watches CNN, MSNBC, PBS, or network news and has at least one college degree, they will probably be somewhat to the left. On the other hand, an apolitical person who listens to Fox News or talk radio will tend to be more to the right. Conservative influences such as some commentators on Fox news and talk radio, especially Rush Limbaugh, Dennis Prager, Larry Elder, Mark Levin, and others have pushed back against leftism.

All of these are general observations, because family upbringing and where one was raised also factor in, so all of this isn't written in stone. Also, people are unique individuals, which is something the left don't understand. Liberals and apolitical people actually have much in common with conservatives, and nothing in common with leftism. Stay tuned!

This is a very tough part of the book for me to write because the entire chapter unavoidably involves politics. I genuinely dislike arguing the subject of politics, so I also don't enjoy writing about it either—especially because it's now so divisive in America. In some cases, family members or friends have stopped speaking to each other because of their vote in the 2016 Presidential Election. So because of this present toxic political atmosphere in our country, I actually considered not including the subject of politics in this book. I figured that, since it is a nice and somewhat informative story about my Army experience and how America was in the early 1960's, why ruin it by discussing politics? But since this book covers the time immediately before and during the beginning of the rapid rise of political and social upheaval in America, it is necessary and relevant to the theme of this book: the end of my innocence, but more importantly, the end of America's innocence into upheaval. So, according to the book's context, it is simply impossible to omit writing about politics. People whom I know and care about may disagree with me, but I hope they don't disown or "cancel" me because of my political beliefs. I have to speak what I believe to be the truth, which is largely based on studying U.S. History in school and living through this era, even though some may consider my views politically repugnant.

Unfortunately, the political climate of today has also made me more cynical regarding politics and politicians than I was ten years ago. It seems to me that politics and staying in office, rather than the welfare of the country, is the most important consideration with many of our so-called leaders on both sides of the aisle.

H.L. Mencken (9-12-1880—1-29-1956) was a journalist, English scholar, satirist, and unrelenting critic of American culture and those who were its prominent citizens. He was sometimes known as the "bad boy of Baltimore" for his ill-tempered and irascible cutting style of writing. Mencken wrote the following about politicians:

> *"The typical lawmaker of today is a man wholly de-*
> *void of principle - a mere counter in a grotesque and*
> *knavish game. If the right pressure could be applied*
> *to him, he would be cheerfully in favor of polygamy,*
> *astrology, or cannibalism."*[1]

I can identify with Mencken's views on politics and politicians although I'm probably less extreme. His writings were often viewed as rants and diatribes containing very insulting rhetorical statements that were considered not very profound by critics. However, his caustic comments were also quite amusing; political correctness did not exist in his day. While some may consider his comments as hyperbole and a little over the top, I wonder what Mencken would say about politics and politicians today?

I was raised in a home that taught me that the Democratic Party is the party of the "little guy" and the Republican Party is the party of "the rich." I don't believe that anymore and my reasons will become quite clear later on in this book. My parents always voted democratic and I did too until the Presidential Election of 1992. Even though most Democrats are probably liberal, the Democratic Party is no longer the liberal party, but has become the party of the left. Presidents Franklin Delano Roosevelt, Harry S. Truman, John Fitzgerald Kennedy, Lyndon B. Johnson, and James Earl (Jimmy) Carter Jr. would not be welcome in today's Democratic Party. I'm not even sure about Bill Clinton, except for his electability.

Even though most Democrats are not true leftists, the agenda of the Democratic Party has decidedly become more and more radical leftist and has become the party of

Barack H. Obama, who ideologically is certainly leftist leaning and possibly even a true leftist. He wanted to fundamentally change America. Michelle Obama said after her husband's election that "for the first time I am proud of my country." Obama's policies and appointments had definitely moved America to the left. This partly explains the election of Donald J. Trump—because most of America is still center-right. Donald Trump was seen as a flawed candidate, but he was the only one who could have won the election of 2016 instead of moderate "Republicans" such as a John McCain or Mitt Romney. The country was ready for a change from Obama's leftism which Trump articulated in his "America First" campaign. As we shall later see, leftism puts America and nationalism last in favor of globalism.

So Trump's election was far more than the fact that he was an outsider, rather than a Washington establishment politician, or that Hillary Clinton was a terrible candidate. Trump's victory was a repudiation of the eight years of leftist policies which would've continued under Hillary Clinton: government control of health care and most everything else; confiscatory taxes; wealth re-distribution; economy killing over-regulation; reducing the military; globalism and loss of American sovereignty through the subservience to the U.N. and ridiculous international climate treaties such as the Kyoto protocol and the Paris accord; weakness towards China, Iran, and other enemies; open borders in order to destroy America's language, identity, and culture; having people dependent on the government (a goal of leftism); and abortion on demand.

Obama was first elected because he was a historical figure, the first black president; he was reelected because he was still carefully portrayed as a moderate by the media and not seen as a leftist, even though his leftism should have been obvious by 2012.

Barack Obama wanted to fundamentally change the present day America we know and turn it into a European type socialist state. So his agenda essentially destroys America and creates a new and different nation. His leftist agenda did harm to the country, but I don't believe he can be placed in the same category as the many true-leftist mentality dictators throughout history. The difference between a true murderous leftist mentality and just leftist leaning ideology involves intent; how that leader uses power and what he or she is willing to do in order to achieve his or her aims. Leftist policies can do harm to a nation, but someone who is truly an evil person and applies the principles of leftism in a ruthless manner always results in not only a changed nation, but a massive loss of life and freedom.

Three major examples of evil people with a true-leftist mentality and a commitment to enforce leftist policies are Adolph Hitler, Vladimir Lenin, and Mao Tse dung. All were initially considered leftists because they overthrew the existing government. Adolph Hitler replaced Paul Von Hindenburg and the Weimar Republic, Lenin overthrew the Czar, and Chairman Mao overthrew Chang Kai-shek. But the fact that they took power and then became the establishment did not suddenly make these men right-wing. Their basic ideology was always leftist: a totalitarian mentality relying on lies, demagoguery, and coercion in order to control the masses. Fidel Castro, Joseph Stalin, Vladimir Putin, Pol Pot, Idi Amin, Robert Mugabe, Kim Jong Il, Hideki Tojo, the Mullahs, and many more can also be added to this list. So, regardless of whether the terms of Totalitarianism, Authoritarianism, Communism, Socialism, Nazism, or Fascism are used—they all can be attributed to the mentality of the left, because the basic deeds of the left are lies, coercion, totalitarianism, and the taking away of guns, Bibles, individual freedoms, especially freedom of speech and religion. History has already proven that fact. If leftism ever becomes the majority view in this country, that sets up the possibility for another Hitler.

I always considered myself a liberal until I began listening to conservative talk radio in October of 1988. At first I hated it and it made me angry listening to the various host's comments which were against everything I believed, or at least what I thought was true. I especially couldn't stand Rush Limbaugh because I thought he was a blowhard and very insulting to people. But I couldn't stop listening to him or Lee Rogers from KGO in San Francisco and a few of the others because these conservative guys were making a lot of sense. I eventually started having a few "aha" moments and finally realized that I was more of a conservative than a liberal. But I actually found that my views were totally incompatible, not with conservatism or liberalism, but with leftism.

The Difference between the Mainstream and Leftism

With all the previous comments said, one of the purposes of this chapter is to bring some perspective in the political debate and also to clear up many misunderstandings between blue state-red state, conservatism, liberalism, and leftism. It's important to know the difference between leftism and conservatism/liberalism (the mainstream) because they're more than just labels. These viewpoints represent opposing positions in America which have very different visions for the country. Notice that I did not refer to the left as liberalism. That's because the term liberalism has been taken over by the left.

On every major issue and foundational belief, vast differences exist between conservatism/liberalism and the left. Much of the following discussion is based on the very important 2017 article by Dennis Prager entitled—'What is the difference between a leftist and a liberal?' Prager is a nationally syndicated radio talk show host and lecturer out of Los Angeles. His thesis is basically that conservatives and liberals have much in common, but neither have anything in common with the left. Knowing the difference between conservatism/liberalism and leftism is vitally important in understanding the important issues of today.

Race

Leftists don't see people as individuals, but as victims of the rich; especially those of white European ancestry—therefore, racial minorities are victims instead of unique individuals with dreams, potential, and talents. Today this "racism" is referred to as white privilege. The so called white supremacist conspiracy or white privilege is nothing more than a fabrication of the left, who are the true racists because they see people in terms of their race, along with class, and gender. They are obsessed with race and the main target of their racism is whites, especially white men. As a conservative, I'm not obsessed with race because I see people as individuals rather than a member of a group. "The essence of the liberal position on race was that the color of one's skin is insignificant. To liberals of a generation ago, only racists believed that race is intrinsically significant. However, to the left, the notion that race is insignificant is itself racist. Thus, the University of California officially regards the statement, 'There is only one race, the human race,' as racist. Liberals were passionately committed to racial integration. Liberals should be sickened by the existence of black dormitories and separate black graduations on university campuses."[2]

Capitalism

The left despise capitalism because they see it as the oppression of the poor where only white people can get ahead and the rest of the people are held down. In reality, they don't care about the poor or any other victim groups, they simply use them to attain power through divide and conquer. Actually, leftist ruled countries around the world are the true oppressors of people where most everybody is poor except the ruling class elites. Here in the Western Hemisphere, Venezuela and Cuba are two of the most blatant examples.

"Liberals have always been pro-capitalism, recognizing it for what it is: the only economic means of lifting great numbers out of poverty. Liberals did often view government as able to play a bigger role in lifting people out of poverty more than conservatives, but they were never opposed to capitalism, and they were never for socialism. Opposition to capitalism and advocacy of socialism are leftist values."[3]

Nationalism

Why did the leftist Obama administration support such things as sanctuary cities, opposition to ICE rounding up illegal aliens, advocating the program of catch and release, and not protecting our southern border? Because leftism fundamentally believes in globalism and hates the idea of nations, flags, national anthems, and borders. According to the left, nationalism really means white supremacy and racism. Many liberals advocate the helping of immigrants through sanctuary cities because they sincerely believe in helping people from other countries enjoy the blessing of America, but they don't recognize that the Sanctuary City policy is misguided and illegal. But leftists don't care one iota for these people; they simply use them as pawns in their game of making America a poor third world country controllable by them and more representative of the third world's racial, ethnic, and cultural diversity—in other words, make America poorer and less white and more dependent on government. Conservatives and liberals are not obsessed with race and class like the left are and mostly believe that a less white America is neither good nor bad. But the left's ingrained racism demands America being less white. In fact, the Left want to destroy America and believe that flooding it with non-whites will do that, which is in itself, racist.

I know lots of liberals and realize they are not leftists at all; they are decent people who love this country as great, unique, and free. "Liberals deeply believed in the nation-state, whether their nation was the United States, Great Britain, or France. The left have always opposed national-ism because leftism is rooted in class solidarity, not national solidarity. The left have contempt for nationalism, seeing in it intellectual and moral primitivism at best, and the road to fascism at worst. Liberals always wanted to protect Ameri-can sovereignty and borders. The notion of open borders would have struck a liberal as just as objectionable as it does a conservative.

It is emblematic of our time that the left-wing writers of Superman comics had Superman announce a few years ago, 'I intend to speak before the United Nations tomorrow and inform them that I am renouncing my American citizenship.' When the writers of Superman were liberal, Superman was not only an American but one who fought for 'truth, jus-tice, and the American way.' But in his announcement, he explained that motto is 'not enough anymore.'"[4] Again, the left are global in their outlook and hate the idea of borders, language, and a distinct American culture.

View of America

"The left's view of America was encapsulated in then-pres-idential candidate Barack Obama's statement in 2008. 'We are five days away from fundamentally transforming the United States of America,' he said. Now, if you were to meet

a man who said that he wanted to fundamentally transform his wife, or a woman who said that about her husband, would you assume that either loved their spouse? Of
course not."[5] The people applauding Obama's speech about
fundamentally transforming America were even more con-
temptible than President Obama's speech because of their
ignorance of how fortunate they are to live in America and
how a fundamental change towards Obama's leftist policies
will make America a less desirable place to live.

In the past, the liberal media had a patriotic attitude towards America, even though they were often critical of its
faults. "Liberals venerated America. Watch American films
from the 1930s through the 1950s and you will be watching overtly patriotic, America-celebrating films—virtually all
produced, directed, and acted in by liberals. Liberals well
understand that America is imperfect, but they agree with
a liberal icon named Abraham Lincoln that America is "the
last best hope of earth." To the left, America is essentially
racist, sexist, violent, homophobic, xenophobic, and Islamophobic. The left around the world loathe America, and it is
hard to imagine why the American left would differ in this
one way from fellow leftists around the world."[6]

Leftists often take offense at having their so-called love of
America doubted, but those previously mentioned left-wing
descriptions of America are reason enough to assume that
the left have more contempt than love for America. Therefore, one unmistakable characteristic of the left is their hatred and contempt for America. Liberals and conservatives
don't hate America—they both see it as the best country on
earth, in spite of its flaws.

Free Speech

To the left, free speech is only allowed for those who agree
with their agenda. Therefore, anyone who opposes the leftist agenda is demonized, shouted down, accused of hate

speech or racism, and not allowed to express their point of view. One of the greatest examples of leftist behavior and thought (besides the editorial page of the New York Times) is on our university campuses, which were once places for the exchange of ideas in teaching students to think critically and decide for themselves. But in recent history, many of our schools and universities have been poisoned by leftism and intolerance towards anything that counters their dogma. When a conservative speaker, such as Ann Coulter or Ben Shapiro, is invited by a university to address the students they are shouted down and not allowed to continue. That's because the left don't want any opposing viewpoints and seek to destroy and vilify those who oppose them. Many of those students who oppose free speech rights of conservative speakers with whom they disagree are probably not true leftists, but they have simply been brainwashed by the many leftist professors in our universities today. They are useful pawns of the Left who call the conservative speakers haters and fascists, but in reality, that describes the mentality of the left; the true haters and ones who force their views on others. When I was in college, some of my professors were leftist, some liberal, and a very few conservative, but the one unmistakable characteristic of the leftist professors was their hatred and contempt for America and conservatives.

None of this is to say that all young people, especially college students, are indoctrinated. America still has a lot of amazing young people and, fortunately, most students, whether they are liberal or conservative, just want to get their degree and don't really have time for such nonsense. We have many young people in this country, whether they attend college or not, who go into the military, become police, firefighters, medical and other front-line workers, teachers, small business owners, hotel and restaurant workers, drive trucks, stock grocery shelfs, pick up garbage, work in business and industry, non-profits, and many other occupations that make the country work.

"The difference between the left and liberals regarding free speech is as dramatic as the difference regarding race. No one was more committed than American liberals to the famous statement, 'I disapprove of what you say, but I will defend to the death your right to say it.' Liberals still are. But the left are leading the first nationwide suppression of free speech in American history—from the universities to Google to almost every other institution and place of work. It claims to only oppose hate speech, but protecting the right of person A to say what person B deems objectionable is the entire point of free speech."[7] So called hate speech is not demonstrated through quoting the Bible or expressing conservative values.

Judaism and Christianity

Leftists hate Christianity and America's Judeo-Christian foundation. Leftist thought, which is post-modern, hates the whole idea of God. "Liberals knew and appreciated the Judeo-Christian roots of American civilization. They themselves went to church or synagogue, or at the very least appreciated that most of their fellow Americans did. The contempt that the left has—and has always had—for religion (except for Islam today) is not something with which a liberal would ever have identified.[8] The left's biggest enemy and their object of hate and contempt are those who possess traditional values, especially Bible-believing Christians. The Bible says, for example, that abortion, homosexuality, and gender re-identification are sins, so the truth of the Bible stands in the way of much of the left's agenda.

Western Civilization

"Liberals have a deep love of Western civilization. They taught it at virtually every university and celebrated its unique moral, ethical, philosophical, artistic, musical, and literary achievements. No liberal would have joined the leftist Rev. Jesse Jackson in chanting at Stanford University: 'Hey, hey. Ho, ho. Western civ has got to go.'"[9] Now, Western civilization is being demonized in many of our universities. For example, the English department of the Ivy League University of Pennsylvania recently took down the mural of William Shakespeare because he was a white European. In other places, Christopher Columbus is also under attack for being white and helping to bring Western civilization to the Americas.

The dramatic turn to the left in the Democratic Party is striking! One only has to look at the difference between the beliefs of FDR and many in today's Democratic Party. "The most revered liberal in American history is former President Franklin Delano Roosevelt, who frequently cited the need to protect not just Western civilization but Christian civilization. Yet leftists unanimously denounced President Donald Trump for his speech in Warsaw, Poland, in which he spoke of protecting Western civilization. They argued not only that Western civilization is not superior to any other civilization but also that it is no more than a euphemism for white supremacy."[10]

Dennis Prager concludes with one final thought: "If the left is not defeated, American and Western civilization will not survive. But the left will not be defeated until good liberals understand this and join the fight. Dear liberals: Conservatives are not your enemy. The left is."[11]

Culture War on the West

Many believe that a culture war exists in America and the world. This culture war is often believed to be the struggle between Christianity/Judaism & Western Culture vs. Islam. That claim is certainly understandable because Islam, according to the Qur'an, is incompatible with Western culture. Earlier verses in the Qur'an that were later abrogated (erased, but still in the Qur'an) are seemingly conciliatory, even friendly toward Christians and Jews. When read in context, they actually are not conciliatory towards non-Muslims, but these verses are deceptive enough to fool most people. These abrogated verses are now used to perpetuate the current lie (seen on many billboards in Florida and elsewhere around the country) that Christianity and Islam are not really that different because, after all, are supposedly worshipping the same God and Islam is a religion of peace. President Obama stupidly declared that the word Islam means "peace," when it actually means "submission" to Allah. So in reality, the Jihadists are actually correct when they make the claim that the Qur'an supports Jihad, Sharia Law, and killing the infidel (See Endnotes on Islam).[12] The abrogated verses are meant to confuse people into believing that the Qur'an is a peaceful book. So the rise of radical Islam is an existential threat to the United States and the world.

The True Culture War

But, with all the preceding said concerning Islam, the true culture war exists internally within America and Western Culture; it's a battle between conservativism/liberalism versus leftism. The sad and most difficult part of this battle is that many liberals and a few conservatives misguidedly have some leftist views, in contrast to the left which have no conservative or liberal views.

Malevolent people exist in America and the world pretending to be fighting on behalf on race, class, and gender victims, but they actually wanted or want to fundamentally change America and Western Civilization into a totalitarian state and use these "victims" as merely pawns to divide and weaken the country so they can take over. Three examples of the many true leftists who wanted or want to change America are George Soros, a billionaire financier of left-wing causes, the late Frank Marshall Davis, who was a Communist and one who influenced Barack Obama while he lived in Chicago, and the late Saul Alinsky, who wrote the book "Rules for Radicals" which is the community organizer's bible for attacking the mainstream and also conducting violent protests. Many more could be named.

The left claim that they desire health care for all, college for all, a minimum wage for all, but that is only a ploy to get votes by giving away free stuff. The popularity of Bernie Sanders, who is one of the advocates of everything for all, illustrates this point. Medi-care and social security are not entitlements because people pay into the system, but the socialists of the left want these for everybody, regardless if they pay into it or not. Of course, doing so would collapse the system, destroy the economy, and cause an economic meltdown (a goal of the left). With an economic meltdown and the resulting chaos, people tend to turn towards anyone promising domestic peace, order, prosperity, and returning to normal; exactly the way some dictators have come to power throughout history. But Bernie Sanders is a true believer in Socialism and really thinks that his policies will make life better for all citizens and foolishly doesn't see the harm these policies would inflict on the country. Therefore, by definition Bernie Sanders is not a true leftist because his

motivation is not to destroy America even though his policies are decidedly leftist and destructive.

Europe: The Model to Avoid

The left generally prefer Europe to the U.S. because it is
even more secular, socialist leaning, and seen as "less judgmental"—all of which the left define as "enlightened." They
also see capitalist America and Israel as the major problem
in the world and standing in the way of a truly global one-
world government. They like to point out how great socialized medicine is in Europe and Canada. But Canadians, who
can afford it, travel to the U.S. because of the shorter waiting time for their serious surgeries. In the UK, health care is
available to all but with a long waiting time. If there are con-
trols on how much doctors and hospitals can earn, that also
results in fewer doctors and hospitals, so nationalization of
any business results in less available product or services. If
less service is available and everybody is on the same single
payer plan, the wait times have to be longer. But the left
don't care about economics or understand that health care
is a business and involves profit (anathema to the left).

Sweden is often given as an example as Socialism that
works, but Sweden isn't really Socialist in the Marxist-Le-
ninist sense and people do pay extremely high income taxes
(around 60%) in paying for their low cost health care. One
problem that would occur here in the U.S. with a single-pay-
er national system, besides government being notoriously
inefficient, is that almost half the population pays little or
no federal income tax.

Europe is also more tolerant which will eventually be
their undoing because it is becoming more and more an
easy target for terrorists. Europe is spiritually dead and in
decline—especially the birthrate. It's too bad because Europe is very beautiful and has many wonderful people and

places to visit and enjoy, but the last thing we want to become is Europe!

Earlier, I mentioned that the Democratic Party is now the party of the left, but I also said that most Democrats and their politicians are not true leftists. So how can that be? It is because, even though most Democrats could really be described as liberal (remember, there is a difference between liberal and leftist), they still support many leftist policies such as increased regulation and high taxes on business, abortion "rights," nationalized health care, open borders, and cutting military spending. But again, it's the motivation behind their views. Even though Jimmy Carter, for example, is very leftist in his views, I don't believe he wanted to destroy the country—even though he was a terrible president. Democratic politicians have to remain somewhat loyal to the leftist party agenda or suffer the consequences, the same as Republicans not supporting the GOP agenda.

What about Conservatives and the Far-right?

So far, only leftism has been discussed which begs the question: "What about conservatives and the far-right?" Conservatism and the so called far-right also have nothing in common in the same way as liberalism and leftism having nothing in common. The reason I hardly mention the far-right as opposed to the far-left is because the far-right are basically irrelevant. They have no real power or influence when compared to the left. The far-right have zero influence in the media (conservative talk-radio is conservative, not right-wing), pop-culture, academia, the courts, or politics. Thankfully, they've been marginalized, so that such extreme right-wing groups like the white-supremacists, neo-Nazis, the KKK, and some so called "Christian Evangelical churches" which advocate the murdering of homosexuals, have little power, especially when compared to the left.

Leftist Rejection of Historic American Ideals

Leftism categorically rejects three foundational American ideals which make this country unique and are printed on U.S. currency—e pluribus unum (from many one), Liberty, and In God We Trust.

Instead of e pluribus unum, leftism uses the term "diversity." Diversity can make a nation strong if it's a melting pot of many groups and cultures into one united nation like America. But the left use "diversity" as a tool in the dividing of people based upon race, class, and gender. Diversity as strictly separate groups without an allegiance to a national identity tends to weaken nations. But again, the left opposes nationalism and borders in favor of globalism.

Leftism denies "liberty;" instead substituting "equality" in the communistic sense that everybody should be equal and it isn't fair that some people prosper while others don't. Equality has supplanted freedom and the pursuit of excellence in favor of coercion and mediocrity. Yes, as much as possible, equality of opportunity should exist, but not equality of result. The reality of humanity is that some prosper and some don't. Some make bad choices which affect their ability for success and happiness, and others make good choices which can increase their chances of success. Some overcome bad circumstances and rise above them, but the left believe that those who fail in society are all somehow victims of capitalism and white privilege. Socialist style equality gives no incentive to excel which guarantees mediocrity and economic failure. The only ones who do well under socialist "equality" are the privileged few at the top. Equality is an unattainable goal which reflects on the left's ignorance of human nature and is why Socialism never works.

Leftism substitutes the phrase "In God We Trust" into either man is his own god, or the state is god. Leftism is actually a religion and the post-modern creed of "there is no God" is the cornerstone of leftism. If there is no God with an absolute standard of truth (the Bible) and right and wrong (the Ten Commandments), then no absolutes exist—instead only numerous gray areas where morality and truth are relative and determined by one's own personal opinion; so no one has the right to judge anyone else and quoting the Bible is considered judgmental hate speech.

Leftism condemns all other religions (except Islam) and claims that religion, especially Christianity, has killed more people than all other wars combined. They point to the Inquisition and the Crusades as evidence that Christianity kills. But the Christianity they are referring to was Roman Catholicism, not true Biblical Christianity. True Biblical Christians were the martyrs killed at the hands of the Popes. Leftists also fail to mention Islam and how many millions they have killed all throughout history, and even today. They also have a blind spot towards Communism, which has killed many millions of people.

The Two Sides of the Left

It's important to make a further distinction regarding leftism. The following are the two basic types of leftism, recognizing these are extreme examples and sometimes one can be a combination of the two. For example, George Soros could fit both types of leftism—using his wealth to gain power as an oligarch (practical leftism) and also having an ideological position of hatred of America in a desire to fundamentally transform the country.

The two divisions of leftism are the following:

Ideological Leftism: Socialism/Communism

Ideological leftism again shows the evidence that leftism is a religion. Ideological leftists are true believers in their cause. Fervor exists concerning such things as climate change, globalism, and the need for a socialist equality as defined by the left. These people consist of academia, many in the media, Alexandra Ocasio Cortez, Elizabeth Warren, Talib, Omar, and others who are basically Socialists. Of course, if asked, they would deny that they hate the country, but like all leftists, they believe in power and control in an ideological manner through a totalitarian system of government. They've been indoctrinated to hate this country and believe that America is a racist unfair country. They are globalists and hate nationalism, borders, one-language, and believe in open borders in order to bring in people they can control in order to remain in power.

Ideological leftism also exists in the violent elements of Socialism-Marxism in such groups as Black Lives Matter and Antifa. They too are the result of youth indoctrinated into hating America and do the dirty work of physically destroying and desecrating the country. Ideological leftism is obvious and easily detected, but a more dangerous and powerful type of leftism exists: practical leftism.

Practical Leftism: Corporate Power and Control

This consists of the oligarchs in media, high tech and other big corporations, Wall Street, and other super rich donors, and other "elites" who want to control the country. So power is also the motivation of these practical leftists. The difference is that they give lip service to racial justice, the environment, and other causes of "religious" leftism, but aren't really that ideological except that they have been indoctrinated in the same universities as the hard core leftists—in that regard, they are also globalists, but for a different reason: power and access to worldwide markets (especially China) without tariffs unless it benefits them. Like religious leftism, they are anti the American worker in favor of the immigration of cheap labor and also the outsourcing of manufacturing jobs.

The great irony is that a complete shift has taken place between Democrats and Republicans regarding business and labor. Under the old reality, the Democrats were the party of labor unions and the Republicans were the party of management. But in 2016 and especially 2020, many rank and file union members snubbed Biden in favor of President Trump because of the great economy and his fight against offshoring jobs.

Practical leftists are far more dangerous than the hard core leftists because they can hide under the banner of respectability. After all, most everybody believes the media are telling the truth and that American corporations care about the American worker, right? The truth is that big business, especially big tech, is in bed with China and has teamed up in an effort to take control of America through disinformation by sources like Google, Facebook, Twitter, and others who now decide what is true and what is "misinformation." Their definition of misinformation is anything from a conservative-pro Trump viewpoint. Even though many of these leftists aren't really ideological, they still take these anti-Trump stands because Donald Trump is a threat to their game of money, power, and control through controlling the narrative of news.

Hopefully, you now have a clearer idea of what leftism really is and the harm it has done and can do if unchecked. This has been an overview of leftism, but the next few chapters will shed more light on this cancer that is destroying America.

Abraham Lincoln once said that America will never be destroyed from the outside. If we falter and lose our freedoms, it will be because we destroyed ourselves. The left is in the process of doing just that. The hope for America and Western Civilization is that more and more people have finally seen the true face of leftism.

Endnotes

[1] bizquotes.com/quote/331096

[2] Dennis Prager The Daily Signal, September 12, 2017.

[3] Ibid

[4] Ibid

[5] Ibid

[6] Ibid

[7] Ibid

[8] Ibid

[9] Ibid

[10] Ibid

[11] Ibid

[12] Robert C. Greer, PhD "What the Qur'an Reveals, Understanding Islam," Advantage Books, Longwood, Florida, (2011), p. 61-63, 163

Verses in the Qur'an which illustrate the Doctrine of Abrogation and Jihad:

"We will make thee recite, and thou shalt not forget, save what God pleases. Verily, He knows the open and what is concealed" (Q 87:6-7)."

(Q 13.39): God blots out what He will, or He confirms; and with Him is the Mother of the Book.

(Q 2.106): "Whatever verse we may annul or cause thee to forget, we will bring a better one than it, or one like it; dost thou not know that God is mighty over all?"

"While he was still in Mecca, Muhammad became aware that maintaining consistency in the often contradictory teachings in his surahs was going to be an increasingly difficult endeavor. He therefore incorporated the Doctrine of Abrogation addressing the question of contradictions within the Qur'an. It states that an earlier statement carrying divine authority is abrogated (erased) by a later contradictory statement which also carries divine authority. Islamic scholar Maulana Muhammad Ali comments that some Islamic scholars place the number of abrogated verses in the Qur'an at five hundred. Other scholars, however, are more conservative, claiming a more correct number to be as few as twenty one.

Christians maintain that the Qur'an is a historical document. It was written in a specific time in history and influenced by the passing of time. Muhammad made changes to his developing theology due to changes in circumstances and his outlook on life. These changes affected specific teachings, such as his views on alcoholic beverages, Jihad, and Jews and Christians (see Q 2.106 and 13.39)."

Also see: *Maulana Muhammad Ali, The Religion of Islam, (Dublin, Ohio: Ahmadiyya Anjuman Ish'at at Islam, 2005), pp 32, 33.*

The doctrine of Jihad and killing the infidel is clearly taught in the Qur'an because the abrogated surahs have replaced the more so called conciliatory ones. This is just one of many surahs:

(Q2.190-191): "Fight in God's way with those who fight with you, but transgress not; verily, God loves not those who do transgress. Kill them wherever ye find them, and drive them out from whence

Boot Camp 1963: Innocence to Upheaval

they drive you out; for sedition is worse than slaughter; but fight them not by the Sacred Mosque until they fight you there; then kill them, for such is the recompense of those that misbelieve."

Chapter 12

Twenty-Six Specific Examples Illustrating the Difference Between the Mainstream and Leftism

We've covered a general overview of leftism including the ideological differences separating leftism from Liberalism and conservativism, but now it's necessary to give some specific examples to those who don't normally pay very much attention to politics. The following comparison gives twenty-six specific examples not in any particular order which define the culture war raging on many fronts and further illustrate the significant differences between the mainstream (conservatism/liberalism) vs. leftism. It's not hard to figure out which example is leftism, and it's not the first. I'm sure more examples could be cited.

Some room for nuance exists—for example, Number One could also include people who deny God's existence, but don't believe that religion necessarily harms or helps society or that Bible believers are stupid.

Number One

It is between those who worship God, or recognize that religion is a positive influence in the country—as opposed to—those who deny God's existence, believe that religion harms society, and think that anyone who believes the Bible is ignorant, as well as anti-science, anti-intellectual, homophobic, and sexist.

Number Two

It is between those who believe that the increase of mass shootings are not the result of too few gun laws, but the breakdown of the family, faith, discipline, an increased tolerance towards evil, and allowing known dangerous mentally ill people to live in society—as opposed to— those who believe that institutionalizing the mentally ill violates their rights, calling evil behavior evil is judgmental, and blame conservatives or the NRA for opposing more gun laws. Many non-leftists also believe this myth that more gun laws or "gun control" will solve the problem of mass shootings. Gun control only serves the left's desire to disarm all the law abiding citizens, which they have done throughout history.

Number Three

It is between those who believe admission to universities, police, and fire departments, etc. should be based on the most qualified candidate—as opposed to—those who believe that admission standards should be lowered and/or preferences given for women and people of color (whatever that means), which in itself is sexist and racist because the left think that women, blacks and other minorities are basically incapable of making it without their help. Martin Luther King, Jr. said that people should be judged "not by the color of their skin but by the content of their character."

Number Four

It is between those who see people as individuals and the potential of their ability to live free and contribute to society—as opposed to—those who see people in terms of

148

race, class and gender victims who need government to take care of them.

Number Five

It is between those who believe in nationalism—borders, language, culture, and think that the immersion in English for immigrants, and especially their children, is better than bilingual education because it promotes their assimilation and is good for America—while bilingual education is bad for immigrants since it causes cultural division, lack of communication-assimilation, and the balkanization of immigrant groups—as opposed to—those who believe "nationalism" means white racism, favor a global community with open borders, and that it is better to embrace many languages and cultures in the name of "diversity" rather than the English language and a unique American culture, which they basically hate.

Number Six

It is between those who believe in the death penalty for heinous murderous crimes as punishment and a deterrent; believe in victim's rights and support building more prisons while opposing the releasing of dangerous criminals in order to ease overcrowding; and believe that abortion is the murder of an innocent human being—as opposed to—those believing that abortion destroys an unviable tissue mass and is a constitutional "right"—while at the same time, believe that murderers should never be put to death and the release of "non-violent felons" because of jail overcrowding is OK while also opposing construction of more prisons.

Number Seven

It is between those who believe that America, with all its faults, is still a decent country and the best hope for the earth—as opposed to—those who believe that America is a racist, sexist, homophobic, xenophobic, Islamophobic nation needing open borders and denationalization in order to integrate into the global community.

Number Eight

It is between those who believe that Communism is one of the great evils of the world—as opposed to—those who believe that it is a good idea, but just hasn't been tried by the right people (them).

Number Nine

It is between those who opposed a nuclear freeze during the cold war and believed that the nuclear arms race led to the defeat of the Soviet Union and the end of the Cold War (historically proven)—as opposed to—those who supported a nuclear freeze, opposed a strong military, and relied on the "good will" of the Soviet Union.

Number Ten

It is between those who peacefully protest, obey the law, and pick up after themselves, such as the Tea Party Movement and Trump supporters—as opposed to—those who violently protest, break the law and cause personal injury, property damage, and a mess for someone else to clean up—such as Occupy Wall Street, Black Lives Matter, Antifa, and protestors on university campuses trying to ban conservative speakers.

Number eleven

It is between those who believe that school choice should be available through vouchers, especially for poor parents, so their children can attend private schools and get an education unbiased by leftism and its political correctness and revisionist history present in many public schools—as opposed to—those who want to force children to attend public schools—especially the teacher's unions who are tools of the Democratic Party. They claim to be protecting the children, but they are condemning them to inferior schools, especially in poor neighborhoods.

Number Twelve

It is between those who believe that God made humans male and female and that marriage should be between a man and a woman as God intended in order to continue humanity, promote healthy families, the socialization of children, and societal stability—as opposed to—those who believe that one's sexual identity is according to "who they think they are;" who believe that marriage can be between same sex or even multiple parents regardless of sex and believe a mother and a father are unnecessary in raising a child; that it maintains the status quo which they find judgmental and unacceptable.

Number Thirteen

It is between those who believe that high taxes and more power centralized in the federal government is a bad thing which leads to a loss of freedom, especially through a potential dictator leading the country; that the founding fathers were wise to distribute power away from a few people at the top and, instead, diffuse power to many through the Senate, House of Representatives, Judiciary, and state and local governments. Who believe it was also wise to create the electoral college rather than majority rule, which can become mob rule (compare the American revolution to the

French Revolution)—as opposed to—those who think that the popular vote should decide national elections (basically California and New York would decide every election); hate the senate because Wyoming has as many senators as California; and believe that redistribution of wealth from the "rich" to the poor distributed through a strong central government somehow makes things more fair.

Number Fourteen

It is between those who believe that Israel has a right to exist in its land and is the only democracy and true friend of America in the Middle East—as opposed to—those who believe the Jews have driven the Palestinians out of a thriving nation in 1948 and have become occupiers of Palestine (a myth); that the Israelis and Palestinians are morally equivalent. My question is: who are the terrorists launching rockets? It's not the Israelis.

Number Fifteen

It is between those who believe that the United Nations is a worthless, anti-American and anti-Israel organization which has done nothing to handle the tyrants of the world; that it is a lackey of China—as opposed to—those who believe that the United Nations is a moral force for good in the world, and since America is not a force for good, it should therefore be subservient to the UN, world courts, and other world-wide organizations and treaties. This is also part of the global outlook of the left in destroying American sovereignty.

Number Sixteen

It is between those who believe that race and gender quotas in schools (and elsewhere), besides being unfair, encourages mediocrity and students who are ill prepared to compete in today's world—as opposed to—those who believe that It is good that high schools and colleges have dropped hundreds of men's sports teams in order to meet gender-based quotas; believe in a trophy for all who compete so that no one's self-esteem will ever be damaged, and that competition is bad and causes some students to feel bad about themselves.

Number Seventeen

It is between those who believe that profiling, racial and otherwise, is a legitimate law enforcement technique and profiling of possible terrorists is a good idea based on common sense—as opposed to—those who believe little old lady grandmothers are as likely to be a terrorist and should be searched as a Middle Eastern young male—which is based on no common sense and the stupidity of political correctness!

Number Eighteen

It is between those who believe that violent crime in the inner city is caused by fatherless families and a lack of guidance, values, and discipline in kids while growing up; that a kid without a father can have the gang become their "father"—as opposed to—those who believe that racism and poverty, not a lack of fathers or values, is the primary cause of violent crime in the inner city.

Number Nineteen

It is between those who believe that a moral difference exists between Western culture (especially in America) and other cultures: Islam, in which women are subjugated and infidels persecuted and murdered; communist ruled countries where people basically have little or no rights; and third-world countries, such as in Africa, in which tribal warfare has resulted in the brutal murder of thousands, especially Christians—as opposed to—those who believe that all cultures are morally equivalent and no moral difference exists between America and Zimbabwe!

Number Twenty

It is between those who believe that God is sovereign over the earth including controlling the climate and climate is mainly influenced by the God created sun through solar activity; that climate has always gone through warm and cool periods naturally and the current warming trend (since 1850) is not unprecedented [e.g. Greenland has actually been green before during the time of the settlement by Erik the Red's Norsemen (Vikings) in the 10th century during the Medieval Warming period from 950-1250 (see chapter 16)—as opposed to—those who believe that man is in control of the earth, not God, and believe that climate change is caused primarily by man's so called carbon footprint and that we are going to destroy the earth because this warming is unprecedented in human history. This is one of the most dangerous leftist myths because it is the leftist idea most believed by people regardless of political beliefs and helps unite millennials to support so called progressivism.

Number Twenty-one

It is between those who believe that the so-called national mainstream media is heavily influenced by the left; that their reporting is biased, and that most newspapers, network news, PBS. CNN, and MSNBC are tools of the Democratic Party, especially regarding efforts to invalidate the

2016 election and get rid of Donald Trump. It's also between those who truly want to know the truth and get beyond the easy headlines and one line teasers—as opposed to—those who believe that the media's reporting (except Fox News and conservative talk radio) is fair and unbiased and represents true journalism.

Number Twenty-two

It is between those who simply want to live their lives in peace without being made to feel guilty or "responsible" for other's misfortunes, including slavery—as opposed to—those who post "hate free zone," "no human is illegal," "Black Lives Matter," and other sanctimonious in your face progressive signs in their front yard; believe that anyone who has the audacity to criticize victim groups of the left such as LGBTQ, the homeless, blacks and other minorities, illegal immigrants, women, etc. is a "hater."

Number Twenty-three

It is between those who believe that political correctness: for example, changing the name "manholes" to "person holes," or "history" to whatever else in order to get rid of the "his," or changing the term "convicted felon" to one who has had a "judicial incident" as is the case in San Francisco, or changing the term "illegal alien" to the PC "undocumented immigrant," or taking down statues of history, changing mascots—so as to not offend the "snowflakes" and victim groups; believe that the left take themselves much too seriously, are juvenile, and need to join the real world and get out of their alternate utopian universe—as opposed to—those that want every victim group to be protected at the cost of destroying American history and free speech.

155

Number Twenty-four

It is between those who see the true cause of the Covid-19 pandemic: China who allowed air travel outside of China, but locked down the rest of China; bought up all the PPE equipment before the pandemic became known and left the rest of the world short; that the lockdown, which at first seemed reasonable because not much was known about the virus, has proven to be unnecessary as long as precautions were taken as more data has shown; who realize that blue state leaders wanted to continue the lockdown to keep the economy from rebounding at the cost of their own citizens which caused great destruction and suffering economically, socially, health wise, and in every other imaginable way for purely political reasons (particularly in the third quarter ending Sept. 30th) to hurt Donald Trump's chances of re-election—as opposed to—the sycophants in the media and academia who believe that China handled the situation well and the pandemic in America was the result of Trump's so called mismanagement of the virus—exactly the position of China and the America-hating worldwide left.

Number Twenty-five

It is between those who believe that America should come first and that endless wars in other countries and giving billions to ingrate countries who hate us makes no sense—as opposed to—those who think America owes the rest of the world and being the only superpower is unfair and dangerous, even though at the same time believing that we should be involved in foreign wars and be the security force for the rest of the world (not all leftists believe this).

Number Twenty-Six

Finally, it is between those who believe that America and Western Civilization must survive—as opposed to—those who want it to cease to exist—the left.

The next eight chapters consist of: Chapter 13, Leftism Applied, Chapter 14, Black Lives Matter, Chapter 15, Covid-19, Chapter 16 & 17, Climate change, Chapter 18, An Independent Voice, Chapter 19, the 2020 Election, and Chapter 20, What about God? All represent the heart of this second edition of Boot Camp 1963. These chapters were written during the pandemic of 2020-2021.

Chapter 13

Leftism Applied

It's easy for some to simply dismiss the following content as nothing more than conspiracy theory and something that can never happen in America. But it's hard to imagine what is happening in our country today and how much the left is destroying it in a relatively short period of time. Anybody who possesses a basic knowledge of history and government in America and in other parts of the world can easily see that history does repeat itself. Unchecked Leftism absolutely will destroy this country as it has others throughout history. The most controversial thesis of this book is that the left are destroying America intentionally to gain power. That doesn't mean that every University, CEO, Democrat, college student, or member of the media hate this country and want to destroy it, but enough of them actually desire that which is causing the country's turn towards leftism. If leftism ever truly dominates our country, the following is what can be expected.

Fascism/Authoritarianism/Power

Fascism, Authoritarianism, and desire for power describe the mentality of the left. As mentioned earlier in this writing, current leftist fascism is attacking free speech by controlling, condemning, and punishing any speech or actions critical of their agenda of totalitarian control and coercion. In other words, leftism is really afraid of the truth because the truth refutes leftism throughout history and exposes it as a destroyer of nations. Yet the great irony is that leftists call conservatives fascists, but they project onto others the actual traits describing them. Leftist fascism/authoritarianism is manifested in the following ways:

Coercion

Leftism is coercive, so the overall goal justifies any method necessary to achieve that goal including the politics of personal destruction, especially from the cancel culture that we see so often today. Followers of leftism, ignorant regarding its destructive and hateful mentality and goals, are completely divorced from reality and think wealth somehow comes from government and more taxes on the rich—in short, they live in a fantasy world and know zero about basic economics. These followers actually have a naïve notion of a utopian world where everybody can coexist peacefully in a one-world community. They apparently don't know much about human nature or history. But the true radical leftist cares nothing about peaceful coexistence or a better life for people because, again, their goal is power and control.

Followers of leftist ideology, especially indoctrinated students, are like immature spoiled brats as evidenced by those "protesting" against Republicans and some of the Trump administration workers in Washington D.C. and elsewhere. These workers were hounded and shouted down, often with profanity, by these brainwashed shrill people. Leftists and their indoctrinated pawns are the true haters and this is also illustrated by the hate mobs and shouting down of those who supported Judge Brett Kavanaugh in

2018. An example was the incident with Senator Ted Cruz and his family not even being able to go out to dinner without being confronted by these mindless dupes shouting "we believe the survivors." It is obvious the brainwashing that the protestors received in the university, the internet, and the "mainstream" media when one hears their rants, even at the doorsteps of the homes of those they harass.

One of the worst examples is Antifa, a supposedly anti-fascist group (are you kidding!) who stormed the home of Fox News commentator, Tucker Carlson, shouting "we know where you sleep at night." He was finally forced to move to a new location for the protection of his family after his home was vandalized. This group is leftist inspired and fits the definition of cowardly, fascist, and terrorist bullies. Behind these mindless protesting malcontents are radical professors and Marxist community organizers; the anarchists of the left who organize these protests. Antifa and other such groups are reminiscent of Hitler's Brown shirts in the 1930's and reflect the true fascism of the left. Where are the conservative mob groups who initiate and organize the stopping of traffic, riot and loot, beat up innocent people, disrupt the speaking events of leftists, and show up at the homes of leftists ranting profanity? The answer is they don't exist.*

*The riots at the Capitol on January 6, 2021 represented the first major riot by Trump supporters, but it was nursery school compared to the 2020 riots by BLM and Antifa which got a free pass from the media.

Political Correctness/Cancel Culture

So much of fascism is accomplished by coercive political correctness and the penalty paid for offending the left's victim group pawns: blacks and other people of color, women, and gays. The left consider any criticism of these groups as racism and hate speech, so the perpetrators have to be cancelled. Even sports team mascots deemed offensive are being cancelled, such as the Cleveland Indians or the Washington Redskins. More and more it seems like we're heading in the direction of becoming a Godless narcissistic victim culture.

But the left's use of political correctness is more than simply preventing people from being offended. Now, to make any criticism deemed critical to the left's victim groups results in retaliation, even being fired from a job. Today, the "cancel culture" is alive and well where people have been cancelled for political incorrectness. For Example, many people have been fired over comments concerning BLM or negative comments concerning players kneeling at NFL games during the national anthem. Two local examples here in the Sacramento area involve Grant Napear, longtime announcer for the Sacramento Kings NBA team and radio sports talk host on KHTK. When asked about his take on Black Lives Matter, Napear tweeted "all lives matter, every single one." That was enough to get him fired from KHTK and he also resigned as announcer for the Kings. If you say "all lives matter" that is considered racist because the true BLM believers who naively think that the movement is actually about racial justice are not after equal justice as they claim, but rather justice strictly for them. They feel like they are owed because of a long history of racism and also historical slavery (demanding reparations), so equal justice isn't enough. But for the true leftist Marxist founders of BLM, it's not about social or racial justice, but rather destruction of society and the attainment of power.

It's sad that the sports world in general is caving in to political correctness and endorsing Black Lives Matter for fear of being called racist. Most sports commissioners, owners, and media are really cowards who are afraid of retaliation and losing sponsors or, in the case of the NBA, losing their lucrative relationship with China. Even Major League Soccer (MLS) recently caved when the LA Galaxy fired forward Alexander Katai for comments his wife made about the BLM demonstrators basically saying they should be killed. This provoked outrage so they fired her husband. Many sports figures warm up in BLM tee shirts without knowing what this group really stands for.

Another local example here in the Sacramento area is a Mr. Pickles sandwich shop franchisee in Davis, California refusing to display a Black Lives Matter sign in his shop. He compared the tactics of BLM to the KKK so his franchise was pulled. But is that really so inaccurate a comparison when you consider what's been happening with the riots and destruction in the country?

Mr. Pickles higher ups and other corporation CEO's are so cowardly that Goodyear Tire Company, for example, bans their employees from wearing "MAGA," or "All Lives Matter" hats but allows "Black Lives Matter," and "LGBTQ" hats. Corporate America are capitulating to the fascism of the left, but even worse, some are joining the movement and support suppressing criticism of BLM because they agree that America is a racist unfair nation. It must be remembered that many CEO's of big business today got their MBA's from universities that have been ideologically corrupted by the left. So even some CEO's in their sixties are young enough to have been indoctrinated by anti-American revisionist history and globalism taught in academia for the last forty or fifty years. So, for example, the hiring of cheap labor for manufacturing in other countries is no problem even if it hurts American workers.

Another example of political correctness is Donald Trump being called a racist for calling Covid-19 a "China virus." The virus came from China and was allowed to spread to the rest of the world, but facts and truth don't matter to the left. He was called racist and xenophobic by Joe Biden and others for his January 2020 ban on all travel from China, which turned out to be a good move.

So through the "cancel culture," the left cause people to be fired from their jobs if they criticize BLM, kneeling before the national anthem, or openly support Donald Trump. Some have been shamed and the weaker among us suffering from white guilt even kneel down and apologize for their "error" of being white. It's disgusting! The left demand submission from anyone not a part of their victim groups or who disagrees with their agenda.

Now that the 2020 election has given the left full power, and the Capitol riot has given them their pretext, they are ramping up their cancel culture persecution of Trump and his supporters. The rhetoric is frightening and reminiscent of Germany in the 1930's towards Jews, Christians, and any dissenters critical of Hitler.

So the fascism of leftism and the resulting loss of free speech through political correctness have already begun. As a result of total leftist control, political correctness will be institutionalized and codified into law. Anything that can be deemed offensive to the left and their victim groups will be enforced as hate speech and punishable by loss of a job (already happening due to the cancel culture), fines, imprisonment, and/or sensitivity training which will be accomplished through reeducation camps similar to those in Red China. In fact, because the left are basically authoritarian, their vision for America is something like Communist China with the government in total control and no freedom. "Hate speech" even goes beyond the victim groups and has now been interpreted by the left as anything that disagrees with their agenda.

But why are some people offended by such terms as, for example, "China Virus" when discussing covid-19? Why do some follow the left in destroying cities and anybody in their way? It's because of years of indoctrination. False narratives, such as "unprecedented" racial Injustice and man-caused climate change, lead to ridiculous ideas like defunding the police and the green new deal. Why do people believe these false narratives? Again, it's because of Indoctrination.

Indoctrination: False Narratives & Propaganda

The left never let a good "crisis" go to waste. They use false narratives to create hysteria and fear among the population and a demand to "do something." The do something usually amounts to loss of freedom and bigger government strengthening its control over the citizens. They either create a crisis out of nothing, such as the hysteria of man-caused climate change (see chapters 16 & 17) and turn it into a catastrophe; or make an existing problem much worse such as Covid-19 forcing extensive lockdowns; or calling America systemically racist—the lie that America is the world's most racist country. The charge that the police are systemically racist is another over the top charge by the left. Yes, there are bad cops and some police reform is necessary to weed them out, but any police brutality today is nothing compared to the 50's and 60's. Racism still exists in America, but race relations are much better than in earlier times when segregation and systemic racism truly existed. Unfortunately, unrevised history and perspective are rarely taught anymore in our schools and universities.

Anything that challenges the dogma, agenda, or lies of the left is simply dismissed as conspiracy theory and false information. Anybody who challenges the PC dogma is cancelled simply by being referred to as racist. "Racism" is now the catch-all accusatory phrase of the left.

The left actually project themselves onto others and they are the true conspirators who use false information and want to destroy the country and take power. Some current true examples of the left's harm to the country are the following: the left use climate change to cripple the economy in order to "solve the problem" making America subservient to the international community through climate treaties, of course this is dismissed as a conspiracy; the Russia investigation and the fake Steele dossier was planned by Clinton, Obama, Biden, and corrupt members of the intelligence community in order to undermine the presidency of Donald Trump, this is also dismissed as a conspiracy; Covid-19 shutdowns, especially in blue states, were engineered to hurt the economy and Trump's chances of re-election; and the distribution of UNSOLICITED mail-in ballots for election fraud by the Democrats, also dismissed as conspiracy theory.

Results of Indoctrination

Revisionist History/Destroying History

Past generations can't be judged by the standards of the world of today, but that's one of the ways the left distorts history. For example, slavery was a major part of the economic system of the world from time immemorial. You can argue about the morality of slavery (it was a great evil), but it still existed everywhere. Leftists regard George Washington, Thomas Jefferson, and some of the other founding fathers as white racist slave owners. Many of our founding fathers were actually anti-slavery, but the left have no sense of historical perspective because history and critical thinking are no longer being taught at most of our schools and universities. Rather than teaching critical thinking, schools

166

and universities have been insidiously indoctrinating students for the last 50 years to hate America. The violence of Black Lives Matter, Antifa, and other violent movements jumping on the BLM bandwagon is a testimony to this indoctrination (see chapter 14 and the discussion on Critical Race Theory and the 1619 Project). The United States has done more to eliminate slavery than any other nation.

Our civil war was fought because the North, especially through the Abolitionist Movement, sought to do away with slavery, which was an important economic necessity in the South's agrarian economy, so the South seceded and the war was then fought to save the union. But in doing so, the war resulted in the slaves being emancipated at great cost to many lives, mostly white. Abraham Lincoln was a Christian and a Republican, not a Democrat—as some teach. The Republicans were the party of abolition, while the Democrats were the party of slavery, the KKK, and segregation. The rioters either don't know history or don't care because they even tore down a statue of General Grant in San Francisco and Abraham Lincoln in Portland, Oregon. Ulysses S. Grant and Abraham Lincoln had more to do with defeating the confederacy than anyone else. Yet the false narrative of systemic racism today in America fuels the haters of this country, most of which couldn't care less about racism or black lives, but only care about destroying America, a nation they have been indoctrinated to hate. To accomplish a totalitarian takeover of a free country, enough of the populace has to be indoctrinated to hate that country and demand change. The media and academia have largely accomplished this brainwashing of much of our society.

White Privilege

Another myth of false indoctrination is white privilege, where only whites can get ahead, and yet we have seen that blacks and other non-whites have so much more opportunity than they did in the 50's or 60's, even including a black president

Part of that myth of white privilege is that only whites live in the best areas of town. But today it's not unusual to see black families living in nice suburban neighborhoods alongside whites. In the 50's or 60's, segregation was the rule of the day in the North and South and very little mixing of the races occurred—whether living in the same neighborhood or having any contact with each other.

Mixed marriages were unheard of in the 50's and 60's and were strictly taboo, especially in the south, where a black man with a white woman would've probably gotten shot or lynched. My litmus test for racism is the view of interracial marriage: any view that opposes interracial marriage is essentially racist, period. But many will try to sugar coat it with such arguments as: it's not fair to the children. It doesn't wash. Some of the most amazing people I have known have been children of interracial marriages. Interracial marriage is much more prevalent now than it was fifty years ago.

White privilege of today is a myth but it is treated as fact and even some of our top industries, such as Sandia Nuclear Labs, have seminars on how white privilege has oppressed people of color. If the left take over, these Chinese style re-education camps will become gulags for indoctrination. Whites in these seminars are supposed to write letters of apology to people of color, bowing in submission admitting their guilt because they are white—which leads us to white guilt.

White Guilt

But why are so many leftists white? It's because they don't fully consider themselves white because they fancy themselves as somehow in solidarity with "people of color," but they are also ashamed of being white. An example would be Elizabeth Warren who claimed to be part native-American. Many have said that she made this claim to get into law school through affirmative action. That could possibly be true, but I believe it is deeper: being part native-American soothes her guilt over being pasty white.

Why are many whites in the media so leftist today? Again, it's because most in the media have grown up in the generations that were indoctrinated in our universities to believe that whites are essentially racist and white people, historically and today, are solely responsible for slavery. The truth is that white guilt is a powerful tool for the race baiting industry in order to attain power.

Many believe that so many whites voted for Barack Obama so they could be excused for their "racism." White guilt is supposed to be deserved because of black victims. Black victimization is harmful to blacks because they've been convinced of their victimhood which robs them of being responsible for themselves; instead white liberals, beginning in the 1960's, convinced blacks that they were victims and government would take care of them which hasn't worked out so well.

A degree in journalism is a certificate of indoctrination. Journalism consists of reporting facts accurately without any bias. But a journalism or liberal arts education in many of our so called "great" universities almost insures that a journalism student will turn to the left. All one has to do is watch CNN, MSNBC, NBC, CBS, ABC, PBS, NPR, and many internet sites, and it's like they are speaking from the same left-wing talking points. Today those talking points are anti-Trump, anti-conservative, anti-Christian, anti-white western culture, anti-family, and anti-America.

Censorship: Suppression of Free Speech

We previously discussed the left's fascistic censorship of conservative speakers on college campuses by shouting them down to suppression of opposing views by Google, Twitter, Facebook, and most media outlets. Unfortunately, many in the media support the leftist agenda, even if most aren't true leftists who want to bring down the country. This is sad because I like our local TV news personalities and reporters here in Sacramento and believe they are basically mainstream people, but their stations are owned or affiliated by networks which are journalistically corrupt. One of the truly great ironies is that even mainstream liberals support this hateful agenda without fully knowing the destruction caused by leftism. The reason is they are victims of revisionist history and indoctrination, mostly through academia. Again, we are now at the point where anything that disagrees with the leftist dogma narrative, especially that America is systemically racist and unfair is deemed "racist" and "hate speech."

The whole point of this censorship is to maintain this false narrative propaganda. This is what all leftist countries have done throughout history. One of the most notable examples was Joseph Goebbels (10-29-1897—5-1-1945) who was the Minister of Propaganda for Hitler and the Nazis. Two of his quotes relating to censorship are: *"Truth is the greatest enemy of the state."* Another quote attributed to Goebbels is: *"If you tell a lie big enough and keep repeating it, people will eventually come to believe it. The lie can be maintained only for such time as the State can shield the people from the political, economic and/or military consequences of the lie."* That's exactly what the media and academia are doing in America. Adolph Hitler burned books, suppressed all dissent and turned his mobs of brown-shirts against businesses owned by Jews. Today, we have the scary possibility of a similar circumstance where Antifa, BLM, and other radical leftist mobs are the brown-shirt thugs of the 1930's. The suppression by the media of conservative viewpoints, especially by high tech firms such as Google, Facebook, Twitter, and other social media represent the burning of the books. The wealth and power these Silicon Valley companies have is scary because of their ability to cause so many people to believe the lies of the Left. The increasing hostility to those questioning the leftist agenda, especially Biblical Christians, mirrors Hitler, Stalin, and Chairman Mao and their attacks on the church. Under absolute rule by the left, Christians, Trump supporters and other dissenters will be the Jews of 90 years ago.

A few Specific Lies of the Left

Everything the left declare is a lie, yet they constantly accuse conservatives of lying. Our only ideologically leftist president, Barack H. Obama, lied repeatedly about Obama care and how you can keep your plan or doctor, which turned out to be untrue. One of the architects of Obama care, Dr. Jonathan Gruber, basically said that the ACA was a wealth redistribution scheme.

> *"Obamacare's opacity was a deliberate strategy"*
> *Gruber made an argument that many of Obamacare's critics have long made, including me. It's that the law's complex system of insurance regulation is a way of concealing from voters what Obamacare really is: a huge redistribution of wealth from the young and healthy to the old and unhealthy. In the video, Gruber points out that if Democrats had been honest about these facts, and that the law's in-*

*dividual mandate is in effect a major tax hike, Obam-
acare would never have passed Congress."*[1]

For people who cannot afford health care, an Obamacare type program would have been OK. But proponents of Obamacare wanted it for everybody and to get rid of all competing private health insurance; that was the problem. Government control of health care (or socialized medicine) gives the left more power—that was the main reason for this push for nationalized Obamacare.

Socialized medicine also limits the amount of health care available because more people are on a single plan and government is inherently inefficient which would lead to rationed care. That creates an ethical and moral problem of who gets health care and who doesn't. I'm afraid that a leftist takeover of health care would result in government designated "less desirable" people not getting health care. Under the Nazis and the Soviet Union, Jews, the mentally retarded, homosexuals, sick elderly, ethnic minorities, and designated enemies of the state were undesirables and it didn't go well for them. In a leftist controlled America, Christians and Trump supporters would definitely be on the enemies of the state list.

The Democrats had both houses of congress and the people were lied to about Obamacare and the negative consequences of a government takeover of all health care. Obamacare passed without a single Republican vote. Joseph Goebbels would be proud of the Democrats!

Obama also lied in sending Susan Rice to appear on all the Sunday network news shows in order to lie concerning the September 11, 2012 attack of the American compound at Bengazi, Libya. Rice and Hillary Clinton blamed the murder of the U.S. ambassador Chris Stevens and several others in the U.S. embassy on a video which mocked Islam that was posted online. In reality, it was a planned attack that happened on Obama and Hillary Clinton's "watch" and was bungled resulting in the death of Stevens and other Americans who fought a heroic battle without help from Obama or Clinton after reinforcements were denied. The Bengazi incident was reduced to election year politics; the purpose of the lie was to protect Obama's reelection, which unfortunately was successful.

Obama's biggest and current lie is that Donald Trump inherited a good economy from his handling of the economy. In this quote from CNN business, the anemic economy under Obama is explained:

> *The U.S. economy grew at an annual rate of 1.6% in 2016, the Commerce Department reported Friday. In the last three months of the year -- between October and December -- the economy grew at an annual rate of 1.9%. It's the slowest pace of growth since 2011.*
> *It reflects how slow the recovery has been for many Americans since the Great Recession, which ended in 2009.*[2]

In what I would consider an unbiased comment, economist Gary Burtless says the following:

> *"Until February 2020, a fair-minded observer would have given the Trump administration a decent grade for U.S. economic performance in its first 36 months in office," said Brookings Institution economist Gary Burtless. "However, a fair-minded observer would have given the administration a failing grade for*

living up to its promise to deliver 4%-per-year economic growth."[3]

The point is that Obama claiming credit for the Trump economy is ridiculous and another lie of the left. The 2009-2016 "recovery" was the worst since post World War II recession in the late 1940's.

Another lie is "Russian collusion" in the 2016 election which was a two and a half year long witch hunt by the Mueller investigation which produced zero evidence. So called Russia collusion to help Trump get elected was a total hoax just like the current "Russian disinformation" declared by the democrats, high-tech, and the media on actual evidence of the Biden family colluding with China. To the left, everything has been "Russia," when the truth is that everything is "China." Why are China downplayed and not mentioned as the real threat to America? It's because corrupt politicians and oligarchs in business and Wall Street are benefiting from Chinese money from doing business in China and the Chinese buying influence with powerful people in the U.S. while stealing technology and collecting data on American citizens. Russia doesn't have the economy of China and can't flood the country with money, but China can.

Does anybody really believe that Russia wanted Hillary Clinton to lose, after her ineptitude as Secretary of State, especially concerning the "Russian Reset?" Shortly after this reset, Russia was emboldened to annex Crimea from the Ukraine.

Another lie of the left is that Trump is the great divider of the country. No, he inherited a divided country thanks to eight years of Barack Obama's leftist politics, specifically, his identity politics which pitted races, classes, and genders against each other. That's what leftism does: it divides and conquers.

And of course, one of the Left's biggest lies: climate change and a 97% "consensus" of scientists who declare that climate change is man-caused. Chapters 16-17 are dedicated to debunking this lie.

To chronicle all the lies of the left, especially the swamp, regarding the Russia investigation of collusion, the Mueller report, Adam Schiff, the impeachment, and others would take a separate very long book, of which a few have already been written.

Demagoguery

Every leftist throughout history has used demagoguery in the stirring up of hatred in order to remain in power by catering to hate. Nero blamed Christians for the burning of Rome; Hitler blamed the Jews for the problems suffered by post world war I Germany; the left today blame Whites, Christians, conservatives, Trump supporters, and Western culture for injustice, racism, poverty, and all the other problems in this country and in the world. It's almost like Paranoid Schizophrenia and fixing blame on another person or thing responsible for one's problems. This is the most dangerous type of mental illness because it can lead one into trying to destroy the person or thing that is the subject of one's ire. Groups such as Antifa and some members of Black Lives Matter have this irrational hatred of white America and western culture resulting from years of indoctrination and revisionist history. Again, if they hadn't received this indoctrination, they would realize that America is much less racist than it was up through the 1960's and is the least racist and freest country in the world. But they are taught hatred of America in many of the schools, universities, and by the media.

Another notable target of the left's demagoguery is Biblical Christianity. Christianity stands in the way of the left's support of homosexuality as an acceptable alternate lifestyle (Genesis 19; Romans 1: 18-32; 1 Corinthians 6:9), unlimited abortion (Jeremiah 1:5), destroying the nuclear family, gender re-identification (Genesis 5:2), and de facto declaration of leftism or secularism as the national religion. One only needs to see the treatment by the left towards churches during the Covid-19 Pandemic. Churches were declared non-essential and were closed down for months; those pastors who fought back have been fined and, in some cases, even jailed. Yet liquor stores, casinos, Planned Parenthood abortion clinics, and other such "essential" businesses were open.

Leftism is godless and secular, so one can't simply blame the internet for the moral breakdown in America. The horrendous news stories we are seeing are happening more and more because God and Biblical principles are abandoned in favor of the "values" of secular leftism: there is no God, therefore, moral standards of conduct or the definition of the family are relative to one's own opinion and anti-social behavior can be justified because of some perceived unfairness suffered. The only statement I will make concerning this subject is the following: when I look at the news headlines today, and also the reaction to those headlines, then compare them with those of the early sixties, that says it all. We were closer to God then.

Today's demagoguery is also directed towards Trump supporters, and now anyone who worked for President trump is singled out in the media as enemies who should never be able to work again in Washington or anywhere else. They have been canceled, just like Hilary Clinton once did in referring to Trump supporters as "deplorables."

Demagoguery also dangerously dehumanizes people, so the object of one's hatred and blame ceases to be a person. Therefore, any atrocities done against that person is justified. This was the mentality for Hitler's murdering six-million Jews, Stalin's murdering millions of Jews and other "undesirables," and the brutal treatment of U.S. and British prisoners of war by the Japanese during World War II. This explains a lot about the riots in the cities: Trump supporters and business owners don't matter, so rioting, physical violence, and looting are justified. The storming of the Capitol by some Trump supporters, possibly egged on by anarchists posing as Trump supporters, has increased the danger of a backlash against Trump supporters and other conservatives thereby strengthened the "justification" for hating them.

Moral Superiority?

True leftists believe in their moral superiority over lesser "deplorables" and consider themselves to be "the morally elite class" which results in possessing a severe case of self-righteousness. Again, leftism is essentially a religion! So not only do they believe in their moral superiority, but a true leftist thinks that he or she is the smartest person in the room and those who would differ with their leftist views, especially Bible-believing conservative Christians who don't share their "enlightenment," are stupid and evil. Of course, those who are "beneath them" need to have leftists rule over them in order to maintain stability. But in reality, the left are all about fear, chaos, division uncertainty, and anarchy, especially internal anarchy against the United States. A stable country that's happy and prosperous is good news for America, but bad news for the left.

True leftists are hypocritical because their behavior and beliefs do not even come close to a high moral standard— actually they are godless and the idea of a sovereign God over the world is laughable to them. Instead, they are humanistic and worship man whom they believe is the controller of the earth and is able to control nature and solve the world's problems.

Anarchy

Anarchy is a useful tool of the left because chaos and social upheaval can weaken a country and make it ripe for a takeover. The mob violence of destruction of statues and government buildings, and the destroying and looting of private business are a great thing to the left. These mobs are controlled and organized by people higher up with a Marxist mentality who really want to destroy the country. They use their BLM and Antifa pawns to do the heavy lifting.

It cannot be emphasized enough that these anarchists, such as Antifa and Black Lives Matter, are the result of the loss of two generations to indoctrination in the false narrative that America is a fascist country with systemic racism. These are the people that have been taught hatred of their own country so rioting, looting, and taking down statues gives them a sense of accomplishment. These violent anarchists are also the people who have co-opted the BLM movement and turned it into violent mobs. The sad thing is that not all of the Black Lives Matter protestors hate America but sincerely believe that changes will create a better country. They too are the result of indoctrination but at least are sincere in their belief of America being an unfair country with systemic racism (true leftists know that's a lie). They are wrong about that, but at least some of them are trying to do what they think is right without destroying the country. Unfortunately, true leftists such as the Marxist community organizers and the radical leftist elements of BLM anarchists are bad people who turn the protests into violence.

Double Standard Regarding Protest

The corrupt leftist influenced media have a notable double standard regarding protests. When people were protesting the Covid-19 lockdown in Michigan and other places, the media were all over them for being lawless. Or their negative reaction to tea party protests in 2009-2010—the Tea party protestors were considered by the media racist because we had a black president. But when BLM, Antifa, and others rioted and looted, those were then apparently legitimate and peaceful protests. Much of the media, except Fox News, deliberately avoided showing videos of rioting, looting, and cops being shot and beaten in order to maintain the false narrative of "peaceful law abiding" protests. If America had an honest press that looked out for the interest of Americans, everyone would know the truth that leftism is destroying America and must be stopped.

Immigration: Borders, Language, Culture

Immigration policy should not be a social-welfare program to help the poor of the world—it should be for the benefit of the host country first, then the immigrant. I constantly hear the argument: "give me your tired and your poor," but America needed many immigrants to homestead and populate an expanding country. After the industrial revolution, U.S. immigration policy of the second half of the nineteenth century and the first two decades of the twentieth century, was geared to benefit the country because jobs were plentiful and America needed workers. Cities were expanding at a fast rate and needed police, firemen, construction workers, sanitation workers, etc. Industry was also booming and needed labor, which was mostly manual; so immigration was economically driven by the need of immigrants as workers in a fast growing nation and economy. Now technology has eliminated many jobs done by manual labor and fewer jobs exist compared to the population so fewer workers are required. Skilled workers are in demand now, but the left want to flood the country with needy, uneducated, unskilled, and they hope, pliable people who will believe their lies and keep them in power.

If you take away a nation's borders, national language, history, culture, and national identity, you've destroyed that nation. One of the key ways the left want to accomplishing this is through the immigration policy of open borders. Part of the left's desire to fundamentally change America was amply demonstrated through Barack Obama's leftist immigration policy with de facto open borders. As previously mentioned, this was to make America less white because leftists truly hate whites and believe they are the major problem in the world. The left also want to bring in poor unskilled people dependent on government; turning America into a third world country ruled by the leftist elites but with no middle class, so everybody else is poor—like most countries in Latin America, Africa, and the rest of the third world. Is there any wonder why so many people want to migrate to America from Mexico, Central, and South America alone? Big business and big tech want more cheap imported labor which will further depress wages and take away jobs from American citizens, especially minorities and the poor. The left claim to be the champions of poor minorities, but like everything else about the left, that's another lie. But why would these people want to destroy the country? It's all about power and if the country is destroyed, they can take over and impose an authoritarian government.

Persecution of the Church

If the Left fully take over, the Biblical Christian church will be attacked and outright banned along with all religious freedom. Once again, America will be more like China which has a state-sanctioned pseudo "Christian" church (three-self church), but the government wants the Bible interpreted as supporting the state's agenda. In the true underground Chinese biblical church, pastors are being murdered. So similar to the Chinese Communist leftists, all religious freedom, except for liberal "acceptable" (non-biblical) churches approved by the government will be banned. Pressure by far left politicians is already underway toward classifying the Bible as hate speech because the Bible clearly calls homosexuality a sin and an abomination. The Bible also clearly declares that God knew each person even before that person was born (Jer. 1:5; Ps. 139:15-16)—which rankles Planned Parenthood and their abortion infanticide industry. The Bible also declares that marriage is between one man and one woman. God's unit of societal stability is the nuclear family, which the Left reject; In fact, biblical Christianity is the opposite of leftism. Also related to this destruction of the nuclear family is re-identification of gender which is opposed to biblical Christianity and creates confusion in children as to their sexual identity. Remember that confusion among society makes them more vulnerable to control by the left.

California governor Gavin Newsom has already declared the church "non-essential." John Mac Arthur, a Los Angeles pastor with a Bible-believing congregation in the San Fernando Valley has courageously battled the fascism of Los Angeles County in their effort to shut down Grace Community Church in Sun Valley, California. Threatening legal battles, jail, and cutting off power and water has not stopped Pastor MacArthur and the church from meeting.

The media and academia are on board in opposition to the biblical Christian church. Paul Schneider, a German pastor who opposed Hitler commented about Germany after Hitler took absolute power in 1933: "The media were in the grip of the Nazi party. Textbooks were rewritten. Human physiology was dominated by the Nazi that some races were 'higher' and that they would eliminate 'lower' races by force. There was a lot of evidence to support what Paul Schneider said at the time: 'National Socialism becomes more obviously opposed to biblical Christianity every day.'"[4] Eerily reminiscent of today!

Getting Rid of Fair Elections

America is still a center-right country and most Americans reject the agenda of the far-left. The problem is that the far-left has co-opted the Democratic Party. Because of that, the Democrats have tried to steal elections in the following ways:

First, they tried to end the Electoral College and instead decide by popular vote which would make cities and large states decide elections. America is actually a constitutional representative republic, not a democracy ruled by majority rule. The founding fathers in their wisdom knew that majority rule would be a problem. Basically, a few states would decide every election. Cities are notoriously liberal or leftist, so naturally the left would want a popular vote. Here in California, there's even an effort that would allow sixteen-year olds the right to vote.

Second, they tried to change the demographics of certain states, especially in the west, through immigration from Latin America because they figure these new immigrants (legal or not) would vote overwhelming Democratic, which has proven to be the case. In fact, the strategy has worked because two states that have turned Democratic and used to be Republican leaning are Colorado and Nevada which Trump lost in 2016 and 2020. Now the left are desperately trying to turn Texas and Arizona into blue states.

Third, voter fraud by fighting against a requirement of having a voter ID card, even though an ID is required for just about everything else. Non-solicited mail-in ballots are championed by the Democrats because they open up the possibility of voter fraud. Democrats also want illegal aliens and prisoners to vote, which should never be allowed. If the left eventually gets entrenched in power, elections will become a sham and eventually banned altogether. America will be like many countries in Latin America and other areas of the world where elections are rigged. If fair elections are no more, America would be destroyed.

Disarming the Public

What do Nazi Germany, The Soviet Union, and Communist China have in common? They all banned weapons in the hands of private citizens. Totalitarian governments don't want the possibility of private citizens being able to defend themselves against criminals (they don't care) or rising up in armed rebellion against a repressive regime. An armed public who can defend themselves makes them less dependent and less controllable by the government. So the Democrats are constantly trying to ban all weapons under the guise of gun control, or the euphemistic term "mandatory gun buyback." The increase of mass shootings are not the result of too few gun laws, but the breakdown of the family, faith, discipline, an increased tolerance towards evil, defunding the police or erasing a police presence in cities like Chicago, and allowing known dangerous mentally ill people to live in society. But the left believe that institutionalizing the mentally ill violates their rights, even though many of the horrible school shootings were done by known mentally ill people who were not dealt with properly but allowed to remain in society. The left blame conservatives or the NRA for opposing more gun laws. An important point previously mentioned is that many non-leftists also believe this myth that more gun laws or "gun control" will solve the problem of mass shootings.

Destroying the family

What constitutes a family is another way that leftism is destroying America. Whether one wants to make a moral judgment regarding the condition of America and the world or not, certainly America and the world have become more dangerous. God's unit of societal stability has always been the family, consisting of one father and one mother. Father-less families, particularly in the ghetto, have produced di-sastrous results. The left want a redefining of the family and desire to get rid of the western nuclear family. In fact, left-ism believes that fatherless families are OK, so no big deal if 10% of households in 1960 had no father compared to 40% today. But leftism hates western culture and the west-ern nuclear family (a position of the BLM movement) and blames it for the oppression of people of color here and in third-world countries. Again, the Marxists who control BLM don't care one bit about third world countries or people of color; they simply use them for their own goal of destroy-ing western culture and gaining their own tyrannical power. Much of the downward trend we've seen in America has resulted from the breakup of the nuclear family, especially in minority communities whom the left supposedly care about.

Destruction of the Justice System

The reason why the mob violence and other crimes have increased is that no consequences exist anymore for their crimes. Two things are happening: First, many places in the country through ill-conceived legislation have turned felonies into misdemeanors because of jail overcrowding; second, because of this and a lack of will by democratic run cities to enforce the law, protestors are arrested then released because of "bail reform" so no consequences result from committing crimes.

Leftists around the country have funded organizations such as The Minnesota Freedom Fund in Minneapolis (Supported by Kamala Harris and others) and The Bail Project which bailed out rioters who were arrested so they could return to the streets. Rich leftist donors, such as George Soros, have funded leftist candidates running for office, including District Attorneys who won't enforce the law and want to let dangerous felons out of jail. A Soros backed District Attorney, George Gascon in Los Angeles, is the latest example. Why would somebody want to have criminals released back to the streets? It's because that will create more crime, chaos, and fear among the public; exactly the desire of the Left. When things get bad enough, eventually the public will clamor for action which will be dealt with by a strong authoritarian government. People will tolerate authoritarianism if the government can maintain peace. Once that government has that power, BLM, Antifa, and other groups will be dealt with harshly in order to maintain order; like Red China and how they deal with agitators.

Another way of destroying the justice system is through packing the Supreme Court. Franklin Roosevelt tried to do that in 1936 as a way to push through his sometimes unconstitutional New Deal reforms, but was rejected by his own party. Unfortunately, today's Democratic Party is not your father's or grandfather's party; it is now the party of the far left. Today, the Democrats are accusing the Republicans of packing the Supreme Court by confirming Judge Amy Coney Barrett to the bench. But packing the court is not replacing a vacancy, as in the case of replacing the deceased Ruth Bader Ginsberg, but packing is actually adding the total of justices to more than the current nine. Yet the Democrats keep using this term as if the American people are too stupid to know the difference, which the left believe.

Destruction of the Separation of Powers

Packing the Supreme Court not only would destroy our justice system, it would destroy the separation of powers and basically abolish the legislative branch by giving legislative power to the Supreme Court; the balance of power which has worked throughout America's history would also be destroyed.

I believe they would pack the Supreme Court because the left hasn't been able to push through their socialist agenda through the legislature; instead they've historically gotten laws passed through the Supreme Court, such as Roe vs. Wade. The left consider the Supreme Court as another legislative body. What packing the Supreme Court would do is make that a reality.

Destruction of the Middle Class

Covid-19 and the George Floyd killing turned out to be the perfect storm in the radical left's plan to destroy the middle class. The middle class, especially small businesses, is the glue that holds America (and all countries) together. If the middle class of any country can be destroyed, then everybody (except the elites) become poor and ripe for a takeover by authoritarianism. The shutdowns, the rioting and looting have destroyed many small businesses and greatly contributed to the destruction of the middle class. What you end up with is a rich elite class and a poor underclass.

In a leftist takeover of America, the elites would consist of those such as powerful politicians and those of the intelligence community, Silicon Valley and other corporate CEO's, huge donors to the cause such as George Soros and other oligarch elites. Everybody else would be the "equal" lower class. That's how authoritarian ruled countries have always been structured and America would be no exception.

The Deep State

The deep state is dismissed as a conspiracy theory, but due to cronyism and corruption in the intelligence agencies, left leaning politicians, big business (especially high-tech), Wall street, billionaire financiers, the media, many believe that the deep state is a reality and constitutes a hidden government with a huge influence in the legitimately elected government and U.S. political system. The left taking complete power through winning the presidency and both houses of congress will be devastating.

Endnotes

[1] Avik Roy Forbes Staff The Apothecary Contributor Group Policy Commentary from Forbes' Policy Editor (2014)

[2] CNN Business Jan 27, 2017

[3] Politifact, the Poynter Institute July 15, 2020,

[4] Victor Budgen, *Paul Schneider and the Nazis,* unpublished manuscript, no date, p.9, idem., Was and Grace, Don Stephens, EP books, 6 Silver Court, Watchmead, Welwyn, Garden City, UK, AL71TS, p. 54.

Chapter 14

Black Lives Matter

The Black Lives Matter Movement & the Truth about Racism in America

The Black Lives Matter Movement (BLM) is a textbook example of the application all of the characteristics of leftism. This chapter will further demonstrate Leftism in action, especially with the current example of BLM. In order to further understand leftism and BLM, the purpose of this chapter is to explain what this movement is really about.

The very first thing necessary to know is that the Black Lives Matter movement is not about black lives, period. It's actually a worldwide Marxist movement dedicated to the violent overthrow of the American government and all of our institutions. It's funded by such people as George Soros and organizations like Act Blue, and unfortunately, many US corporations and sports owners who are either afraid of the left and the accusation of racism, or have decided that the left will prevail and want to be on the winning team. Even more insidious, many BLM supporting corporations, especially high tech oligarchs whom have amassed a huge amount of wealth and influence, are global in outlook with no national allegiance to America. One of the main sources of their power is information (or misinformation) over the internet and social media which gives their version of "truth." From Facebook, Google, Twitter, Instagram, and others, they have the power to censor points of view in which they disagree which are usually conservative and pro-American.

We are heading towards a system much like Russia, for example, where a few rich businessmen oligarchs have enormous power and influence. Again, the American middle class are disappearing, which as we have seen, is the goal of Marxists and other totalitarians. They want to destroy the economy and middle class, concentrate wealth and power at the top, and overthrow our existing government and all of its institutions. The oligarchs running most of our U.S. corporations have decided that the left will eventually take over the country which will give them even more power. These corporate CEOs, especially high-tech oligarchs, are basically anti-American nationalism, pro-Chinese, anti-Christian, and anti-freedom of speech.

The BLM movement distorts America's history regarding slavery and racism refusing to acknowledge how much less racist America is today while giving everybody else in the rest of the world a free pass concerning the history of racism and slavery. Some legitimate peaceful protestors in BLM are sincere but misguided and indoctrinated into believing the big lie of the left that America is the most racist country in the world and the police are out to kill as many blacks as they can. Other BLM protestors are violent and want to overthrow the government and establish a utopian socialist society. Racism still exists in America and some of the protestors have experienced racism. You add to that the propaganda they've received from this Marxist organization, plus suppression of the truth by the media & academia. and it's no wonder they are protesting, rioting, killing, and looting even though the rioting and looting are still inexcusable.

Up through 1960's, America was very racist but much progress has occurred. But the left and their sycophants in the media and academia don't mention that progress. Instead they use the killing of George Floyd, plus alleged and real incidents of mistreatment of other blacks at the hands of the police, as an excuse to claim the "systemic racism" of the police. Of course it's considered racist to say that blacks who make up 13% of the U.S. population commit around 40% of the crime—some surveys say a little higher and some say a little lower of a percentage. So, on a per capita basis, police are likely to have more contact with blacks in dangerous situations than with other races, yet actual murders of blacks are very low—in 2019, a total of 10 blacks were killed at the hands of the police, but many more blacks are killed at the hands of other blacks.

Martin Luther King would be appalled at the violence of the BLM movement today. His speech in Washington D.C., appropriately delivered on the steps at the Lincoln Memorial in Washington D.C. August 28, 1963, illustrated that racism was prevalent in the country at that time and before. He wanted everybody to work together peacefully in order to end it. See his speech in chapter 5.

History of Slavery and Racism

Before we can talk about slavery and racism in America, we need some historical context which unfortunately isn't taught much anymore in our schools and universities. The true history of slavery and racism in this country has to be understood in the world of the seventeenth, eighteenth, nineteenth, & twentieth centuries. Everybody can agree that slavery and racism are a great evil in the world which proves that the world is basically corrupt and man is a sinner and a fallen creature. Slavery, genocide, conquering indigenous peoples, and racism have been around since man has been on the planet. It's also not strictly limited to Western Europeans conquering and practicing racism against indigenous people of color as leftist historians like to emphasize. Muslims, Russians, and hordes from Asia have practiced the same throughout history. This whole idea floating around the media that Western culture and white people in America somehow created racism and slavery is part of the false narratives of the left.

In the 17th century, African slaves began coming to America and many other places, such as the West Indies and South America, and slavery was a key economic part of the worldwide economy. The slave traders were akin to the present day human traffickers and it was a lucrative business. The difference though is that slavery, as evil an institution as it was, at least served an economic purpose, whereas human traffickers just line their own pockets and serve no useful purpose—they only destroy innocent lives. It's also an inconvenient truth that slave traders didn't invade Africa and take people captive; they were aided and abetted by the local tribal leaders selling their own people into slavery for their own profit.

Abolishing Slavery

Another historical fact completely ignored in our schools is that America did more to end slavery than any other nation on Earth. To be clear, the cause of the civil war was succession by the South, not slavery itself, but slavery was the underlying cause of that succession. Slavery was the elephant in the room decades before the civil war. It actually started with the 1803 Louisiana Purchase and vast new territory added to the country. Manifest Destiny and westward expansion were the mentality in the 19th century. Unfortunately, Native Americans were in the way. The eradication of the Native Americans is the only arguable example of

America practicing genocide on another people, although blacks falsely make the same claim.

The one key issue was the following: since slavery was legal in parts of the United States, would a new state carved out of a territory become a slave or free state? The Whigs, and later the Republicans and other anti-slavery forces in the north opposed new territories being added as slave states, while the Democrats in the south advocated for the new states added to be slave states. The Missouri Compromise was a major example of the battle between abolitionists and pro-slavery politicians and shows how slavery was dealt with before the civil war:

> *"Deadlock in Washington was at length broken in 1820 by the time-honored American solution of compromise—actually a bundle of three compromises. Courtly Henry Clay of Kentucky, gifted conciliator, played a leading role. Congress, despite abolitionist pleas, agreed to admit Missouri as a slave state. But at the same time, free-soil Maine, which until then had been a part of Massachusetts, was admitted as a separate state. The balanced between the North and South was thus kept at twelve states each and remained there for fifteen years. Although Missouri was permitted to retain slaves, all future bondage was prohibited in the remainder of the Louisiana Purchase north of the line of 36° 30'—the southern boundary of Missouri."*[1]

Modern History of Racial Riots

As noted earlier, America's upheaval really began to increase in 1964; the year following my 5½ month period of training at Fort Ord. I talked about 1964 as the year that the beginning of the War in Vietnam and the rise of the radical left took stage. But the year 1964 was also when the long hot summers in America began. It started with the Harlem Riot and spread to more cities. I was overseas in Germany and received news either through Armed Forces Radio, The Stars and Stripes Newspaper, or the BBC. A lot of the news in 1964, even the Presidential Election, I didn't pay that much attention to, but the Harlem riot really affected us all, even being overseas.

> *"Harlem race riot of 1964, a six-day period of riot-ing that started on July 18, 1964, in the Manhat-tan neighbourhood of Harlem after a white off-duty police officer shot and killed an African American teenager. The rioting spread to Bedford-Stuyvesant and Brownsville in Brooklyn and to South Jamaica, Queens, and was the first of a number of race riots in major American cities—including Rochester, New York; Jersey City, Paterson, and Elizabeth, New Jersey; Dixmoor (near Chicago), Illinois; and Philadel-phia—in that year alone, not to mention the notori-ous Watts riots of 1965."*[2]

The racial atmosphere when I was overseas in 1964 was tenser than it had been prior to the summer of that year and what occurred was a polarization and taking of sides. Many southern whites were against the blacks; but surpris-ingly, I learned that some of the most bigoted whites came from places like Chicago, Detroit, New York, Philadelphia, and other places outside the South. Some blacks were the militant type who hated "whitey." Many of us, black and white, were in the middle. We got along well and did not want to take sides and join the racial prejudice bandwagon.

From 1964-1968, rioting took place every "long hot summer." The worst riots were the Watts riot in Los Ange-les in 1965, and the 1967 riots in Detroit and Newark, N.J.

The riots today are nothing new except for one distinction: the racial violence during the sixties was much more under-standable because of the years of segregation and Jim Crow laws and the institutionalized racism existing in parts of the country. Racism existed everywhere, but it was more overt in the South during the sixties.

The consequences of the riots were profound. After Lyndon Johnson won the landslide victory over Barry Gold-water in the 1964 Presidential Election, he basically had a mandate which resulted in a massive increase in the size of the federal government. The so called "War on Poverty" or "Great Society" resulted in trillions of dollars spent to fight poverty and other problems with very little results as far as ending poverty. Much of the motivation came as a result of the riots and the perceived need to help minorities. Gov-ernment handout programs referred to as "entitlements" eventually created an underclass and basically gave away a lot of free stuff which today is largely driving our nation-al debt and the unchecked expansion of government. The handouts, seen by many as being cynical, paternalistic, and condescending, seemed to be saying: "behave yourselves and we will reward you."

Ironically, in one sense, blacks were better off in the 50's and early 60's because the black family was largely in-tact with a father in the house, and black middle classes existed in many places, especially in New York (Harlem) and Washington, D.C. Blacks had to make it on their own and didn't depend on government handouts. To be sure, every-thing was segregated both in the North and the South, but blacks were not a huge poverty-stricken underclass. Then the white liberal took over to "help them."

Today, poor schools and living conditions exist in the ghetto and some racism still exists in America, but much more opportunity exists for African Americans today than in the 1960's. African Americans and whites get along much better today than in the sixties, in spite of the left's attempts to divide the races through reverse racism and identity politics. So, unfortunately, today race relations are taking a turn in the wrong direction thanks to those on the left who divide and conquer through such movements as Black Lives Matter.

The Black Lives Matter violence, besides the fact that it is based on the proven lie of "hands up, don't shoot," doesn't make sense, especially when compared to the 1960's. Many of these so called protestors never lived in the sixties and don't realize how fortunate they really are to live in America today. Unfortunately, these young protestors don't know any of this history because, not only have they not been taught true history, they've been indoctrinated into the lie of a systemic racist America. But again, up until recent events, race relations are one area where things have definitely gotten better.

Some people living here in the U.S. including bad cops are racist, but America is not a racist country anymore; especially compared to most other countries in the world. But the race grievance industry of Jesse Jackson, Al Sharpton, Jeremiah Wright, and others are having a field day dividing blacks and whites. The left depend on division and social unrest; it's where they get power and influence.

Beginnings of BLM

The rioting of 2014 in Ferguson, Missouri is an example of how the left can use a false narrative to create a whole new movement. The false narrative was of course that Officer Darren Wilson supposedly shot Michael Brown while he was pleading for his life with his hands up in surrender and yelling "don't shoot." After the testimony of some honest witnesses who witnessed the event, it was clear that Darren Wilson was under attack by Michael Brown, a large 6'4" man who was trying to take Officer Wilson's gun away from him. The killing of Michael Brown was an act of self-defense. Even an investigation by the Obama-Holder justice department came to the following conclusion:

"As discussed above, Darren Wilson has stated his intent in shooting Michael Brown was in response to a perceived deadly threat. The only possible basis for prosecuting Wilson under section 242 would therefore by if the government could prove that his account is not true—i.e., that Brown never assaulted Wilson at the SUV, never attempted to gain control of Wilson's gun, and hereafter clearly surrendered in a way that no reasonable officer could have failed to perceive. Given that Wilson's account is corroborated by physical evidence and that his perception of a threat posed by Brown is corroborated by other eyewitnesses, to include aspects of the testimony of Witness 101, there is no credible evidence that Wilson willfully shot Brown as he was attempting to surrender or was otherwise not posing a threat. Even if Wilson was mistaken in his interpretation of Brown's conduct, the fact that others interpreted that conduct the same way as Wilson precludes a determination that he acted with a bad purpose to disobey the law. The same is true even if Wilson could be said to have acted with poor judgment in the manner in which he first interacted with Brown, or in pursuing Brown after the incident at the SUV. These are matters of policy and procedure that do not rise to the level of a Constitutional violation and thus cannot support a criminal prosecution. Cf. Gardner v. Howard, 109 F.3d 427,430-31 8th Cir. 1997) (violation of

internal policies and procedures do not in and of itself rise to violation of Constitution).

Because Wilson did not act with the requisite criminal intent, it cannot be proven beyond reasonable doubt to a jury that he violated 18 U.S.C. 242 when he fired his weapon at Brown.[3]

Conclusion: For the reasons set forth above this matter lacks prosecutive merit and should be closed.

Ferguson effect

The Ferguson effect and the attack on the police in other cities, notably in New York City, Dallas, and other places, have resulted in police backing off from proactive policing in the black ghettos. As a result, violent black on black crime rose significantly. The most notable example is Chicago, where drug gang violence is claiming many black lives each year. When police leave a neighborhood, crime goes way up and the victims are usually blacks and other minorities. This is why the leftist idea of "defund the police" makes no sense until you realize that BLM is not about black lives any more than feminism is about women, of LGBTQ is about gays. Defunding the police makes perfect sense if your goal is to destroy society and cause social upheaval in America. Remember, true radical leftists are the hierarchy of BLM and want to destroy America! If Black Lives Matter was truly about black lives and racial justice, then they would be demanding three things:

First, they would advocate for school choice through vouchers so poor black families in the inner city could have the choice of going to a non-pubic school instead of being forced to attend the mostly inferior public schools in the inner city.

198

Second, they would not be in favor of defunding the police which hurts people in poor neighborhoods the most. Blacks who are stuck in the inner city ghettos are often killed by other blacks, especially with the absence of police.

Third, they would be against abortion and the common placing of Planned Parenthood abortion clinics in black neighborhoods. Abortion is the single greatest genocide committed against blacks, not the police.

The Cowardly "Mainstream"

The biggest difference between the riots in the 60's and BLM protests now, is that many so called mainstream people are on board with BLM and other leftist causes because of pressure to conform and the threat of being called racist. Democrat politicians support BLM for power and votes; Silicon Valley CEOS for ideological and practical reasons; big business in general for fear of being labeled racist and suffering financially; sports because of black athletes and cowardly owners; entertainment because of rampant leftism in Hollywood and pressure to conform or else not work in Hollywood. The left's big trump card is labeling anybody who disagrees with them a racist, but ironically, it is the left who are the true racists and see everything through the prism of race.

Indoctrination

Years of Indoctrination of "hate America" in the schools has been mentioned throughout this book as a cause why BLM protesters and Antifa riot, loot, burn American flags, commit violence, destruction of property, and seemingly want to destroy the country as we know it. Much of this indoctrination comes from what is generally called "social justice" curriculum taught in the schools and universities. The latest example and proof of this indoctrination is the changing of the names of Lincoln, Jefferson, Washington, and other schools by the San Francisco school board be- cause "Lincoln or other presidents didn't demonstrate that they cared about black lives" whatever that means. This is more evidence of a total disregard of historical context and unfairly judging history by today's standards. They're even replacing the name of an elementary school named after Diane Feinstein, a key figure in San Francisco historically and today, because of a controversy of her involvement regard- ing a Confederate flag flying over city hall. This kind of fool- ishness is not limited to San Francisco. Cowardly and indoc- trinated school administrators allowing such things are as despicable as the BLM fascists.

Antifa, in particular, is the most obvious proof of this indoctrination because many are white young people from affluent backgrounds who have never experienced racism because of their color and should know better as to how fortunate they are living in the U.S. But a hate America in- doctrination of youth through social justice curriculum has created a group of violent irrational anarchistic ingrates.

Critical Race Theory (CRT)

Two examples of the social justice curriculum taught in schools and universities are Critical Race Theory and the 1619 Project. Critical Race Theory or CRT, begun in the ear- ly 70's, is the view that the law and legal institutions are racist and that race is not biologically defined and natural, but instead, is a socially constructed concept used by white people to further their economic and political interests at the expense of people of color. So they believe that America is basically a zero-sum nation where one man's gain (a white person) is another man's loss (a person of color). Schools in Buffalo, NY and many other places are teaching this hateful nonsense.

CRT argues that racism is ingrained in the fabric and system of the American society. This is the analytical lens that CRT uses in examining existing power structures. CRT identifies that these power structures are based on white privilege and white supremacy, which perpetuates the marginalization of people of color.

Legal scholar Roy L. Brooks has defined CRT as "a collection of critical stances against the existing legal order from a race-based point of view," adding that:

"It focuses on the various ways in which the received tradition in law adversely affects people of color not as individuals but as a group. Thus, CRT attempts to analyze law and legal traditions through the history, contemporary experiences, and racial sensibilities of racial minorities in this country. The question always lurking in the background of CRT is this: What would the legal landscape look like today if people of color were the decision-makers?"[4]

The answer is that the legal landscape would look pretty much the same—especially after two terms of a black president and many more blacks in positions of power today.

Major themes of CRT include a critique of liberalism: CRT scholars favor a more aggressive approach to social transformation, as opposed to liberalism's more cautious approach—which basically seems to call all of the progress made over the years worthless—at least it never seems to be acknowledged by CRT. Another critique of liberalism by CRT is a race-conscious approach to change by rejecting liberal embrace of affirmative action, color blindness, role modeling, or merit and instead, favor an approach that relies on political organizing in contrast to liberalism's reliance on rights-based remedies. In other words, everything is on the table including rioting, looting, and destroying property, especially in black neighborhoods. These criticisms of liberalism underscore the fact that liberalism and leftism have nothing in common. Things that have worked are being discarded by CRT in favor of community organizing and coercion.

Another CRT theme is storytelling, counter-storytelling, and "naming one's own reality." Naming your own reality is classic postmodernism; the idea that there is no absolute truth and what's true for you may not be true for someone else. It is a key feature of leftism which is nihilistic and anti-God. Presumably, naming your own reality uses narratives to explore experiences of racial oppression. So naming your own reality leads to creating your own truth. "CRT uses "revisionist interpretations of American civil rights law and progress: Criticism of civil-rights scholarship and anti-discrimination law, such as Brown v. Board of Education. Derrick Bell, one of CRT's founders, argued that civil rights advances for blacks coincided with the self-interest of white elitists. Others contend that civil rights legislation wasn't passed for the benefit of blacks or other minorities, but rather, it was enacted in order to improve the image of the United States in the eyes of third-world countries the US needed as allies during the Cold War with the Soviet Union."[5] Apparently Derrick Bell doesn't believe the truth that advances in civil rights benefit all of society. Today, the leftist white elitists are the largest contributors to BLM.

Another theme is called "Intersectional theory:" the examination of race, sex, class, national origin, and sexual orientation, and how their combination plays out in various settings, e.g., how the needs of a Latina female are different from those of a black male and whose needs are the ones promoted.[6]" So people can't simply be people anymore, they have to be a designated by race or gender. It tells a lot about the left's view towards rejecting individualism and exceptionalism in favor of group identity—which always results in mediocrity.

Another theme is "Essentialism: Reducing the experience of a category (gender or race) to the experience of one sub-group (white women or African-Americans). In essence, all oppressed people share the commonality of oppression. However, such oppression varies by gender, class, race, etc., and therefore, the aims and strategies will differ for each of these groups.[7]" You can't make this stuff up! Again, it proves that the left see everything in terms of race, class, and gender.

Another "idea" is Structural determinism: "Exploration of how 'the structure of legal thought or culture influences its content,' whereby a particular mode of thought or widely shared practice determines significant social outcomes, usually occurring without conscious knowledge. As such, theorists posit that our system cannot redress certain kinds of wrongs."[8] It's called prejudice and our system has made great progress, but prejudice will always be a part of humanity because man is a sinner.

And of course the big one: white privilege: "Belief in the notion of a myriad of social advantages, benefits, and courtesies that come with being a member of the dominant race (i.e. white people). A clerk not following you around in a store or not having people cross the street at night to avoid you, are two examples of white privilege.[9]" Maybe the reason a clerk follows a black person around in a store or crossing the street at night is because the crime rate among blacks is so much higher than that of whites. Yes it's terrible that people do that, but black on white crime is higher than the reverse.

Micro-aggression: "Belief in the notion that sudden, stunning, or dispiriting transactions have the power to mar the everyday of oppressed individuals. These include small acts of racism consciously or unconsciously perpetrated, whereby an analogy could be that of water dripping on a rock wearing away at it slowly. Micro-aggressions are based on the assumptions about racial matters that are absorbed from cultural heritage."[10] Anything can be seen as racism, but CRT is not about solving the problem of racism, it's about indoctrinating victim groups to remain victims "protected" by big government which is all about attaining more power for government and less freedom for the individual.

Empathetic fallacy: "Believing that one can change a narrative by offering an alternative narrative in hopes that the listener's empathy will quickly and reliably take over. Empathy is not enough to change racism as most people are not exposed to many people different from themselves and people mostly seek out information about their own culture and group.[11]" Again, to the left, people are not individuals but members of different identity groups, which in itself, is dehumanizing.

This is the kind of psycho-babble that is being taught in many of our schools today. Again, it's no wonder that so many people are confused and believe the nonsense that America is the most racist country on earth and are willing to riot, loot, and destroy society.

President Donald Trump has rightly attacked the corrupted educational viewpoint known as CRT, which again looks at American society and institutions from the perspective of race and racism, calling it "toxic propaganda" and "ideological poison" and to his credit signed an executive order banning CRT from being taught in federal institutions. Trump also wants to have patriotic and traditional American history curriculum restored in schools.

CRT advocates claim that "Critical race theory is a body of scholarly thought aimed at dismantling racism on a structural level by examining how race affects dominant institutions and culture and holds that old systemic racism continues to affect society today. But Trump says that it is an attempt by "the radical left" to paint all whites as racist and that, if not removed, will "dissolve the civic bonds that tie us together."[12] President Trump is absolutely correct!

1619 Project

The 1619 project is a current and blatant attempt by the left to rewrite American history, to denigrate America, and distort history in trying to make the case that America is an evil racist oppressive country. Donald Trump nailed it when he said the following: "'The left have warped, distorted, and defiled the American story with deceptions, falsehoods, and lies. There is no better example than the New York Times' totally discredited 1619 Project,' he said, during his speech at the National Archives Museum on Thursday, according to the New York Daily News.' This project rewrites American history to teach our children that we were founded on the principle of oppression, not freedom.'"[13] The great irony is that, if the left ever get total control, America will indeed become a country based on oppression because all freedoms will vanish.

The following commentary by historian Jack D. Warren Jr. says it all regarding the 1619 project.

"As teachers get ready for the fall, thousands will be tempted to make use of the 1619 Project curriculum offered online by the Pulitzer Center, which has formed a partnership with the New York Times to distribute lesson plans built around the essays in the 1619 Project, which were originally published in the New York Times Magazine in August 2019. Teachers and school administrators should resist this temptation, since academic reviewers, including some of the nation's leading historians, have been unyielding in their criticism of the 1619 Project, pointing to numerous errors of fact and interpretation and rejecting its fundamental claim that the nation is defined by racism and was conceived in oppression. There are better ways to teach students about the history and ordeal of slavery—an important subject that deserves our finest efforts.

Those same academic critics, unfortunately, have not turned their attention to the 1619 Project curriculum, which is the means by which the poisonous errors and coarse misinterpretations of Nikole Hannah-Jones and her colleagues will be transmitted, like a disease, to young Americans. Having issued their learned responses in the pages of the Atlantic or the Wall Street Journal, they may find it sufficient that the 1619 Project curriculum is the fruit of a poison tree, and not bother to examine it.

That's not a wise position to take. The radical ideologues promoting Nikole Hannah-Jones' grotesque view of America aren't after the mature readers of the Atlantic or the Wall Street Journal. Despite their recent, rapid gains, they're sticking to the long game they've been playing for decades, going after young, impressionable minds. Their method is not to persuade. It is to propagandize.

Their method has been working for some forty years. Their patron saint, the late Howard Zinn, aimed his subversive, error-packed People's History of the United States at teenagers, most of them ill-equipped to see through his irrationality, misuse of sources, and politicized misinterpretations. Indeed Zinn never tried to disguise his aims when addressing mature audiences, to which he said many times that objective truth does not exist and that teaching history is nothing more than a means to advance a political agenda by confecting and presenting interpretations to support it.

The simplicity of the radical dialectic—a bipolar world of oppressors and oppressed, without the complexity or confusing contradictions of a more nuanced, realistic, view of the past—appeals to many young people. It also simplifies the task of overburdened teachers faced with the challenge of equipping students to interpret a complex and confusing world. The radical history of Howard Zinn and Nikole Hannah-Jones addresses present-day dilemmas, and seems more relevant, and certainly more accessible, than the nuanced history writing of serious scholars like Gordon Wood, Mary Beth Norton, Sean Wilentz, and James McPherson. But the fact remains that history is complicated and requires patient study, a willingness to weigh and assess confusing, fragmentary, and sometimes contradictory evidence, and the sophistication to understand that historical events and actors are shaped by many factors, of which race, while often important, is only one. Students really ought to be taught to emulate scholars who understand this, rather than to follow a venomous twenty-first-century Madame Defarge intent on reducing American history to a dismal story of racists and their victims.

The 1619 Project curriculum is actually worse than the dishonest and deceptive material on which it is based. A mature adult reader of the 1619 Project may be equipped to apply critical reasoning to its claims—particularly Hannah-Jones' claim that the purpose of the American Revolution was to perpetuate slavery. We cannot reasonably expect middle school and high school students, to whom we ought to be teaching critical reasoning skills, to bring the same kind of skepticism to their reading of works we assign them. The 1619 Project curriculum goes out of its way to avoid a critical reading of Hannah-Jones central claims. It expects student to accept her conclusions about the nature of American history and culture without critical inquiry and asks them to regard the world around them from Hannah-Jones' perspective, rather than treat Hannah-Jones as one of many interpreters, much less recognize her as a journalist with no credentials or standing as an historian.

The premise of the curriculum is that Nikole Hannah-Jones has discovered a fundamental truth about American history that has eluded the historical profession: that the central, defining feature of American history and culture is racism. The exercises that make up this curriculum are all based on this premise.

None of those exercises invite students to challenge the premise. Every exercise involves asking students a loaded question—a question that presupposes the relevant facts and serves the questioner's agenda. The effect is the same as asking an innocent man if he has stopped beating his wife. The only sensible response is to dispute the premise by saying "I have never beaten my wife." But students are rarely welcome to dispute the premise of their teachers' questions.

Indeed in the current cultural climate, a student brave enough to challenge the Hannah-Jones premise is quite likely to be accused of being a racist—the fastest route to such a charge at this time being to challenge the thesis that something called "systemic racism" is the defining characteristic of American history and culture. The truth of this thesis has quite suddenly become an article of faith, not subject to scrutiny or consideration using the traditional canons of evidence. The Pulitzer Center's curriculum is not a tool for intellectual exploration or discovery. It is a catechism.

Like a catechism, it presupposes the articles of the faith—one of which is the irrational and indefensible absurdity that the American Revolution was conducted to per-petuate slavery. This is, in fact, the main pillar of the faith. If, as a generation of historians from Edmund S. Morgan and Bernard Bailyn, to Gordon S. Wood have made clear, the American Revolution was a pivotal moment in the develop-ment of human freedom, the central premise of the 1619 Project is revealed as pernicious nonsense.

Under no circumstances do the creators of the 1619 Project curriculum suggest students entertain this possibil-ity. There is no room for questioning the new revelation. This is nowhere clearer than in the centerpiece of the 1619 Project curriculum, a lesson entitled "Exploring 'The Idea of America' by Nikole Hannah-Jones." In it, students are asked to read Hannah-Jones' error-choked essay and then respond to a series of questions based on the assumption that Hannah-Jones' claims are fact and that any assertion to the contrary is, by definition, racist.

"What examples of hypocrisy in the founding of the United States does Hannah-Jones supply?" is the lead—and leading—question. That the founding of the United States was an exercise in hypocrisy is taken for granted—because Hannah-Jones says so. The follow-up question is contorted to require students to recapitulate Hannah-Jones' errors about the Revolution as if they were facts: "What evidence can you see for how 'some might argue that this nation was founded not as a democracy but as a slaveocracy?'"

At no point in the lesson are students asked to weigh the validity of what Hannah-Jones says about the American Revolution, nor to judge the evidence she presents, because a perceptive student would recognize that she presents no evidence at all. Neither here nor anywhere else in this so-called curriculum are students asked to read and consider any of the several carefully reasoned critiques of "The Idea of America," including those written by important historians and published in major magazines, like the one by Sean Wilentz in the Atlantic.

'What picture does Hannah-Jones paint of the major figures in classical U.S. history such as Thomas Jefferson and Abraham Lincoln?' Jefferson and Lincoln were racists is the answer programmed into this catechism—students need only refer to "The Idea of America" to validate that claim. 'Did you learn new information about them from her essay?' Yes, the student is led to answer, followed by something like 'I learned how despicable they truly are.' And since you learned this new information, the catechist concludes, 'why do you think this information wasn't included in other resources from which you have learned about U.S. history?'

You get the idea. Susan or Johnny are supposed to respond 'because the history books from which I've learned about U.S. history were written by systemic racists,' and gets extra credit for blessing Nikole Hannah-Jones for opening their eyes to the true faith. Woe unto the student who responds 'I don't think I learned that Jefferson and Lincoln were despicable from the books I've read because they were written by distinguished historians who devoted many years to research, carefully documented their assertions, and faced the scrutiny of professional peer review. They don't think what Nikole Hannah-Jones has written is correct. In fact, with respect to Jefferson and Lincoln, the preeminent authorities think she's totally wrong.' Few sixteen- and seventeen-year-old U.S. history students are prepared to serve up that answer, and a teacher who's embraced the 1619 Project curriculum with the zeal of a convert is not likely to respond favorably to those who can. Such a teacher might be prepared to quote Ms. Hannah-Jones, who disdains her critics as "old, white male historians" and sneers, for example, at James McPherson, the most respected Civil

War historian of our time. 'Who considers him preeminent?' Hannah-Jones asks. 'I don't.'

To put this sneer in context: James McPherson spent a distinguished career as an historian at Princeton. His book, The Struggle for Equality, is a standard work on the fight for black emancipation and empowerment in the Civil War and Reconstruction. His succeeding volume, The Abolitionist Legacy: From Reconstruction to the NAACP, carries the story of civil rights activism down to 1910. W.E.B. DuBois called that crusade 'the finest thing in American history.' Professor McPherson's history of the Civil War era, Battle Cry of Freedom, put conflicting ideas about freedom, including the freedom of African-Americans, at the center of the story. The book won the Pulitzer Prize and was praised by Ms. Hannah-Jones own New York Times as perhaps the best one-volume history of the Civil War ever published. His many important books include Abraham Lincoln and the Second American Revolution and Ordeal by Fire: Civil War and Reconstruction.

A student who suggested we rely on James McPherson's view of Lincoln, elaborated in collected works spread over nearly sixty years of patient scholarship, instead of the view of Nicole Hannah-Jones, whose collected works on Lincoln fill a few skimpy paragraphs, risks being labeled a racist by the new inquisition. The 1619 Project curriculum does not admit the possibility that 'other resources from which you have learned about U.S. history—the collected works of James McPherson, perhaps—could be right and the 1619 Project wrong.' That would be heresy.

The whole dismal exercise bears comparison with the work of a German pedagogue of the 1930s, Werner May, whose German National Catechism asked leading questions in the same style: 'How has the Jew subjugated the peoples?' The answer: 'With Money . . . Thousands and thousands of Germans have been made wretched by the Jews and been reduced to poverty.' And another: 'What other guilt does the Jew bear?' The answer: 'While the German people was fighting a life and death battle during the World War, the Jew incited people at home and seduced them into treason. . . . He corrupted Germans through bad books . . . Everywhere, his influence was destructive.' The cost to a young German of challenging the premise of these questions was high, and few students dared. Most, of course, dutifully repeated the dogmas as they were told to do.

Like the grotesquely distorted view of American history and culture framed by Nikole Hannah-Jones in her essay, "The Idea of America," the catechism devised by the Pulitzer Center is an anti-intellectual exercise, scorning historical scholarship and elevating an error-riddled newspaper essay above interpretations of the American past carefully constructed by serious scholars over more than fifty years. The 1619 Project curriculum is not an educational enterprise. It is tool of political indoctrination. No school system should endorse it. No teacher should use it. And no student should be misled by it, nor punished for rejecting its fatally flawed premise."[14]

More and more, we are losing our young people to this kind of leftist indoctrination. Some textbooks in California want to define capitalism as white racism. Again, it's no wonder that BLM, Antifa, and others are in the streets rioting and looting. Critical Race Theory and its hideous new step child the 1619 Project are indoctrinating young people to hate America. That and the breakdown of family, faith, and guidance are the reasons for the rioting and looting, not systematic racism in America. Like the previously mentioned Werner May and his indoctrination against the Jews in 1930's Germany, today's youth are being indoctrinated by CRT and the 1619 project into becoming the Hitler Youth and Brown Shirts of today.

Two simple questions to ask concerning the charge of systematic racism in America are: First, America is racist compared to whom? If compared with the rest of the world, America is the least racist and most free country. Second, Is America more or less racist than it was in the 1960's and before? It is much less racist.

Most blacks today have probably experienced racism, so because what many of them have been taught through historical revisionism, they probably regard America as being systemically racist. But America is much less racist because of much progress made in the last fifty years. Yes, some racism still exists and will always exist, but growing up in the 1950's and 60's, racism was much worse then. Unfortunately, our youth are not being taught that fact.

One More Example

If black Lives matter, they should include black babies who are aborted, or black cops who are killed. Bringing this up is considered racist and dealt with through the fascism of political correctness. Illustrated in the following of many examples shows the dynamic of how the left have weaponized political correctness and the sanctimonious and obsequiousness responses, especially regarding BLM.

North Penn School District Special Education Supervisor Ashley Bennett has been placed on administrative leave, following a public post on Facebook denouncing the Black Lives Matter movement. The now-deleted post, which was shared by Bennett on Wednesday night, said in part:

"I see signs all over saying #BlackLivesMatter. I'm just trying to figure out WHICH black lives matter. It can't be the unborn black babies – they are destroyed without a second thought. It's not black cops – they don't seem to matter at all. It's not my black #Conservative friends. They are told to shut the **** up if they know what's best for them by their black counterparts. It's not black business owners. Their property, their business and their employees don't mean anything. So which black lives matter again?"[15]

Frankly, I couldn't have said it better! That statement is entirely correct! It points out the hypocrisy of BLM and their true intent of destroying this country and anybody who gets in their way without any real regard for black lives. But any criticism of BLM is considered racist.

Bennett's post continues its focus on the Black Lives Matter movement, before taking aim at the coronavirus response, mainstream media coverage, Democrats and others. The post then wraps up with a prayer that God will heal the country.

In reading this book, by now you know that I would agree with any criticism concerning coronavirus response, the Democrats, and the media.

By Thursday morning, Bennett's post had made its way through several local Facebook groups, including Black Residents of Lansdale Area United, where the statements were near-universally decried as insensitive and unacceptable. It also drew the attention of North Penn School District officials, who condemned the post as being out of alignment with the district's views and values.

In response to a request for comment from North Penn Now, district officials provided the following statement:

"The comments that were brought to our attention do not align with the North Penn School District's core values. The views expressed are in direct conflict with our work to develop a community that values diversity. We strive to acknowledge, respect, understand, and celebrate the dynamics of racial and cultural differences. Through the development of a culturally proficient staff, the establishment of structures that promote equitable opportunities, and partnerships with families and students, our school district seeks to create an environment of respect where all members of the school community are empowered to learn, grow, and appreciate one another."

What sanctimonious hogwash!

Officials said that Bennett has since been placed on administrative leave while they conduct an investigation into her actions. When asked for the district's official stance on racial inequality and the Black Lives Matter movement, officials referenced a prior joint statement made by the North Penn Board of School Directors in late May. The district later added the following addition to their statement:

"A school district should be a reflection of its community, and the overwhelming support at numerous events for Black Lives Matter across the diverse and vibrant North Penn community aligns with our district's goals to make genuine, sustainable change. The school district stands 100% behind the values and character demonstrated during this past week-

end's community-wide, peaceful and unifying Soli-
darity March organized by North Penn students and
graduates."

Efforts by North Penn Now to reach Bennett for comment have been unsuccessful at this time. However, Bennett did post a public apology to Facebook on Thursday night, stating that she used poor judgement and taking responsibility for her actions.[17]

Of course, one is forced to listen to their lecturing about how morally pure they are, especially in their adherence to diversity, and how Bennett committed the great sin of an honest assessment of BLM and their hypocrisy. These school district members, like so many others around the country, are self-righteous fools and cowards. Now Bennett is forced to bow down to political correctness. It's disturbing that in the following statement, she chose to bow down and admit her "error," when she was perfectly correct in what she said. There was nothing inappropriate about the post except that the victim culture gets offended by anything now and the action is to cancel such politically incorrect heretics who would post the truth. Yes, she should've known that any truth concerning BLM would be deemed racist and that she would be cancelled. Now she has to somehow come back from the attack of personal destruction by the left:

"All: I shared a post a few days back that was in-
appropriate. I didn't realize at the time how it was
going to be interpreted. I should have. It was some-
thing on my page and I should have been more
aware. Up until recently, [Facebook] has always just
been a way to keep up with my friends, their kids and
dogs. I allowed all of the negativity to get to me and

used poor judgement. Anything that I posted that was interpreted as racist was not my intent. A very wise person made me see that I was wrong. Anyone who was offended...I apologize. I plan to learn and grow from this experience so that my apology is not just words. I take responsibility for my poor actions and hope those of you who know me can eventually forgive me. I will be going off [Facebook] for awhile (sic), so I can focus on the positives. [Thanks] for listening."[18]

Once again, her "error" of judgment was not realizing that anything critical of Black Lives Matter is considered racist. But, in bringing up the inconsistencies of which black lives matter, she simply exposed the truth: black lives don't really matter to BLM. These types of incidents are happening all over the country and point to the fascism of political correctness.

Woke is a Joke

The Black Lives Matter movement born in Ferguson, Missouri and "Woke," are the product of years of ignorance of history and downright indoctrination through such lying propaganda as Critical Race theory and the 1619 Project. "In the six years since Brown's death, "woke" has evolved into a single-word summation of leftist political ideology, centered on social justice politics and critical race theory."[19] Woke and BLM are anti-white western culture and based on a lie concerning Michael Brown's death in Ferguson Missouri. So the origin of woke being based on a lie is only fitting because truth is the enemy of the left. If the left take absolute power in America, the joke will be on woke because they won't be needed anymore.

Endnotes

[1] The American Pageant, David M. Kennedy, Lizabeth Cohen, Thomas A. Baily, Houghton Mifflin Company, Boston, New York (2006), p. 247.

[2] https://www.britannica.com/topic/Harlem-riot

[3] Progressive Management, 2015, p. 86

[4] "What Is Critical Race Theory?". UCLA School of Public Affairs. November 4, 2009. Retrieved 11 March 2012.

[5] Ibid

[6] Ibid

[7] Ibid

[8] Ibid

[9] Ibid

[10] Ibid

[11] Ibid

[12] https://www.bet.com/news/national/2020/09/18/trump-critical-race-theory-patriotic-education-schools.html

[13] Ibid

[14] Slavery, Rights, and the Meaning of the American Revolution ...www.americanrevolutioninstitute.org ›slavery-rights-a commentary by Jack D. Warren, June 16, 2020

[15] Keith Heffintrayer• Fri, Jul 31, 2020, 9:19 AMN orthPennNow.com.

[16] Ibid.

[17] Ibid.

[18] Ibid.

[19] https://www.vox.com/culture/21437879/stay-woke-woke-ness-history-origin-evolution-controversy

Chapter 15

Covid-19

Overview

It has to be remembered that at the beginning of the virus outbreak nobody knew very much about Covid-19. I can remember during the beginning of the news about the Corona Virus in December, 2019 and January, 2020, the World Health Organization (WHO) and China both declared that the virus was non-contagious. That turned out to be a lie. Based on that false information, Dr. Anthony Fauci, President Trump, Andrew Cuomo, Nancy Pelosi, the CDC, and others were saying that the virus was no big deal. Nancy Pelosi even had a crowded party with no masks in San Francisco's Chinatown to show that it was no big deal. Dr. Zeke Emanuel initially said masks probably wouldn't work, but now thinks everybody should wear a mask. But, with Covid-19, the left cannot see or apply a historical context remembering that in the beginning no one knew what we were dealing with. So they now blame President Trump for not acting quickly enough even though they were criticizing him for taking early action in banning flights from China and Europe.

On January 6, the CDC offered in a letter to Chinese officials to send a team of CDC scientists to assist China. China didn't accept the offer for several weeks delaying the U.S. access to vital information about the virus. This important information would have been very helpful in developing diagnostic testing and a vaccine much earlier. In mid-January, the WHO announced that the virus was indeed contagious.

Meanwhile, China had bought up much of the world supply of the PPE equipment before the extent of the pandemic became known and left the rest of the world short. In mid-January, 2020, the news showed Wuhan, China with everybody wearing a mask to prevent the spread of Covid-19, so it became clear that the virus was very contagious. China closed Wuhan off from the rest of China, but allowed air travel outside of China which guaranteed a world-wide pandemic which I believe was intentional.

Were Lockdowns Necessary?

As more scientific data became available, it was apparent to many that maintaining the lockdowns were unnecessary providing that reasonable precautions were taken. Many doctors questioned some of the extended shutdown measures taken further into the pandemic and were criticized. With the spikes in cases even after severe lockdowns, it became apparent that lockdowns certainly haven't worked here in the U.S. Countries such as Spain and Italy which had severe lockdowns early still had huge outbreaks later on and at the present still showing that lockdowns in those countries and others were not very effective. Sweden, on the other hand while practicing minimal caution, kept their economy open and is doing much better than other countries. Their schools and businesses stayed open. Half of their Covid-19 deaths occurred in nursing homes.

A lot of confusion existed, and still does, concerning masks, outdoor safety, testing, opening up the economy, schools, and how to approach this problem. Dr. Scott Atlas of Stanford Medical Center and a fellow at the Hoover Institute claimed that real science showed that shutdowns were unnecessary especially when considering all the harm lockdowns did to the country. He was attacked by the media and some other doctors at Stanford in an "open letter" which claimed that Dr. Atlas' views didn't represent real science. Dr. Atlas threatened a defamation lawsuit unless the letter was rescinded.

When one considers the catastrophic damage to our country physically, economically, and mentally, it validates the claims of Dr. Atlas and many other doctors that the long extended lockdown experienced in America and elsewhere did more harm than good. Basically, the "cure" became worse than the virus.

A lot of discussion and confusion still exists concerning the science, which has become politicized mainly by the WHO, CDC, NIH, AMA, the media, and the Democrats. But again, one thing is for sure: we absolutely know that the damage to America has been catastrophic, but are less sure about the effectiveness of measures to control the virus because it has been so politicized.

It also has become apparent that this politicicalizing of the pandemic was worse because it was an election year and the blue state leaders wanted to continue the lockdown in order to keep the economy from rebounding and hurt Donald Trump's chances of re-election.

Democratic leaders also liked idea of a lockdown because it gave them more power and control over people's lives and livelihood. Compare the measures taken between Democratic run cities and Republican cities and states, the results are revealing. The Democrats simply put politics and exercising of power ahead of the country. The leftist leaders in the blue states are still using Covid-19 to expand their power and control. They claim to follow science, but science has already shown that lockdowns don't solve the problem.

The corrupt media, especially CNN and MSNBC, whom Donald Trump rightly calls "fake news," believed that China handled the situation well and blamed President Trump's so-called mismanagement of the virus—exactly the position of China, the Democrats, and the America-hating worldwide left.

The media also created hysteria by misreporting the extent of shortages of ICU beds. They cherry picked some cases where that was true, but overlook other examples where plenty of ICU beds were available. An example is Utah where in early December, 86% of ICU beds statewide were occupied. But Utah has many universities in the greater Salt Lake City area plus smaller colleges which were open. So Utah's spike really began with the new school year and the opening of universities. College kids are not known for taking precautions. Yet elementary through high schools, small businesses, and churches are always blamed for any spike.

The use of therapeutics such as Hydroxychloroquine and Vitamin D had also been politicized as not being effective and a fake cure touted by President Trump even though many physicians, including Nigerian-American doctor Stella Immanuel of Houston, said it works if used in the early stages of Covid-19. Many studies have shown that Hydroxychloroquine is not effective if used in the later stages of the virus when it's probably too late, or if the patient has extreme health issues. So critics only seemed to cite studies of patients with health problems that would make Hydroxychloroquine ineffective and then ignored testimonies by many doctors that Hydroxychloroquine with Zinc is effective if used in the early stages of the virus. Dr. Immanuel has been attacked by the media and others because going against the dogma of "consensus" within the medical community is demonized as misinformation. No consensus existed concerning Hydroxychloroquine; pro and con views existed among doctors. But more evidence has come out showing that a greater use of therapeutics could have saved many lives of people if used early in their illness, but non-treatment by therapeutics caused them to get much sicker and finally end up on a ventilator when it was too late for many. The politicizing of therapeutics as not very effective probably costed many lives.

Fall Surprise?

Was the large spike of Covid-19 cases in the Fall of 2020 really a surprise? No because it was predicted months ago, that with the beginning of the flu season, cases would go up because the weather would be much colder and people would spend more time indoors. This was one of the few things that predictors got right except now nobody has heard of the flu, it all seems to be Covid-19 which is odd. One possible explanation is that precautions and the flu vaccine have greatly cut down cases of the flu, but I wonder if the flu cases are also attributed to Covid-19. Adding to the total of Covid-19 cases feeds the narrative that the pandemic is even worse than anybody realized. Because nobody seems to be dying from the flu anymore, one can be too cynical.

Overestimating Deaths

The preceding question about flu cases leads to asking how many Covid-19 cases and deaths reported were actually from the virus? Are these figures inflated for financial gain by the hospitals and political gain for the Democrats? Some dismiss this as conspiracy nut and flat-lander lies, but the following is interesting:

"According to the US Department of Health and Human Services [HHS] which oversees the Centers for Medicare & Medicaid Services, under the federal coronavirus aid relief bill known as the CARES Act, hospitals get an extra 20% in Medicare reimbursements on top of traditional rates due to the public health emergency. That's for COVID-19 related admissions, which can include deaths. The pay-out amount varies, according to a Medicare spokesperson who said 'Medicare adjusts hospital payment based on geographic variation in local costs'. Also, earlier this month, HHS announced a second round of federal relief for hospitals in high impact areas, totaling $10 billion. Of that second-round money, HHS reported that 63 California hospitals received $50,000 for each eligible coronavirus patient they admitted between Jan. 1 and June 10, 2020. That's a combined total of more than $607 million.'"[1]

Numerous accounts on Fox news (nobody else will cover these stories) by some doctors and at least one traveling nurse in Dallas declared that they were pressured by the hospital to report cases and deaths as Covid-19 when some were not.

Late 2020 to Early 2021 Spike in Cases

So why did more cases occur and spike in the fall and early winter 20-21?

First, the colder weather in most of the country caused people to meet together indoors, especially during the holiday season, which increased chances of exposure.

Second, much more testing was done which identified more cases of infection.

Third, there was some irresponsible behavior consisting of large gatherings with no masks or social distancing. Medical experts still disagree regarding the effectiveness of masks and now many are saying that only the n95 mask really works, but any mask probably should be worn if there are indoor gatherings with no social distancing. Any mask is better than nothing and, if nothing else, it makes some people feel safer.

Fourth, when outbreaks occurred on our university campuses, many students were sent home only to infect family members; they and their families would've been better off if these students had stayed on campus.

Fifth, as previously mentioned, over-reporting of cases and ICU visits for political and financial gain; even declaring deaths as Covid-19 when they might have been from other causes, especially when people are already health compromised. Two unreported statistics are the number of cases that are from the flu or another sickness and not Covid-19, and the percentage of death vs. Covid-19 cases, which, again, in America is around the 2% range, which is pretty good.

Please, No More Shutdowns

The worst thing we could ever do now is to panic and shut down the nation again. One thing that has been clear throughout much of this virus crisis is that shutting down the nation has had catastrophic results. Once again, the cure was worse than the virus. Besides all of the physical, financial, mental, and social damage, shutdowns have greatly increased the power and influence of government over the people, which is never a good thing. Los Angeles County had shut down indoor and outdoor dining at all restaurants. This was a blatant example of government coercively exerting its power over the people. The science didn't support this action and LA County's own research showed that restaurants were not a huge source of the spread of Covid-19; instead, the spread was worse, twice as bad, in government buildings. The California Restaurant Assn. sued LA County and finally we saw some common sense in the Judge's ruling against the county which stated that:

"Los Angeles County's health director acted "arbitrarily" and didn't prove the danger to the public when she banned outdoor dining at restaurants as coronavirus cases surged last month, a judge ruled Tuesday in a case other businesses may use to try to overturn closures and restrictions. The county failed to show that health benefits outweigh the negative economic effects before issuing the ban, Superior Court Judge James Chalfant wrote. He also said the county did not offer evidence that outdoor dining presented a greater risk of spreading the virus. 'By failing to weigh the benefits of an outdoor dining restriction against its costs, the county acted arbitrarily and its decision lacks a rational relationship to a legitimate end,' the judge wrote. Chalfant limited the outdoor dining ban to three weeks and said once it expires Dec. 16 the Department of Public Health must conduct a risk-benefit analysis before

trying to extend it. It was the first victory for California restaurants challenging health orders that have crippled their industry. But there was no immediate relief for LA county restaurant owners because a more sweeping shutdown ordered by Gov. Gavin Newsom now is in effect. The California Restaurant Association, which brought the lawsuit, had hoped the judge would lift the ban but still was pleased with the result. 'I do think that this is going to hold the county's feet to the fire when they decide to close down an entire sector of economy,' association lawyer Richard Schwartz said. 'You can't have a cure that's worse than the disease.'"[2]

The whole issue of shutdowns should be based on risk vs. reward. The Judge correctly factored in the negative of economic damage resulting in shutdowns. Risk vs. reward should have been applied everywhere, because extensive shutdowns have proven beyond any doubt that shutting down the country was not worth the risk. The surgeon general, head of CDC, and Dr. Fauci, among others have since stated that outdoor lockdowns at not necessary.

Currently here in California at the end of 2020 and into early 2021, cases were spiking even though we've been under the strictest lockdown in the nation. California and New York, states have the most stringent lockdowns yet in December 2020, had the highest death rate per 100,000 cases. By contrast, Florida had a lower death rate than California and New York and yet did not shut down, in fact, businesses were open, schools were open, and Disney World was open. Florida did it right, so why do the media still viciously attack Florida? First, Trump won Florida by about four points; second, Florida has a great Republican governor in Ron DeSantis who has been outspoken against the politicization of Covid-19 by the media and Democrats; third, Florida tried to vaccinate the most vulnerable first, those over 65, in order to follow the real science; and fourth, Florida had resisted attempts by the left to corrupt their election process.

To the Left Covid-19 is the best thing that ever happened in a long time because it gave government more power. Leftist authoritarian governors like Kate Brown of Oregon created more fear in people and even pitted one side against the other in further dividing the country by advising people to rat out their neighbors if more than six people gathered inside during the holidays. That's what the Nazis encouraged in the 30's and 40's if a neighbor was suspected of hiding Jewish people.

Many believe that ICU visits and deaths went down, even after the economy was finally cautiously opened up back in June. The spikes in infections, especially after the 4th of July weekend, caused further shutting down. Again, it's important to note that people acting irresponsibly by going back to pre-pandemic behavior and gathering mostly unprotected in large crowds, especially in bars, protests, and colleges, had largely caused the spikes, not churches, restaurants, and other small businesses. But the left hate small business and churches because they are institutions that the left don't control and they represent freedom to succeed or fail. Small businesses are the backbone of this country which is reason enough for the left to hate them. Small business is also the heart of the middle class, which the left seek to destroy. Leftists also hate the true biblical church because it opposes leftism in every way and always has throughout history.

With the Biden administration, further shutdowns are still on the table and are being threatened or have been implemented. However, the death rate per 100,000 continues to decline and America has done much better in comparison with most of the rest of the world, which is ignored by most of the media. Again, with the exception of Fox News and talk radio, the media never mention the low U.S. death rate, which is around 2 per cent and far lower than most other countries. This can change, especially if people gather together irresponsibly. But we don't need any more shutdowns.

Intellectually and morally reprobate comments on low rated cable networks, plus postings on social media have suggested that Trump has "blood on his hands" because of what he knew in February and should've locked down then. Yet, at the end of January, President Trump banned all flights from China and was immediately attacked as racist and Xenophobic by Joe Biden and other Democrats. Once again, the lockdown of America at first seemed reasonable because not much was known about the virus, but it turned out to be an overreaction with catastrophic consequences for the country in so many ways. Yet lockdowns continued even after evidence demonstrated that they didn't work.

Catastrophe

Because of the following catastrophic damage, Covid-19 is America's twenty-first century Vietnam! Many have lost their livelihood as businesses closed and unemployment rose. This caused financial hardship, loss of homes, a rise in domestic violence, alcohol and drug abuse, crime, suicides, divorce, and damage to families. Children were kept out of school which affected their learning as well as missing important socialization with other kids while spending too much time in front of a screen which may be affecting their eyesight. A collateral health crisis was also created because people were afraid to go to the doctor for routine checkups, many of which can detect serious health problems before it's too late for treatment. Americans are also a social people and want to meet in groups. Social isolation is damaging and caused all kinds of emotional problems. Yes, over 400,000 deaths is a tragedy, but the sheer devastation done to this country, especially by unnecessary lockdowns for political motives along with questionable science is even a bigger tragedy.

New Year's Surprise: A New Strain

Now the year 2021 has greeted us with another Covid-19 twist: new strains of the virus which are touted as more contagious than the current one. Unfortunately, due to the present political atmosphere with all of the lies and half-truths we've heard during this pandemic here and abroad, this begs question such as: "What's behind this?" Are these simply a mutations or another virus released by China? Are these new viruses another media hoax like the Russia collusion scandal? Although these questions sound conspiratorial, the fact is that America is the current victim of a true conspiracy: the radical socialist left's attempt to destroy our economy, society, and all of our institutions. A weakened and frightened country makes that goal much easier to attain.

Did China Intentionally Release the Virus to the Rest of the World?

I believe the answer is yes because China wants to be the dominant power in the world. What better way to further that cause than through weakening the rest of the world economically, especially the U.S? China is also a leftist country, meaning that it is a totalitarian ruled nation where the individual has no rights and the end justifies the means. Maintaining that kind of control over people requires lies, propaganda, and suppression of the truth. Ominously, the

Left of this country in media, academia, high tech, and other corporations are doing just that!

By their lies and propaganda, China has followed the historical footsteps of Nazi Germany and the Soviet Union and did what all leftist countries do: they lied and accuse their critics of the same lies. After it became known how contagious the virus was, they blamed the U.S. Army for bringing the virus into China then later blamed Italy. Both claims turned out to be lies. One of the most frustrating aspects of this pandemic is the way the media and others have blamed President Trump, yet given China a free pass.

Whistleblower

Dr. Li-Meng Yan, a virologist from Hong Kong University and author of many highly regarded papers, was forced to flee China after studying the early outbreak of COVID-19 and publishing a report asserting that she believed COVID-19 could have been "conveniently created" within a lab setting over a period of six months. Her report also asserted that the current SARS virus shows biological characteristics that are inconsistent with a zoonotic virus, which occurs naturally in animals as in the earlier SARS-CoV-2 virus. She studied some of the available data on COVID-19 and became a whistleblower on an open access digital platform. She wrote that the early reports stating the origin of the virus as originating in a wet market in Wuhan sometime in late 2019 lacks substantial support. Of course, her report was strictly censored on peer-reviewed scientific journals.

In a Fox News interview with Tucker Carlson in September 2020, Yan said she believed the Chinese government had intentionally released the Covid-19 virus to the rest of the world. Instagram and Facebook flagged all posts of the interview as false information about COVID-19, saying that they repeated information "that multiple independent fact checkers say is false." Politi-fact described her claims made on Carlson's show as "inaccurate and ridiculous," and gave their strongest rating of "Pants on Fire." But who are these "fact checkers" that the tech companies employ? It needs to be remembered that Facebook, Instagram, Twitter, Politi-fact, and their "fact checkers" are very left leaning and not friends of Donald Trump or conservatives.

On September 15, 2020, Yan's Twitter account was suspended, although the reason for the suspension was unclear. I think the answer is clear: the tech companies suppress the truth so as not to offend China because they make a lot of money from business and manufacturing in China. They also suppress the truth to give themselves power in deciding what is true or not true. Yan challenged Facebook and their deciding what's true or not. The left always refers to information from sources that disagree with their narrative as "conspiracy theory." Note the bias of the Newsweek Magazine reporter in an article concerning Yan's charges, especially in using the terms "spreading the conspiracy," "spreading theories," and questioning "why Yan's Twitter account remains active" in describing Yan's claims:

"A Chinese academic spreading the conspiracy that China was responsible for creating and releasing SARS-CoV-2 says Facebook is "scared of the facts" about COVID-19 after her claims on the platform were flagged as false. Li-Meng Yan, a former post-doctoral fellow at Hong Kong University who has spread theories about the origins of the virus via two non-peer reviewed papers, hit out at the social media giant Wednesday after it placed a fact-checking warning over a link to an interview she conducted with India-based news outlet WION in September.

'Since when could Facebook judge the validity of scientific evidence?' Yan wrote after the news publication complained that its content had been censored. 'Dare anyone represent Facebook to discuss with me point-to-point in a live broadcast, based on my two reports on the lab-origin of COVID-19 by CCP regime?' she added, challenging the flag. 'Why is Facebook so scared of the facts of COVID-19?' But Yan is right: Since when could Facebook judge the validity of scientific evidence?

The researcher has amassed more than 36,000 followers on a second Twitter account after her first was suspended by the platform in September. It remains unclear why the account remains active, as its existence seemingly violates Twitter's own policy."[3]

"Yan believes her life is in danger. She fears she can never go back to her home and lives with the hard truth that she'll likely never see her friends or family there again. Still, she says, the risk is worth it. 'The reason I came to the U.S. is because I deliver the message of the truth of COVID,' she told Fox News from an undisclosed location. She added that if she tried to tell her story in China, she "will be disappeared and killed."'[4]

Why would Dr. Yan lie when you consider the consequences for anyone who defies an evil totalitarian regime like Communist China? This fascist regime has murdered many of its own people, especially whistleblowers regarding Covid-19, and Chinese Christian Pastors for proclaiming the gospel. Leftism is Godless and hates the truth, especially the truth of the Gospel of Jesus Christ—proving the evil of leftism.

"Dr. Li-Meng Yan, now in hiding, claims the government in the country where she was born is trying to shred her repu-

tation and accuses government goons of choreographing a cyber-attack against her in hopes of keeping her quiet. Yan's story weaves an extraordinary claim about cover-ups at the highest levels of government and seemingly exposes the obsessive compulsion of President Xi Jinping and his Communist Party to control the coronavirus narrative: what China knew, when it knew it and what edited information it peddled to the rest of the world. China Churches were ordered to praise XI Jinping's handling of Coronavirus before reopening, a watchdog says.

Yan, who says she was one of the first scientists in the world to study the novel coronavirus, was allegedly asked by her supervisor at the University/WHO reference lab, Dr. Leo Poon, in 2019 to look into the odd cluster of SARS-like cases coming out of mainland China at the end of December 2019. 'The China government refused to let overseas experts, including ones in Hong Kong, do research in China," she said. 'So I turned to my friends to get more information.' Yan had an extensive network of professional contacts in various medical facilities in mainland China, having grown up and completed much of her studies there. She says that is the precise reason she was asked to conduct this kind of research, especially at a time when she says her team knew they weren't getting the whole truth from the government. One friend, a scientist at the Center for Disease Control and Prevention in China, had first-hand knowledge of the cases and purportedly told Yan on Dec. 31 about human-to-human transmission well before China or the WHO admitted such spread was possible. She reported some of these early findings back to her boss, Yan said. 'He just nodded,' she recalled, and told her to keep working.

A few days later, on Jan. 9, 2020, the WHO put out a statement: 'According to Chinese authorities, the virus in question can cause severe illness in some patients and does not transmit readily between people...There is limited infor-

mation to determine the overall risk of this reported cluster.'

Yan said she and her colleagues across China discussed the peculiar virus but that she soon noted a sharp shift in tone. Doctors and researchers who had been openly discussing the virus suddenly clammed up. Those from the city of Wuhan--which later would become the hub of the outbreak--went silent and others were warned not to ask them details. Supervisors, renowned as some of the top experts in the field, also ignored research she was doing at the onset of the pandemic that she believes could have saved lives. She adds that they likely had an obligation to tell the world, given their status as a World Health Organization reference laboratory specializing in influenza viruses and pandemics, especially as the virus began spreading in the early days of 2020. *The doctors said, ominously, 'We can›t talk about it, but we need to wear masks,' Yan said.*

Then the numbers of human-to-human transmission began to grow exponentially, according to her sources, and Yan started digging for answers. 'There are many, many patients who don›t get treatment on time and diagnosis on time,' Yan said. 'Hospital doctors are scared, but they cannot talk. CDC staff are scared.' She said she reported her findings to her supervisor again on Jan. 16 but that›s when he allegedly told her *'to keep silent, and be careful.' 'As he warned me before, "Don›t touch the red line," Yan said* referring to the government. *'We will get in trouble and we'll be disappeared.'* She also claims the co-director of a WHO-affiliated lab, Professor Malik Peiris, knew but didn't do anything about it. Peiris also did not respond to requests for comment. The WHO website lists Peiris as an "adviser" on the WHO International Health Regulations Emergency Committee for Pneumonia due to the Novel Coronavirus 2019-nCoV.

Yan was frustrated, but not surprised. 'I already know that would happen because I know the corruption among this kind of international organization like the WHO to China government, and to China Communist Party,' she said. 'So basically I accept it but I don't want this misleading information to spread to the world.' The WHO and China have vehemently denied claims of a coronavirus cover-up. The WHO has also denied that Yan, Poon or Peiris ever worked directly for the organization. 'Professor Malik Peiris is an infectious disease expert who has been on WHO missions and expert groups - as are many people eminent in their fields,' WHO spokeswoman Margaret Ann Harris said in an email. 'That does not make him a WHO staff member, nor does he represent WHO.'

Yan says despite any pushback, she has been emboldened by a sense of right and wrong and says she had to speak up despite the personal and professional consequences. 'I know how they treat whistleblowers,' she said.

Like so many before her, once Yan decided to speak out against China, she discovered her life was apparently in jeopardy, as well as that of those closest to her. It was a fear directly relayed to her and seemingly confirmed by U.S.-based Hong Kong blogger Lu Deh, she says. After she shared some of her theories and suspicions with him, he told her she would need to relocate, perhaps to the United States, where she wouldn't have to constantly look over her shoulder. Only then would she be safe and have a platform to speak, he said. Yan made the decision to leave, but things got complicated when her husband of six years, who also worked at her lab, discovered the telephone call between his wife and the blogger. Yan told Fox News she begged her husband to go with her, and says while her spouse, a reputable scientist himself, had initially been supportive of her research he suddenly had a change of heart. 'He was totally pissed off,' she said. 'He blamed me, tried to ruin my confidence. He said they will kill all of us.' Shocked and hurt,

Yan made the decision to leave without him. She got her ticket to the U.S. on April 27. She was on a flight the next day. When she landed at Los Angeles International Airport after her 13-hour journey, she was stopped by customs officials. Fear gripped her and Yan didn't know if she would end up in jail or be sent back to China. 'I had to tell them the truth,' she said. 'I'm doing the right thing. So I tell them that 'don't let me go back to China. I'm the one who came to tell the truth here of COVID-19. And please protect me. If not, the China government will kill me.' The FBI was allegedly called in to investigate. Yan claims they interviewed her for hours, took her cell phone as evidence and allowed her to continue to her destination. The FBI told Fox News it could neither confirm nor deny Yan's claims; however, Fox News was shown an evidence receipt that appeared to confirm an interaction.

As Yan was trying to find her footing in America, she says her friends and family back home were being put through the wringer. Yan claims the government swarmed her hometown of Qingdao and that agents ripped apart her tiny apartment and questioned her parents. When she contacted her mother and father, they pleaded with her to come home, told her she didn't know what she was talking about and begged her to give up the fight. The University of Hong Kong took down her page and apparently revoked access to her online portals and emails, despite the fact that she says she was on an approved annual leave. In a statement to Fox News, a school spokesperson said Yan is not currently an employee. 'Dr Li-Meng Yan is no longer a staff member of the University,' the statement read. 'Out of respect for our current and former employees, we don't disclose personal information about her. Your understanding is appreciated.'

The Chinese Embassy in the United States told Fox News they don't know who Yan is and maintain China has handled the pandemic heroically. 'We have never heard of this person,' the emailed statement read. «The Chinese government has responded swiftly and effectively to COVID-19 since its outbreak. All its efforts have been clearly documented in the white paper 'Fighting COVID-19: China in Action' with full transparency. Facts tell all.'

The WHO has also continued to deny any wrongdoing during the earliest days of the virus. The medical arm of the United Nations has been taken to task recently by scientists challenging its official view of how the virus spreads. The WHO has also altered the coronavirus timeline on its website, now saying it got information about the virus from WHO scientists and not the Beijing authorities--as it has claimed for more than six months.

Fox News has also reached out to the Chinese Ministry of Foreign Affairs and the scientists Yan accuses of suppressing her concerns for comment. Yan says she'll continue to speak out--but knows there›s a target on her back.[5]"

Virus Timeline: Is the WHO in China's pocket?

Earlier, I mentioned that when the virus initially became known, the WHO and China lied and declared that the disease was not contagious human to human. I believe the following commentary by Brett D. Schaefer, who is a Jay Kingham Senior Research Fellow in International Regulatory Affairs at Heritage's Margaret Thatcher Center for Freedom, really nails it concerning the corrupt WHO and their allegiance to China. He gives important insight to the timeline of the virus and the corruption and misinformation involved. He also gives insight into China's influence worldwide:

The World Health Organization Bows to China
April 28th, 2020
COMMENTARY BY
Brett D. Schaefer

"The lack of transparency by Beijing directly enabled CO-VID-19 to spread. The experience of China, the WHO, and COVID-19 should leave the world with no illusions. As the saying goes, crisis reveals character. It has become abundantly clear in recent months that China has no interest in supporting the international system, even when such cooperation could have saved lives.

For decades, the United States and other Western nations encouraged China's integration into international organizations and the global economic order, reasoning that this would "normalize" China—that it would come to appreciate the value of observing international rules and norms and become freer economically and politically. This perception had shifted dramatically in the U.S. over the past couple of years, but the recent experience with the coronavirus pandemic and the World Health Organization should leave everyone convinced that China is influencing the international system far more than the reverse, and that its influence is harmful. It is now clear that Beijing's response to COVID-19 enabled its spread, to the detriment of public health and economies throughout the world.

COVID-19 was first detected in Wuhan in late November or early December. Chinese authorities reacted by suppressing details of the disease and punishing doctors who tried to alert the public and the world. China did not inform the WHO about the virus until Dec. 31, weeks after it had detected the disease. Even after informing the WHO, Beijing continued to suppress information about human-to-human transmission.

The lack of transparency by Beijing directly enabled CO-VID-19 to spread. The mayor of Wuhan admitted that as many as 5 million Chinese had left the city before imposition of a lockdown, allowing infected individuals to travel abroad well into January. On Jan. 14, the WHO declared, "Preliminary investigations conducted by the Chinese authorities have found no clear evidence of human-to-human transmission." A week later, on Jan. 22, the WHO reversed its position and confirmed that there was "evidence of human-to-human transmission." Despite this evidence, however, the WHO strongly opposed travel restrictions and, on Jan. 23, tweeted: "For the moment, WHO does not recommend any broader restrictions on travel or trade. We recommend exit screening at airports as part of a comprehensive set of containment measures." In February, after the U.S. imposed travel restrictions on China, WHO Director-General Tedros Adhanom Ghebreyesus publicly chastised countries for adopting the policy.

It was not until mid-February, after weeks of negotiations with Beijing, that a WHO expert team was able to travel to Wuhan to examine the situation first-hand. By mid-February, 28 countries had COVID-19 cases, and deaths from the disease had surpassed the total from an earlier coronavirus, the 2003 severe acute respiratory syndrome, which had also originated in China There is no disputing the fact that China bears primary responsibility for the COVID-19 disaster besetting the world. As Nicholas Eberstadt of the American Enterprise Institute observes, "Had the [Chinese Communist Party] placed its population's health above its own—had it behaved like an open society or followed international transparency norms—there is no question that the global toll from the COVID-19 pandemic would only be a fraction of what has been exacted to date." But China is not an open society, nor does it feel obliged to follow international norms. If it had felt such an obligation, it would have provided timely and transparent notification to the WHO about the potential outbreak and cooperated fully to assess the risk. These commitments are clear under the International Health Regulations, which were amended in 2005 after China's previous lack of cooperation and transparency in the SARS outbreak.

Tedros has argued that the WHO needs to moderate its tone to obtain cooperation from Beijing. However, his comments go beyond moderation into obsequiousness, without noticeable gains in cooperation. After visiting China in late January, Tedros announced that Beijing had set "a new standard for outbreak control" and praised Chinese actions that "bought the world time, even though those steps have come at greater cost to China itself." Beijing blocked a WHO expert team visit for weeks thereafter. Worse, the WHO may have facilitated the spread of the disease by ignoring a warning from Taiwan about human-to-human transmission in December because the WHO does not recognize Taiwan due to Chinese objections.

Such is the corrupting influence of China that the WHO holds it to a different standard than it does the organization's biggest funder, the U.S. After all, the WHO felt free to criticize the U.S. government for calling COVID-19 a "Chinese virus" and called on governments not to politicize the disease after President Trump criticized the organization's credulousness in echoing Beijing. Meanwhile China, Russia, and Iran orchestrate propaganda disinformation campaigns asserting that the "novel coronavirus is an American bioweapon."

COVID-19 has put the WHO front and center, but China also corrupts other parts of the United Nations system. Under Chinese leadership: The International Civil Aviation Organization has supported Chinese political priorities, even at the expense of the organization's mission. This includes denying Taiwanese participation and concealing Chinese

*cyberespionage. The U.N. Industrial Development Organiza-
tion has robustly endorsed China's Belt and Road Initiative
and provided funding and official commendation for China's
response to COVID-19. The International Telecommunica-
tion Union has provided a forum for proposals by China for a
"radical change to the way the internet works ... which critics say will also bake authoritarianism into the architecture
underpinning the web."*

*In addition, there are numerous reports of Chinese of-
ficials intimidating U.N. staff in violation of the body›s rules
and harassing nongovernmental organizations critical of
Chinese policies. If there is one benefit to the disastrous CO-
VID-19 pandemic, it's that it has forced governments to confront the implications of Chinese influence in international
organizations and its manipulative foreign policy. In recent
weeks:*

*The French foreign minister summoned the Chinese am-
bassador due to an outrageous blog post that "defended
China's handling of the health crisis and accused Western
democracies of reckless behavior, including allegations that
French health care workers left old people to die in nursing
homes." The United Kingdom is reportedly reconsidering its
relationship with China, including its willingness to let China's Huawei participate in the nation's 5G network.*

*African governments are outraged over the "treatment
of African citizens living in China» and frustrated "at Beijing's position on granting debt relief to fight against the
outbreak."*

*China has attempted a public relations coup by publi-
cizing shipments of medical equipment to countries hit by
COVID-19, but it has boomeranged as country after country
finds out that Chinese equipment is faulty or substandard.*

*The experience of China, the WHO, and COVID-19 should
leave the world with no illusions. It has become clear that
China wants one thing: to undermine, coopt, and reshape*

the international system to advance China's interests. If Beijing succeeds, it will not only be the U.S. that suffers."[6]

This piece originally appeared in the Washington Examiner
I decided to include the previous two internet posts and others in this book while they were still available for fear that they would eventually be censored "disappeared" by the high-tech suppression of free speech.

Virtual Society

What the Covid-19 pandemic accomplished has greatly accelerated the virtual society almost overnight. This is one of the most destructive consequences of Covid-19— Zoom has filled the void and is now replacing interpersonal relationships. People are social and need in-person contact. As already noted, social isolation has led to the increase of mental health issues and their catastrophic results, especially the increase of alcohol and drug abuse.

The virtual society makes people more dependent on their electronic devices and has given more power and control to big high-tech and government. A society that's more dependent and socially isolated is easier to control which is great news to the left.

Related to high tech, Covid-19 has also encouraged the technology of tracking people and their locations in the name of contact tracing. Although a legitimate searching tool for use during the pandemic, it's also a perfect development for any totalitarian government's tracking of citizens.

Vaccines

Now that the vaccine is here the left even politicize this remarkable achievement by a public/private partnership between the federal government and the pharmaceutical industry. As of mid-January 2021, over 20,000,000 doses of the vaccine have been delivered to the states, yet only one third of the vaccine has been used. Yet the federal government and the Trump administration have been blamed, when in reality, the state's lack of administration of the vaccine, especially in states with incompetent governors like Gavin Newsom and Andrew Cuomo, are the reason. Florida is doing fine, but California and New York are lagging behind in the administering of the vaccines.

Covid-19 Conclusions

I can only conclude:

(1) China is responsible for intentionally spreading the virus worldwide; the Chinese people are a great people but are under the tyranny and indoctrination of an evil government who want to be the dominant power in the world. But Chinese and other Asian Americans shouldn't be singled out for racist persecution by the thuggish worst elements of society, an unfortunate effect of honesty concerning the Chinese origin of the virus.

(2) The Democrats have played politics and used the virus to shut down the economy for political gain in an election year.

(3) Irresponsible pre-pandemic type of behavior—mainly close social contact with zero precautions have greatly contributed to the spread of the disease rather than restaurants and most other small businesses and churches.

(4) The Media (with the exception of Fox News, Talk Radio, and a few websites and newspapers) have been negligent in telling the truth about the virus and are nothing but an arm

of the Democratic Party which benefitted politically from Covid-19.

(5) Much of what has been said about the "science" of the virus has been contradictory and untrue. Some studies have shown that masks are worthless, others say the opposite; some say shutdowns work, but the evidence shows otherwise. Like everything else, the science has also been politicalized. No wonder people are even skeptical about the benefits of vaccines.

About the only thing we know for sure about the virus itself is that it's extremely contagious but less deadly than previous viruses; it mainly kills those who are elderly, those who are immunosuppressed, and those with serious health conditions such as diabetes, heart and respiratory conditions; it is practically non-existent in young children, and it is spread mainly through the air and spreads easier inside than outside.

People need to live their lives and not be hunkered down at home. They also need to work and provide for their families. The lockdown restrictions have largely destroyed both of these. One thing that should be clear: Justified or not, the Covid-19 government restrictions placed on the people gives a glimpse of what the country would be like under more government control. Under complete control by the left, life in this country will be much worse. This is what we should all be concerned about.

Endnotes

[1] KXTV ABC Sacramento news report, July 30, 2020

[2] by: Associated Press, Courtney Friel, Carlos SaucedoPosted: Dec 8, 2020 / 12:46 PM PST / Updated: Dec 8, 2020 / 10:11 PM PST

[3] Dr. Li-Meng YAN (@DrLiMengYAN1) October 13, 2020 Why is Facebook so scared of the facts of COVID-19? Why is Facebook so scared of the facts of COVID 19? https://t.co/zPU9nE3GBNhttps://t.co/zPU9nE3GBN BY JASON MURDOCK ON 10/15/20 AT 8:33 AM EDT

[4] Barnini Chakraborty on Twitter@Barnini.

[5] Ibid.

[6] www.heritage.org global-politics comentary

Part Five:
Climate Change

Chapter 16

Man Caused Climate Change?

The next two chapters deal with climate change. Since I'm not a climatologist, much of the following content consists of footnoted evidence rather than any expertise on my part. I also tried to connect the dots in order to present this evidence in an understandable manner. The scientific facts presented rebut the fraudulent claim by the world-wide left of man-caused climate change resulting in a future global catastrophe.

The left have dishonestly labeled those who deny man-caused climate change as "climate change deniers," but skeptics of the current climate change propaganda don't deny climate change; they simply deny unprecedented man-caused climate change through the increase of CO_2 emissions, or the so-called "Greenhouse Effect." Science has recorded the fact that the earth's climate has always had periods of warming and cooling which demonstrates the falsehood that CO_2 emissions in the last few years has caused an unprecedented global warming. In fact, science tells of a past warming period that was even warmer than the modest warming of today.

Climate change has historically been recorded in a number of ways. Even before the invention of the printing press, ancient peoples still had different forms of written communication and anecdotal accounts of their different observations and experiences living in different climates.

Modern science has also been able to chronicle the changes in the earth's climate with real science through such tools as studying tree-rings; fossilized pollen which show changes in vegetation; fossil records showing the migration of humans, animals, and vegetation based on climate change; stalagmites and stalactites; cross sections of Arctic and Antarctic ice cores; slight variations in the 23 degree tilt in earth's axis; the earth's elliptical orbit around the sun; solar changes through different levels of energy linked to sunspot activity; satellite technology; locations of weather stations measuring temperature, and many other scientific indicators. All of this information taken together gives a picture of a natural cycle of climate change.

Is Climate Change Real?

The answer is yes. Climate changes and throughout earth's history there have been climate cycles of warming and cooling. But man-caused climate change and the assertion that it has never been warmer than the present is the biggest fraud since Darwin's theory of Macro-Evolution. It is based on flawed computer models and self-serving agendas, but not real science. The widespread belief in man-caused unprecedented climate change demonstrates the effectiveness of the propaganda from the mostly leftist controlled media, academia, pop-culture, UN, and high-tech.

Climate change is a powerful tool used by the left to economically control the world, especially America. Look at the proposed Green New Deal which will destroy the U.S. economy and millions of jobs in the fossil fuels industry. But that's the point: the left want to cripple the economy so they can create a crisis and then take over power. Climate change alarmism also creates fear, which is one of the left's greatest tools for controlling people.

False Claims in Recent History

Climate change alarmists were proven wrong in the mid 1970's when alarmist scientists were concerned about pollution particles in the upper atmosphere deflecting the sun's rays and causing global cooling into another ice age. They also asserted that deflection of the sun's rays would hinder photosynthesis thus causing massive crop failures and world-wide starvation. However, in 1976, our current warming cycle started and the narrative changed from particles in the upper atmosphere to so called climate change and warming of the planet resulting from the greenhouse effect caused by excessive CO_2 emissions.

Today, I believe one of the biggest factors turning young people to the left is this so-called crisis of man caused climate change and the fact that, again, it has been accepted as fact by so many people regardless of their politics. But real science has concluded that climate change is cyclical and has happened before and it's largely based on a 1500 year climate cycle. So this claim by the worldwide left that the climate warming trend currently being experienced is unprecedented and dangerous is ridiculous. Throughout history, a warmer climate has always been beneficial: "Why is there such a fear of a warmer climate? Why are fear mongers predicting world-wide famines as a result of climate change? A warmer climate has always been good for the world's farmers. The northern plains in Canada and in Russia will become warmer and will produce more food. Modern society can help make tropical farming high-tech, or transport more food from Siberia to people with new nonfarm jobs in India or Nigeria. Any future famines will be humanity's fault—caused by war, corrupt governments, or irrational opposition to new technologies—not the fault of the climate."[1]

So climate change is indeed real and we've been in an overall warming trend since 1850, but as part of a natural cycle. My main sources are the books Unstoppable Global Warming Every 1500 years by Dr. Fred Singer and Dennis Avery and The Politically Incorrect Guide to Climate Change by Marc Morano. Also, within these books are many footnotes taken from numerous studies by many scientists and documented data resulting from extensive research. It's impossible for me to do justice to all the evidence of historical climate change in two chapters, so I'm barely scratching the surface. The best way to organize these two chapters is mention the sun's importance to climate change and evidence through tree ring studies; then deal with each historical climate period and apply the evidence.

The next chapter will deal more with the fraudulent claims within this movement like the so called Greenhouse Effect, Arctic meltdown, the demise of the polar bears, catastrophic rising sea levels, fraudulent computer models, unprecedented extreme weather, and other fraudulent claims. Also covered will be the corruption within the climate change community and, again, it barely scratches the surface.

The Earth is warming

Since 1850, at the end of the Little Ice Age, the Earth has been on an extended warming period. "The Earth has recently been warming. This is beyond doubt. It has warmed slowly and erratically for a total of about 0.8 C since 1850. It had one surge of warming from 1850 to 1870 and another from 1916 to 1940. The official thermometers suggest the net warming since 1940 is only about 0.3⁰ C. If we correct the thermometer records for the effects of growing urban heat islands, for widespread intensification of land use, and the recently documented cooling of the Antarctic continent over the past thirty years, the net warming since 1940 would be even less."[2]

So the evidence simply doesn't exist that CO_2 emissions have warmed the earth to an alarming level or that the earth will continue to warm until it becomes unlivable. "Physical evidence from around the world tells us that human-emitted CO_2 (carbon dioxide) has played only a minor role in the planet's recent temperature increases."[3] Certainly not a threat that will destroy the planet, as climate change alarmists proclaim.

The Biggest Cause of Climate Change

The Sun

Up until sixty years ago, scientists believed in a "solar constant," meaning that sun provided an unchangeable constant source of energy. But in the 1960's, satellite technology was able to accurately measure the variations of the sun's energy emitted. Much of the variation has been linked to sunspot activity; with little or no sunspots being a weak sun, and more sunspots being a stronger sun. This was a game changer because changes in the sun's energy level delivered to the earth have a direct effect on the warming or cooling of the planet.

How do changes in the sun's irradiance make a difference in the earth's climate? "The key amplifier is cosmic rays. The sun sends out a "solar wind" that protects the Earth from some of the cosmic rays bombarding the rest of the universe. When the sun is weak, however, more of the cosmic rays get through to the Earth's atmosphere. There, they ionize air molecules and create cloud nuclei. These nuclei then produce low, wet clouds that reflect solar radiation back into outer space. This cools the Earth. Researchers using neutron chambers to measure the cosmic rays have recently found that changes in Earth's cosmic ray levels are correlated with the number and size of such cooling clouds."[4]

One more important factor regarding the sun's effect on climate is ozone chemistry. "When the sun is more active, more of its ultraviolet rays hit the Earth's atmosphere, shattering more oxygen (O_2) molecules—some of which reform into ozone (O_3). The additional ozone molecules absorb more of the near-UV radiation from the sun, increasing temperatures in the atmosphere. Computer models indicate that a 0.1 percent change in the sun's radiation could cause a 2 percent change in the Earth's ozone concentration, affecting atmospheric heat and circulation. "[5]

So, when the sun's radiation was discovered not to be constant, scientists did extensive research based on this fact. "In 1961, the University of Washington's Minze Stuiver (called the second-most cited scientist in geosciences) was able to publish a correlation between solar activity and carbon-14 variations in the tree ring records of the past 1000 years. He concluded that when an active sun created more solar wind to shield the Earth from cosmic rays, less carbon-14 was available to be absorbed by the trees.[6]"

Scientists came to the one obvious conclusion: "The earth continually warms and cools. The cycle is undeniable, ancient, often abrupt, and global. It is also unstoppable. Isotopes in the ice and sediment cores, ancient tree rings, and stalagmites tell us it is linked to small changes in solar activity. The temperature change is moderate. Temperatures at the latitude of New York and Paris moved about 2°C above

the long term mean during warmings, with increases of 3°
or more in the polar latitudes. During the cold phases of the
cycle, temperatures dropped by similar amounts below the
mean. Temperature changes little in the lands at the equator, but rainfall often does.

The cycle shifts have occurred roughly on schedule
whether CO_2 levels were high or low. Based on this, the
Earth is about 150 years into a moderate modern warming
that will last for centuries longer. It will essentially restore
the fine climate of the Medieval Climate Optimum."[7]

Another Major Source of Scientific Evidence That Doesn't Lie: Tree Ring Studies

Tree-ring studies have demonstrated two truths: First, that
climate changes and has for centuries and tree-ring findings
correspond to the different climate cycles of the past; second, that changes aren't limited to a certain area, but world-
wide. "In mountainous northwestern Pakistan, more than
200,000 tree-ring measurements were assembled from 384
long-lived trees that grew on more than twenty individual
sites. The 1,300 year temperature proxy shows the warmest
decades occurred between 800 to 1000, and the coldest periods between 1500 and 1700."[8] The time period from 800
to 1000 corresponds to the Medieval Warming period and
1500 to 1700 corresponds to the Little Ice Age.

Many other studies around the world show evidence
of the different climate cycles. From northwest Pakistan
to California, the evidence is related: "Lisa J. Graumlich of
Montana State University combined both tree rings and
tree lines to assess past climate changes in California's Sierra Nevada. The trees in the mountains' upper tree lines
are preserved in place, living and dead for up to 3000 years.
Graumlich says: *'A relatively dense forest grew above the*

current tree line from the beginning of our records to about 1000 B.C., and again from A.D. 400 to 1000, when temperatures were warm. Abundance of trees and elevation of tree line declined very rapidly from A.D. 1000 to 1400, the period of severe multi-decadal droughts. Tree lines declined more slowly from 1500 to 1900 under the cool temperatures of the Little Ice Age reaching current elevations around 1900."[9]

"A study of foxtail pine and western juniper in the southern Sierra Nevada Mountains indicates a warmer period than the 20th Century from 1100 to 1375 and a cold period from 1450 to 1810, corresponding to the Little Ice Age."[10] "Gaumlich's tree evidence confirms both of the last two 1,500-year cycles: the Roman Warming/Dark Ages climate cycle and the Medieval Warming/Little Ice Age. Severe drought, which has been documented in California during the latter part of the Medieval Warming, obscured the timing of the shift from the Medieval Warming to the Little Ice Age. However, both events were clearly evident."[11] This evidence proves that droughts in California and other places are not unprecedented. So the fear of the 2011-2016, California drought supposedly caused by excessive CO_2 build up is simply unfounded.

Warming and Cooling Periods Throughout History

This section chronicles scientific evidence that proves the existence of distinct periods of historical climate change. These climate periods are general and sometimes overlap. The following illustrates that the current slight warming of the planet cannot possibly be linked to modern industrial era increases in greenhouse gases.

600 B.C. to 200 B.C.—Unnamed Cold Period Preceding the Roman Warming period

The ancient civilization of Egypt kept accurate records of events. "Egyptian records document an unnamed cooling about 750 to 450 B.C.—just before the founding of Rome. The Egyptians had to build dams and canals to deal with a decline in the beneficial Nile floods resulting from the cooler, drier climate. Decreasing flood levels are also recorded in Central Africa, where sediments show that the level of Lake Victoria progressively declined."[12] But the effect of this cool period was felt in other places outside of Egypt: "Early Roman authors wrote of a frozen Tiber River and of snow remaining on the ground for lengthy periods. Those events would be unthinkable today. We also know that the European glaciers advanced in the early part of the Roman civilization."[13] Water being trapped in glaciers lowers the sea level: "The resulting drop in sea level [due to more water being trapped in glaciers and ice sheets] is borne out by many cultural features. Port facilities were constructed and conditioned to a sea level lower than that of today. Evidence from the Mediterranean area is also found in Egypt, where the Sweetwater Canal, built as a response to lowered sea level, became silted," says John E. Oliver, author of *climate and man's environment*."[14]

200 B.C. to 600 A.D.—Roman Warming Period

The early Roman period corresponded to the end of the unnamed cooling period, but after around 100 B.C., the Romans began to notice a change: "After the first century B.C., Romans were writing of a warmer climate with little snow or ice, and with grapes and olives growing farther north in Italy than had been possible in earlier centuries. By 350 A.D., Oliver concludes, 'the climate had become milder in northern realms while in tropical regions it appears to have become excessively wet. Tropical rains in Africa caused high-level Nile floods and temples built earlier were inundated. At this time, too, Central America experienced heavy precipitation and tropical Yucatan was very wet.'"[15] Again, we see the worldwide consequences of climate change occurring in the past. "Hubert Lamb, who founded the Climatic Research Center at Great Britain's University of East Anglia, was the first to document changes in the world's climate over the past 1,000 years. He says the Romans reported grapes first being cultivated at Rome about 150 B.C. Other reports also seem to confirm that through the Roman times the Italian and European climate was becoming warmer; there was 'a recovery from a period around 500 B.C. which was colder than now. By late Roman times, particularly in the fourth century A.D., it may have been warmer than now.'"[16]

According to historian H.W. Allen, Columella, a Roman who wrote during A.D. 30-60, quoted earlier writers who said that in their time "the vine and the olive were still slowly working their way northwards up the leg of Italy. ... Columella added that Saserna concludes that the position of the heavens has changed—regions which previously, on account of the regular severity of the weather, could give no protection to any vine or olive stock planted there now that the former cold has abated and the weather is warmer, produce olive crops and vintages in great abundance."[17]

The Mediterranean climate of today is characterized by cool wet winters and warm dry summers, but during the Roman Warming period, it was quite different: "'The Mediterranean climate itself differed from today,' says Oliver. Weather records kept by Ptolemy in the second century A.D. show that precipitation occurred throughout the year, in contrast to the winter maximums of today."[18]

North Africa (what's now Tunisia, Algeria, and Morocco) "was moist enough to grow large amounts of grain, first for the Carthaginians and then for the Roman Empire. Central Asia experienced strong population growth when the climate there began to warm around A.D. 300, according to Robert Claiborne."[19]

600 A.D. to 900 A.D.—Cold Period of the Dark Ages

The cooling of the Dark Ages was a world-wide event: "A major climate catastrophe ushered in the Dark Ages. Professor Michael Baillie of Queens University in Northern Ireland says tree ring studies verify the major cooling. Moreover, he points to a particular period that he calls the "A.D. 540 Event" when the "trees stopped growing." He discovered that flooded bog oaks and timber from this era display narrow rings indicating that trees suddenly and inexplicably stopped growing around the world. Temperatures dropped. He noted that snow fell during the summer in southern Europe and in coastal China while savage storms swept from Sweden to Chile. 'The trees are unequivocal that something quite terrible happened,' asserts Baillie. 'Not only in Northern Ireland and Britain, but right across northers Siberia, North and South America, a global event of some kind {occurred}.'"[20] "There seems to have been comets, meteors, earthquakes, dimmed skies and inundations and, following the famines of the late 530s, plague arrived in Europe in the window A.D. 542-545, notes Baillie."[21]

"Byzantine historians recorded many frightening comets in the sky "Close call" comets can raise cosmic dust, which we now know can temporarily change the Earth's climate patterns. The historian Procopius, describing the weather in Constantinople at that time, reported that " {t}he sun gave forth its light without brightness, like the moon during the whole year and it seemed exceedingly like the sun in eclipse, for the beams it shed were not clear, nor such as it is accustomed to shed."[22]

900 A.D. to 1300 A.D.

The Medieval Warming Period

"Hubert H. Lamb notes, "{W}here there is no reasonable doubt is that, over the next three to four centuries, {after A.D. 800}} … we see that the climate was warming up, until there came a time when cultivation limits were higher upon the hills than they have ever been since. … Certainly the upper tree line in parts of Central Europe was 100 to 200 meters higher than it became by the seventeenth century. … On the heights in California, the tree ring record indicates that there was a sharp maximum of warmth, much as in Europe, between A.D. 1100 and 1300."[23]

The most amazing aspect of the Medieval Warming Period was the cultivation of grapes in England, which was at the northern end of the past Roman Empire. "The cultivation of grapes for wine-making was extensive through the southern portion of England from about 1100 to around 1300. This represents a northward latitude extension of about 500 km from where grapes are presently grown in France and Germany … With the coming of the 1400s, temperatures became too cold for sustained grape production, and the vineyards in these northern latitudes ceased to exist. It is interesting to note that at the present time the climate is still unfavorable for wine production in these areas.

In this warm time, vineyards were found at 780 meters above sea level in Germany. Today they are found up to 560 meters. If one assumes a 0.6 to 0.7° C. change/100 meter vertical excursion, these data imply that the average mean temperature was 1.0 to 1.4° C. higher than the present."[24] What all of this proves, besides that climate changes, is that the climate of the Medieval Warming Period was even warmer than today.

The Vikings in Greenland

One of the most striking examples of historical evidence of the Medieval Warming Period and past climate change involves Greenland. Much is made by climate alarmists today about the ice melting in Greenland. The following is a chilling story of the experience the Vikings encountered during the Medieval Warming Period and the change into the Little Ice Age: "When Eric the Red led Norse families to settle on Greenland at the end of the tenth century, he had no idea that he and his descendants were about to demonstrate dramatically the Earth's long, moderate climate cycle. Sailing their long ships west from Iceland in circa 985, the Vikings had been pleased to find a huge new uninhabited island, in shores covered with green grass for their cattle and sheep, surrounded by ice-free waters where codfish and seals abounded. They could grow vegetables for their families and hay to feed their animals through the winter. There was no timber but they could ship dried fish, sealskins, and tough rope made from walrus hide to other Norse ports to trade for what they needed. The colony thrived, growing by the year 1100 to three thousand people with twelve churches and its own bishop. The initial settlement split into two: one of the southwestern coast and one further north also on the west coast.

The Vikings did not realize that they were benefiting from the Medieval Warming, a major climate shift that lasted approximately four hundred years that had made

Northern Europe about 2°C warmer than it had been previously. Nor did they realize that after the warming ended, their grassy domain was doomed to five hundred years— the Little Ice Age—of icy temperatures unmoderated by the Gulf Stream that warmed the Norse settlements in Norway and Iceland.

As the Little Ice Age progressed, the colonists were increasingly hard-pressed to survive. The pack ice moved closer to Greenland. Supply ships had to take a more southerly route to avoid the deadly ice. Less and less hay could be harvested in the shorter, cooler summers to feed the livestock through longer and colder winters. The storms got worse.

By 1350, glaciers had crushed the northern Greenland settlement. The last supply ship got through to the southern settlements in 1410; then they were cut off. There was fighting with Inuit hunters pushed south by the encroaching ice to compete with the Norse for the seals. The codfish followed the warm water south, away from the colonies. Skeletons in the settlements' graveyards show the people growing shorter—indicating poor nutrition."[25]

Today's notion that the ice on Greenland is melting at an alarming rate is rebutted by ample scientific evidence: "Greenland has also been growing colder, particularly in southwestern with a statistically significant cooling, particularly in southwestern coastal Greenland. Sea surface temperatures in the nearby Labrador Sea also fell. The studies were made by Edward Hanna of Britain's University of Plymouth and John Capellan of the Danish Meteorological Institute using data from eight Danish weather station on Greenland, plus three stations collecting data from the surface of the nearby sea."[26]

1300 to 1550 the Little Ice Age—Phase One

During the Little Ice Age, the climate was often unstable and unpredictable with warm and very dry summers in some years to very cold and wet ones in other years. The instability showed a remarkable increase in storms and winds in the North Sea and English Channel. "A Modern European transported to the height of the Little Ice Age would not find the climate very different, even if winters were sometimes colder than today and summers very warm on occasion. There was never a monolithic deep freeze, rather a climactic seesaw that swung constantly backwards and forwards. There were Arctic winters, blazing summers, serious droughts, torrential rain years, often bountiful harvests, and long periods of mild winters and warm summers. Cycles of excessive cold and unusual rainfall could last a decade, a few years or just a single season."[27]

"For most of Europe, the end of the good, predictable weather came suddenly. The weather had begun to deteriorate in Eastern Europe in the 1200s. By the 1300s, there was a string of wet years for all of Europe, especially summers, between 1313 and 1321. The worst was the year of 1315, when the grain failed to ripen across Europe. Catastrophic rains affected an enormous area from Ireland to Germany and north into Scandinavia. In parts of northern England, huge tracts of topsoil were washed away, leaving rocks and gullies."[28]

1550 to 1850 the Little Ice Age—Phase Two

During this time, America was founded and the Revolution took place. One of the notable facts about early American history was the cold weather. Many accounts are recorded of the hardships faced by Washington's army which were greatly exacerbated by the cold weather.

"During the exceptionally cold winter of 1684, Fagan reports a three mile wide belt of ice formed along the salt-water coast of the English Channel."[29] "China had a series of severe winters between 1654 and 1676, forcing orange groves that had existed for centuries to be abandoned in Kiangsi Province. Again, we find vegetation patterns among the most powerful evidence of climate change. Oak forests were reported in Mauritania in the 17th century, indicating a cooler and wetter climate south of the Sahara Desert than in recent times. Lake Chad was about 4 meters higher than today."[30]

"In southern Ontario: Ian Campbell and John Mc Andrews of Environment Canada did a pollen study of successive forest changes as the Little Ice Age cooled the climate, finding that a predominance of warmth-loving beech trees shifted to a predominance of cold-tolerant oaks, then to cold-adapted pine."[31]

1850 to the Present

Since 1850, at the end of the Little Ice Age, there has been a warming trend with the exception of the relatively cool period from 1940 to 1975. Since the end of that brief thirty-five year cooling trend, the Earth has, once again, been warmer. In 1976-1978, a sudden spike in warming was recorded. I can remember in California, there was a two-year drought during that period from late 1975 through 1976 and into 1977. In the year 1976, San Jose received less than half of its normal rainfall, although ironically, on February 5, 1976, it actually snowed in the Bay Area and San Jose received a rare snowfall of about ½ to 1 inch, while San Francisco received about 2 inches. In 1979, after this three-year warming spike, the earth began to experience a moderate warming trend.

Additional Scientific Evidence of Historical Global Climate Change and What Causes This Change

One thing that is clear: evidence of warming and cooling has been global, not local. "A chronology of ring widths in the very long-lived bristlecone pine trees on the California-Nevada border extends back to 3431 B.C. From A.D. 800 to the present century, "its hundred-year averages correlate statistically with the temperatures derived for central England."[32]

In Africa—"Researchers from the Weizmann Institute in Israel climbed to Hausberg Tarn, more than 14,000 feet up the mountainside, with their boat and drilling equipment. They retrieved a six-foot core of sediment that had accumulated on the lake bottom between 2250 B.C. and A.D. 750. The team analyzed the ratio of oxygen isotopes in the algae skeletons (called bigenic opal). When the water was cooler, the opal contained less of the heavier exyen-18 isotopes. The largest anomaly was a rapid warming—4° C—between 350 B.C. and A.D. 450, reflecting a warmer climate in equatorial East Africa. Was this the Roman Warming? The Weizman researchers noted warming during the same period in the Swedish part of Lapland and in the northeastern St. Elis Mountains of Alaska and the Canadian Yukon."[33]

"On December 1, 1992, the *New York Times* reported that both the Medieval Warm Period and Little Ice Age were "global climate phenomena, not regional temperature variations." The paper quoted researchers who had compiled "a detailed record of the year-to-year variations in temperature and precipitation over the last thousand years" and found the "unmistakable signatures of the Medieval Warm Period, an era from 1000 to 1375 A.D. when, according to European writers of the time and other sources, the climate was so balmy that wine grapes flourished in Britain and the

Vikings farmed the now-frozen expanse of Greenland; and the Little Ice Age, a stretch of abnormally frigid weather lasting from 1450 to 1850."[34]

I could give example after example of the evidence of warming and cooling periods throughout the world, and chose some of the examples from the west, especially California. California politicians are so inclined to blame so called CO_2 caused climate change for every natural disaster, yet California is one of the greatest examples of historical climate change, including droughts much worse than those of recent history. The point is that climate change has occurred historically before any possible huge buildup of CO_2 emissions.

Endnotes

[1] Unstoppable Global Warming-Every 1500 years by Dr. S Fred Singer, PhD and Dennis T. Avery, Rowman & Littlefield publishers,4501 Forbes Blvd. Suite 200, Lanham, Maryland 20706, (2007), p.9

[2] Ibid. p. 6

[3] Ibid.

[4] Ibid.

[5] Ibid.

[6] M. Stuiver, Journal of geophysical Research 66 (1962): 273-276. Idem., Unstoppable Global Warming-Every 1500 years by Dr. S Fred Singer, PhD and Dennis T. Avery, Rowman & Littlefield publishers,4501 Forbes Blvd. Suite 200, Lanham, Maryland 20706, (2007) p 30.

[7] Unstoppable Global Warming-Every 1500 years by Dr. S Fred Singer, PhD and Dennis T. Avery, Rowman & Littlefield publishers,4501 Forbes Blvd. Suite 200, Lanham, Maryland 20706, (2007), p.3-4

[8] J. Esper et al, "1300 Years of Climate History for Western Central Asia Inferred from Tree rings," *The Holocene* 12 (2002): 267-277. Idem., Unstoppable Global Warming-Every 1500 years by Dr. S Fred Singer, PhD and Dennis T. Avery, Rowman & Littlefield publishers,4501 Forbes Blvd. Suite 200, Lanham, Maryland 20706, (2007), p.63-64

[9] L.J. Graumlich, "Global Change in Wilderness Areas: Disentangling Natural and Anthropogenic Changes," U.S. Department of Agriculture Forest Service Proceedings RMRS-P-15-Vol 3, 2000..Idem. Unstoppable Global Warming-Every 1500 years by Dr. S Fred Singer, PhD and Dennis T. Avery, Rowman & Littlefield publishers,4501 Forbes Blvd. Suite 200, Lanham, Maryland 20706, (2007), p.64

[10] Ibid.

[11] Unstoppable Global Warming-Every 1500 years by Dr. S Fred Singer, PhD and Dennis T. Avery, Rowman & Littlefield publishers,4501 Forbes Blvd. Suite 200, Lanham, Maryland 20706, (2007), p.65.

[12] Ibid.p.41-41.

[13] Ibid. p.42.

[14]John El Oliver, *Climate and Man's Environment* (New York: Wiley, 1973, 365, Idem. Unstoppable Global Warming-Every 1500 years by Dr. S Fred Singer, PhD and Dennis T. Avery, Rowman & Littlefield publishers,4501 Forbes Blvd. Suite 200, Lanham, Maryland 20706, (2007), p.42.

[15] Ibid.

[16]H.H. Lamb, *Climate, History and the Future* (London: Methuen, 1977), 156. Idem, Unstoppable Global Warming-Every 1500 years by Dr. S Fred Singer, PhD and Dennis T. Avery, Rowman & Littlefield publishers,4501 Forbes Blvd. Suite 200, Lanham, Maryland 20706, (2007), p.42

[17]H.W. Allen notes shared with Lamb, referred to in Allen's *history of Wine* (London: Faber & Faber, 1961) 75. Idem. Unstoppable Global Warming-Every 1500 years by Dr. S Fred Singer, PhD and Dennis T. Avery, Rowman & Littlefield publishers,4501 Forbes Blvd. Suite 200, Lanham, Maryland 20706, (2007), p.43.

[18]John El Oliver, *Climate and Man's Environment* (New York: Wiley, 1973, 365, Idem Unstoppable Global Warming-Every 1500 years by Dr. S Fred Singer, PhD and Dennis T. Avery, Rowman & Littlefield publishers,4501 Forbes Blvd. Suite 200, Lanham, Maryland 20706, (2007), p.43

[19]Robert Claiborne, *Climate, Man and History,* (New York: Norton, 1970), 344-47. Idem Unstoppable Global Warming-Every 1500 years by Dr. S Fred Singer, PhD and Dennis T. Avery, Rowman & Littlefield publishers,4501 Forbes Blvd. Suite 200, Lanham, Maryland 20706, (2007), p.44

[20]"Tree Rings Challenge History," BBC News, 8 September 2000. Idem Idem Unstoppable Global Warming-Every 1500 years by Dr. S Fred Singer, PhD and Dennis T. Avery, Rowman & Littlefield publishers,4501 Forbes Blvd. Suite 200, Lanham, Maryland 20706, (2007), p.44

[21] Ibid.

[22]H.H. Lamb, *Climate History and the Modern World,* (London: Routledge, 1982), 159 idem. Unstoppable Global Warming-Every 1500 years

Chapter Sixteen- Man Caused Climate Change?

by Dr. S Fred Singer, PhD and Dennis T. Avery, Rowman & Littlefield publishers,4501 Forbes Blvd. Suite 200, Lanham, Maryland 20706, (2007), p.44

[23] Ibid., p.46

[24] R.D. Tkachuck, "The Little Ice Age," *Origins 10 (1983); 51-65.* idem. Unstoppable Global Warming-Every 1500 years by Dr. S Fred Singer, PhD and Dennis T. Avery, Rowman & Littlefield publishers,4501 Forbes Blvd. Suite 200, Lanham, Maryland 20706, (2007), p.47

[25] Unstoppable Global Warming-Every 1500 years by Dr. S Fred Singer, PhD and Dennis T. Avery, Rowman & Littlefield publishers,4501 Forbes Blvd. Suite 200, Lanham, Maryland 20706, (2007), p.xvii-xviii.

[26] E. Hanna and J. Capellan, "Recent cooling in coastal southern Greenland and relation with the North Atlantic Oscillation," *Geophysical Research Letters* 30 (2003); 10/29/2002L015797.

[27] B. Fagan, *Floods, Famines and Emperors: El Nino and the Fate of Civilizations* (New York: Basic Books, 1999), 197. idem. Unstoppable Global Warming-Every 1500 years by Dr. S Fred Singer, PhD and Dennis T. Avery, Rowman & Littlefield publishers,4501 Forbes Blvd. Suite 200, Lanham, Maryland 20706, (2007), p.52.

[28] H.H. Lamb, *Climate History and the Modern World,* (London: Routledge, 1982), 195, Idem. Unstoppable Global Warming-Every 1500 years by Dr. S Fred Singer, PhD and Dennis T. Avery, Rowman & Littlefield publishers,4501 Forbes Blvd. Suite 200, Lanham, Maryland 20706, (2007), p 53

[29] B. Fagan, *Floods, Famines and Emperors: El Nino and the Fate of Civilizations* (New York: Basic Books, 1999), 197, Idem. Unstoppable Global Warming-Every 1500 years by Dr. S Fred Singer, PhD and Dennis T. Avery, Rowman & Littlefield publishers,4501 Forbes Blvd. Suite 200, Lanham, Maryland 20706, (2007), p 55

[30] H.H. Lamb, *Climate History and the Modern World,* (London: Routledge, 1982), 235, idem., Unstoppable Global Warming-Every 1500 years by Dr. S Fred Singer, PhD and Dennis T. Avery, Rowman & Littlefield publishers,4501 Forbes Blvd. Suite 200, Lanham, Maryland 20706, (2007), p 57

Boot Camp 1963: Innocence to Upheaval

[31] Campbell and Mc Andrews, "Forest Disequilibrium," Nature 366 (1993) 336-338, idem Unstoppable Global Warming-Every 1500 years by Dr. S Fred Singer, PhD and Dennis T. Avery, Rowman & Littlefield publishers,4501 Forbes Blvd. Suite 200, Lanham, Maryland 20706, (2007), p.88.

[32] V.C. LaMarche, "Paleo-climatic Inferences from Long Tree ring Records." *Science* 183 (1974): 1043-48. Idem. Unstoppable Global Warming-Every 1500 years by Dr. S Fred Singer, PhD and Dennis T. Avery, Rowman & Littlefield publishers,4501 Forbes Blvd. Suite 200, Lanham, Maryland 20706, (2007), p.88

[33] M. Rietti-Shati et al., "A 3000-year Climatic Record from Biogenic Silica Oxygen Isotopes in an Equatorial High-Altitude Lake." *Science* 281 (1998): 980-982, Idem. Idem. Unstoppable Global Warming-Every 1500 years by Dr. S Fred Singer, PhD and Dennis T. Avery, Rowman & Littlefield publishers,4501 Forbes Blvd. Suite 200, Lanham, Maryland 20706, (2007), p.89

[34] Marc Morano, "The Politically Incorrect Guide to Climate Change," Regnery Publishing, A division of Salem Media Group, 300 New Jersey Ave. NW, Washington, D.C. 20001 (2018), 85.

Chapter 17

Fraud, Falsehood & Indoctrination in the Climate Change Hustle

Radical Environmentalism

This fraudulent movement is one of the many ways the left started its war on America by declaring that America is destroying the planet through pollution, even though the worst polluters are the so called developing nations of China and India, which get a free pass. The environmental fear mongering indoctrination from the left, which began in the 1960's, is now referred to as man-caused climate change.

So much of the radical environmentalism of the left comes from indoctrination in the schools and universities. Even though colleges were less left-leaning in the late sixties and early 70's, a negative attitude still existed with many professors concerning industry, Capitalism, and their effect on the environment. The key word used back then regarding the environment was "ecology." At that time, most of the professors were liberal, some were leftists, and a few professors were conservatives. One class I attended at San Jose State University during the spring semester of 1971—Geography of Natural Resources—was taught by an avowed leftist who basically thought that America was the meanest, most racist, and worst country to ever exist. According to him, America was using up most of world natural resources and was mainly responsible for the pollution that was "destroying the planet." At that time, I was concerned about pollution too and had the same sense of dread that many people have today over climate change. Since God was not in my life, the world was all I had because I didn't really believe in an after-life.

Science Combats Fraudulent Scientific Claims

I cannot possibly cover the fraud of the climate change movement in one chapter, but I will focus on the science in rebutting most of the common arguments claiming the demise of the Earth through global warming and the false narratives behind such claims.

Why "Climate Change" Instead of "Global Warming?"
"

Remember a few years back when the man-caused climate change narrative was referred to as "global warming?" Why is it now referred to as "climate change" and not "global warming?" Because climate change is something that is real and undeniable, it exists. But global warming is something that can be proven wrong if the earth begins to cool. "'Global Warming' means something actually falsifiable: the climate establishment may hide and manipulate the evidence, as we have seen them do, but if the warming pauses, or— worse—if temperatures actually drop, that messes up the "global warming" narrative. Any and all weather events, on the other hand—hotter weather, colder weather, wetter weather, drier weather, any kind of storms—can be attri-

274

bute to "climate change." So now the media jump on every heat wave, cold snap, hurricane, tornado, drought, floods, or other example of weather in the news to claim that the "unprecedented" weather is due to human activity. Blizzards and record cold temperatures are now caused by global warming—or what used to be "global warming," but is now "climate change." No matter what climate or weather event occurs, it seems that climate change predicted it. Climate science has evolved to predict all possible outcomes—so no matter what happens they can claim they predicted it."[1]

Moving the Goalposts

The fraudulent narrative of man-caused climate change has a unique way of moving the goalpost: "Predictions of less snow were ubiquitous by global warming scientists. But once that prediction failed to come true, the opposite of what they predicted instead became—what they expected. How did global warming scientists explain record snow after predicting less snow? Easy. More snow is now caused by global warming."[2] Climate activists simply invent their own reality as it suits them. The lies of the left, especially regarding the man-caused climate change industry, could make Machiavelli blush!

More goalpost moving has occurred in declaring the "hottest year." "When 2014 was declared the "hottest year" based on surface data, the claim, which was within the margin of error from previous "hottest years," did not impress climatologist Judith Curry. 'With 2014 essentially tied with 2005 and 2010 for hottest year, this implies that there has been essentially no trend in warming over the past decade. This 'almost' record year does not help the growing discrepancy between the climate model projections and the surface temperature observations,' Curry told the *Washington Post.*' Since then, 2016 was also declared the "hottest year."[3]

Foundation of the Fraud: The Greenhouse Effect

The so called Greenhouse Effect of excessive CO_2 warming of the planet has been thoroughly discredited, but fake science still pushes this narrative. "The fourth and latest report (2007) of the UN-sponsored intergovernmental Panel on Climate Change proclaims near-certainty that the cause is human. But a US Climate Change Science Program (CCSP) report, published in April 2006, presents clear evidence to the contrary. Specifically, the best available observations show a global warming pattern (in latitude and altitude) that differs dramatically from the pattern calculated by state-of-art greenhouse models. In other words, *the observed and theoretical fingerprints don't match.* We can therefore state with confidence that the human contribution to current warming is not significant and is outweighed by natural climate variability."[4]

Climate change alarmists are forced to deny science that clearly demonstrates historical global warming (before industrial CO_2 emissions were present) and that the current warming trend is not unprecedented: "The greenhouse theory does not explain recent temperature changes. Most of the current warming occurred before 1940, before there was much human-generated CO_2 in the air. After 1940, temperatures declined until 1975 or so, despite a huge surge in industrial CO_2 during that period."[5]

Over-heating and climate catastrophe predictions have come and gone and never happened which demonstrate they were false claims. How many different predictions of flooding of our coastal areas due to the heating of the planet have been false? All of them! They never happened. "The early and supposedly most powerful increases in atmospheric CO_2 have not produced the frightening planetary

276

overheating that the theory and climate models told us to expect. We must discount future increments of CO_2 in the atmosphere, because each increment of CO_2 produces less warming than the unit before it. The amounts of CO_2 already added to the atmosphere may already be close to saturation levels."[6]

Climate change activists claim that heating at the poles is an indication of global warming which is why they are always trying to make the case of any melting polar ice as a smoking gun. But real science proves them wrong: "the greenhouse theory predicts that CO_2-driven warming of the Earth's surface will start, and be strongest, in the North and South Polar regions. This is not happening. A broadly scattered set of meteorological stations and ocean buoys show that temperature readings in the Arctic, Greenland, and the seas around them are colder today than in the 1930's. Alaska has been warming, but researchers say this is due to the Pacific Decadal Oscillation (PDO), not a broader Arctic warming pattern. The twenty to thirty year cycle of the PDO seems to have recently reversed again, so Alaska may now cool with the rest of the Arctic."[7]

What about the various methods and locations involved in measuring temperature, do they make a difference?— "we must discount the "official" temperature record to reflect the increased size and intensity of today's urban heat islands, where most of the official thermometers are located. We must take account of the changes in rural land use (forests cleared for farming and pastures, more intensive row-crop and irrigated farming) that affects soil moisture and temperatures. When meteorological experts reconstructed U.S. official temperatures "without cities and crops"—using more accurate data from satellites and high-altitude weather balloons—about half of the recent "official" warning disappeared."[8]

Which warms first?—"the Earth's surface thermometers have recently warmed faster than the temperature readings in the lower atmosphere up to 30,000 feet. Yet the greenhouse theory says that CO_2 will warm the lower atmosphere first, and then the atmospheric heat will radiate to the Earth's surface. That is not happening either."[9]

"Ice cores have revealed that temperatures and CO_2 levels have tracked closely together during the warmings after each of Earth's last three ice age glaciations. However, the CO_2 changes have lagged about 800 years behind the temperature changes. Global warming has produced more CO_2, rather than more CO_2 producing global warming. This is consistent with the reality that the oceans hold the vast majority of the planet's carbon, and the laws of physics declare that when oceans warm, they must release some of their gases to the atmosphere."[10]

What about excess water vapor in the atmosphere causing global warming?—"the greenhouse theory requires that the warming effect of additional CO_2 be amplified by increased water vapor in the atmosphere. But there is no evidence that the upper atmosphere is retaining more water vapor. A team of researchers from NASA and MIT recently discovered a natural climatic heat vent in the Earth's atmosphere that apparently increases the efficiency of rainfall when sea surface temperatures rise above 28° C. This effect seems to be big enough to vent all the heat the models predict would be generated by a doubling of CO_2."[11]

Unprecedented Arctic Ice Melt?

So where is the Arctic Sea ice melt? "Arctic sea ice was 22 percent greater in 2016 than in 2012, a record low year in the satellite monitoring era."[12]

"The 2016 Arctic sea ice minimum was part of a ten-year 'hiatus" in the melting of sea ice with 'no significant change in the past decade,' according to climate analyst David Whitehouse of the UK Global Warming Policy Forum. 'There is no general decrease in minimal ice area, by this measure, between 2007-2016—ten years! The case can be made that the behavior of the Arctic ice cover has changed from the declining years of 1998-2007.'"[13]

"One of the most inexplicable claims about Arctic ice came from Obama science czar John Holdren, who in 2009 claimed that winter sea ice could soon disappear—'if you lose the summer sea ice, there are phenomena that could lead you not so very long thereafter to lose the winter sea ice as well. And if you lose that sea ice year round, it's going to mean drastic climactic change all over the hemisphere.'"[14] Holdren's claims of a year round ice free Arctic did not sit well with scientists. 'Oh my, unless the continents really diverge away so that the Arctic is no longer enclosed you will have winter sea ice. So that's not going to happen,' noted climatologist Judith Curry."[15]

Unprecedented Antarctic Ice Melt?

"In the Antarctic, only the thin finger of the Antarctic peninsula, which juts up toward Argentina, has been warming. Temperatures over the other 98 percent of the Antarctic continent have been declining slowly since the 1960's, according to a broad array of Antarctic surface stations and satellite measurements."[16]

Dire stories that are warning of irreversible melting of the Antarctic ice always talk about the west Antarctica Peninsula: "But the focus on West Antarctica angers scientists, who see it as cherry picking. Al Gore, for example, has warned, 'The West Antarctic Peninsula is warming about four times faster than the global average.'"[17] "Climate scientist Ben Herman, past director of the Institute of Atmospheric Physics and former head of the Department of Atmospheric Sciences at the University of Arizona, explained; 'It is interesting that all of the AGW [anthropogenic global warming] stories concerning Antarctica are always about what's happening around the [western] peninsula, which seems to be the only place on Antarctica that has shown warming. How about the net 'no change' or 'cooling' over the rest of the continent, which is probably about 95% of the land mass.'"[18]

"If the greenhouse theory were valid, temperatures in the Arctic and the Antarctic would have risen several degrees Celsius since 1940 due to the huge emissions of man-made CO_2. The icy bad news for the theory is that the temperatures at and near the North and South Poles have been cooling instead."[19] So the overwhelming truth against the man-caused climate change fraud is that if the Earth was warming at a catastrophic level as activists claim, then Antarctica would show significant melting, which it hasn't. "Antarctica is failing to follow the predictions of man-made global warming activists. In recent years, Antarctica sea ice has been at or near all-time record high extent in recent years. 'Antarctic sea ice yearly wintertime maximum extent hit record highs from 2012 to 2014 before returning to average levels in 2015.' NASA reported. In 2016, Antarctic sea ice dropped to record low levels in the past forty years of satellite monitoring due 'in part due to a unique one-two punch from atmospheric conditions.'"[20]

Demise of Polar bears?

"The photogenic polar bear has been the icon for the modern global warming movement. 'They are looking for poster children' explains geologist Bob Carter. 'It suits that advertising purpose. It has nothing to do with science.'"[21]

"The fact is that polar bear populations are at or near historic highs. Scientists point out that the computer models predicting polar bear population collapse simply do not reflect reality or account for the adaptability of these animals."[22]

"Polar bears have survived several episodes of much warmer climate over the last 10,000 years than exists today.' Evolutionary biologist and paleo-zoologist Susan Crockford of the University of Victoria explains: 'There is no evidence to suggest that the polar bear or its food supply is in danger of disappearing entirely with increased Arctic warming, regardless of the dire fairy-tale scenarios predicted by computer models.'"[23]

Catastrophic Effect on Sea Levels?

"For the last 5000 years or so, the rate of rise has been about seven inches per century. Tide gauge data from the past century show a rise of about six inches—even after the strong warming period between 1916 and 1940."[24] "When the climate warms, ocean waters expand and glaciers melt, so sea levels rise. But a warmer ocean evaporates more water, some of which ends up as snow and ice on Greenland and on the Antarctic Continent where they don't melt. That makes sea levels fall. More warming and more evaporation is currently thickening the masses of the Greenland ice sheet and the Antarctic ice cap, even as they exhibit some minor melting around their edges. Thus, there is no reason to expect any big acceleration of sea level increase in the 21st century. Researchers say it would take another 7,000 years to melt the West Antarctic Ice Sheet—a small fraction of all the South Pole's ice—and we're almost sure to get another ice age before then."[25]

"A 2017 study published in the journal *Science of the Total Environment* found that the Antarctic Peninsula has been cooling and that the previous warm period during the end of the twentieth century was "an extreme case." The earlier warm period has now shifted to a cooling period on the peninsula between 1999 and 2014. The Antarctic peninsula has been touted by climate activists as one of the fastest warming places on the planet."[26]

It's Never Been Warmer?

One of the basic scare tactics climate alarmists deploy is often repeating the lie that "It's never been warmer." The year 2016 was touted as the hottest year ever by such climate hustlers as Al Gore. In a January 18, 2017 article in the New York Times it was claimed that 2016 was the hottest year on record. But is that really true? "According to several analyses, global temperatures have been essentially holding steady for almost two decades. Not that you'd know it from the media and climate activists."[27] But curiously, the actual numbers for the "hottest year" claim did not appear in the *Times* piece. Hmm! "A 2017 analysis by astrophysicist David Whitehouse of the Global Warming Policy Foundation, said, 'According to NOAA, 2016 was 0.07° F warmer than 2015, which is 0.04° C. Considering the error in the annual temperature is +/-0.1°C this makes 2016 statistically indistinguishable from 2015, making any claim of a record using NOAA data specious."[28]

James Varney, writing at Real Clear Investigations, noted, "NOAA fixed the 2016 increase at 0.04 degrees Celsius. The British Met Office reported an even lower rise, of 0.01C. Both increases are well within the margin of error for such calculations, approximately 0.1 degrees, and therefore are dismissed by many scientists as meaningless."[29]

What all of this evidence means is the following: "global temperatures are holding basically steady. The media and climate activists are hyping supposed "record" temperatures that are not even outside the margin of error of the dataset as somehow meaningful. It is a fancy way of saying the "pause" or "slowdown, "hiatus" or "standstill" in temperatures is continuing."[30]

In a 1999 quote, James Hansen, a NASA lead global warming scientist wrote: "The U.S. has warmed during the past century, but the warming hardly exceeds year-to-year variability. Indeed, in the U.S. the warmest decade was the 1930's and the warmest year was 1934. In the U.S. there has been little temperature change in the past 50 years, the time of rapidly increasing greenhouses gases—in fact, there was a slight cooling throughout much of the country."[31]

Fires in the west

"The Mainstream media seem to be very sure that wildfires are getting worse because of man-caused global warming. *ABC World News Tonight* warned in 2014 that "here in America, more wildfires, intense burns" have arrived courtesy of climate change. *CBS This Morning* features climate fear promoter Michio Kaku, predicting 'hundred-year droughts, hundred-year forest fires' and claiming that 'something is very dangerously happening with the weather.'"[32]

Here in California and other parts of the West, wildfires have been very devastating, especially in the last five years, so does that mean that climate change is causing fires to seemingly be worse? The answer is no. Part of the reason for recent catastrophic fires in California was a five-year drought (2011-2016 not related to climate change) which weakened trees. Forests were not thinned so more trees were competing for less water. In addition, trees were dying of a Borer Beetle infestation. Unfortunately, because of environmental groups such as the Sierra Club and others, these forests were not thinned. Dead or dying trees and ground debris were also not removed. As a result, wildfires had plenty of dry fuel to burn causing massive fires. I could cite numerous scientific evidence, but in the cause of brevity, I'll cite the following—"in the United States, wildfires are also due in part to a failure to thin forests or remove dead and diseased trees. In 2014, forestry professor David B. South of Auburn University testified to the U.S. Senate Environment and Public Works Committee that 'data suggest that extremely large mega fires were four-times more common before 1940,' adding that 'we cannot reasonably say that anthropogenic global warming causes extremely large wildfires.' As he explained, 'To attribute this human-caused increase in fire risks to carbon dioxide emissions is simply unscientific.'"[33]

"The evidence is so strong that even the *Los Angeles Times* featured an article rebuking Governor Jerry Brown for his claims that California's 2015 wildfires were 'a real wakeup call' to reduce carbon dioxide emissions, which he claimed were 'in many respects driving all of this.' The *Times* article noted, 'But scientists who study climate change and fire behavior say their work does not show a link between this year's wildfires and global warming, or support Brown's assertion that fires are not unpredictable and unprecedented. There is not enough evidence, they say.'"[34]

Extreme Weather?

In this section, we will explore claims of extreme weather due to climate change. Thomas Friedman, one of the leading proponents of extreme weather due to climate change, has actually touched upon a truth although he doesn't realize it: In his following quote, he is actually describing what happened in phase one of the little ice Age, which contained weather that was often extreme and unpredictable: "'What actually happens in climate change is the weather gets weird. The hots get hotter, the dries get drier and longer and wider, the rains get heavier, etc. the snows get thicker.' Friedman claims."[35] In other words, no matter what kind of weather occurs, it can be claimed as extreme and unprecedented and blamed on climate change. But is that claim true? "History and paleontology tell us warmer periods have experienced more human-favorable and more stable weather than the cool periods. There has been no increase in the frequency or severity of hurricanes, blizzards, cyclones, tornadoes, or any other kind of storms during the warming of the past 150 years. That makes sense because storms are driven by the temperature differential between the Equator and the Polar Regions. Since greenhouse warming should boost the temperatures at the poles much more than at the Equator, warming will reduce the differential and moderate the storms."[36] So, even if greenhouse gases building up in the atmosphere were warming the earth to unprecedented levels, which they're not, that warming wouldn't be the cause of so-called unprecedented severe weather climate alarmists attribute to those greenhouse emissions.

Tornados

There's been a lot of hype over some severe tornadoes that have occurred in the last ten years, but science says: "tornadoes have been at or near record level lows and tornadoes in the region known as "tornado alley" are not proof of man-made climate change. But record low tornado and declining strength does not fit the narrative that "polluters" are making the weather worse. As Climatologist Roger Pielke Sr. has explained, 'To try to attribute a given weather event, due to added CO_2 or whatever, is impossible...and I think we're misleading the public by telling them that we know why climate is behaving the way it is.'"[37]

The assertion by climate alarmists that tornadoes are stronger and deadlier than in the past is nonsense. The deadliest tornado in American history occurred back in the 1920's. The Tri-State Tornado of March 18, 1925, also called the Great Tri-State Tornado, traveled from the town of Ellington, located in southeastern Missouri through southern Illinois and into southwestern Indiana. The storm completely destroyed a number of towns and caused 695 deaths.

"The tornado materialized about 1:00 PM local time in Ellington, Missouri. It caught the town's residents by surprise, as the weather forecast had been normal. (To prevent panic among the public, tornado forecasting was not practiced at the time, and even the word "tornado" had been banned from U.S. weather forecasts since the late 19th century.) The storm moved quickly to the northeast, speeding through the Missouri towns of Annapolis, Biehle, and Frohna and killing 11 people before crossing the Missis-sippi River into southern Illinois, where it virtually destroyed the towns of Gorham, De Soto, and Murphysboro, among others. Murphysboro was the hardest-hit area in the tornado's path, with 234 fatalities. After killing more than 600 people in Illinois, the tornado crossed the Wabash River into Indiana, where it demolished the towns of Griffin, Owensville, and Princeton and devastated about 85 farms in between. Having taken 71 lives in Indiana, the storm dissipated about 4:30 PM approximately 3 miles (5 km) southwest of Petersburg.

With winds of roughly 300 miles (480 km) per hour, which would classify it as an EF5 tornado in the Enhanced Fujita Scale, the tornado lasted 3.5 hours and traveled 219 miles (352 km)—setting records for both duration and distance. Its width of up to 1 mile (1.6 km), average speed of almost 62 miles (100 km) per hour, and peak speed of 73 miles (117 km) per hour also make it one of the largest and fastest tornadoes in U.S. history. In addition to the 695 casualties, there were more than 2,000 injured survivors, as well as thousands who were left homeless and without food. Fires, looting, and theft in the tornado's aftermath exacerbated its effects."[38]

Even factoring in the lack of early warning, this was still an undeniably massive and deadly tornado and one of many that occurred before larger amounts of CO_2 was present in the atmosphere.

Hurricanes

"In 2017, the National Oceanic and Atmospheric Administration stated that it was 'premature to conclude that human activities—and particularly greenhouse gas emissions that cause global warming—have already had a detectable impact on Atlantic hurricane or global tropical cyclone activity.' The United States went from Hurricane Wilma in 2005 to Hurricane Harvey in 2017 with no Category 3 or larger hurricanes making landfall. That twelve-year period was the longest hiatus since at least 1900 and possibly even back to the U.S. Civil War."[39] "The worst decade for major (Category 3, 4, and 5) hurricanes was the 1940's, according to National Oceanic and Atmospheric Administration data."[40]

One thing that is clear: higher CO_2 doesn't cause more frequent or intense hurricanes: "Meteorologist Tom Wysmuller formerly with NASA explained that severe weather has actually decreased. "Precipitation over the last hundred years is relatively flat world-wide...If you match CO_2 and tornado counts, they are down. If you plot CO_2 versus hurricane strikes, as you increase CO_2, hurricane strikes go down. Does that mean more CO_2 means less hurricanes? No because correlation is not necessarily causation. But all these claims about more hurricanes, more intense hurricanes, they're false."[41]

Historical Catastrophic Hurricanes

So climate alarmists claim that hurricanes are more frequent and deadly than in the past and blame climate change. Earlier in this book, I brought up Hurricane Flora of 1963 to show that some of the deadliest hurricanes occurred before more modern times with larger amounts of greenhouse gases in the atmosphere. Two other examples worth noting are the Galveston hurricane of September 8, 1900, also called Great Galveston hurricane (tropical cyclone) and the Labor Day Hurricane of 1935.

The Galveston hurricane: "one of the deadliest natural disasters in U.S. history, claiming more than 8,000 lives. As the storm hit the island city of Galveston, Texas, it was a category 4 hurricane, the second strongest designation on the Saffir-Simpson hurricane scale.

The storm was first detected on August 27 in the tropical Atlantic. The system landed on Cuba as a tropical storm on September 3 and moved on in a west-northwest direction. In the Gulf of Mexico the storm rapidly intensified. Citizens along the Gulf Coast were warned that the hurricane was approaching; however, many ignored the warnings. On September 8 the storm reached Galveston, which at the time had a population of approximately 40,000 and benefited economically and culturally from its status as the largest port city in Texas. The storm tides (storm surges) of 8–15 feet (2.5–4.5 meters) and winds at more than 130 miles (210 km) per hour were too much for the low-lying city. Homes and businesses were easily demolished by the water and wind. Some 8,000 lives were lost, according to official estimates, but as many as 12,000 people may have died as a result of the storm. From Galveston the storm moved on to the Great Lakes and New England, which experienced strong wind gusts and heavy rainfall. After the hurricane, Galveston raised the elevation of many new buildings by more than 10 feet (3 meters). The city also built an extensive seawall to act as a buffer against future storms. Despite the reconstruction, the city's status as the premier shipping port was lost to Houston a few years after the disaster."[42]

"The Labor Day Hurricane of 1935 was the third strongest Atlantic Hurricane in history, and the strongest ever to make landfall. The storm began its formation east of the Bahamas during the last few days of August 1935. At the time, there were no sophisticated weather forecasting tools. Despite this, the US Weather Bureau issued its first storm advisory on August 31, 1935. A day later on September 1st, the storm grew and reached hurricane status, mainly due to the slow movement over the warm shallow waters approaching the Florida Keys.

On September 2, 1935, Labor Day, the stormed reached its peak intensity of 892 mb and sustained winds of 185 mph as it made landfall between Miami and Key West. The exact spot of landfall was hard to determine, but it is believed to be around the Long Key area. The damage it left in its wake was devastating. The destruction path was 40 miles wide from Key Largo to Marathon. Buildings and trees were leveled and destroyed. Even the railroad was destroyed and was never rebuilt. The death toll was staggering – 485 people perished, half of which were World War 1 veterans hired to work on the railroad. The cause of death for most was drowning, but rumor has it that some died by sandblasting, a mixture of sand and high winds.

The initial forecast by the Weather Bureau said the

storm would pass through the Florida Straits which pre-vented early evacuation. This error proved to be fatal as the late warning contributed to considerably higher death tolls. Gale force winds and flooding continued into Tuesday as the storm moved into the Gulf of Mexico, continuing to burden rescue efforts. The storm continued up the gulf along the west coast of Florida and weakened significantly before making landfall again near the town of Cedar Keys, Florida on September 4, 1935.[43]

The point of mentioning these natural disasters is that the "scientific" and political left continue to propagate the lie that storms today are stronger than ever before. The 1940's actually saw the most frequent hurricanes ever. Again, claims of today's climate being unprecedented are simply false.

Climategate

Hacked emails from the University of East Anglia's (UK) Climate Research Institute have revealed the fraudulence of the whole man-caused climate change narrative. Once again, the UN IPCC has been exposed for the fraud it is, and frankly, along with the entire UN. This became known as "Climategate." "The Climategate emails showed that the UN IPCC scientists were holding together the global warming narrative and the supposed scientific "consensus" that sup-ported it by subterfuge and intimidation. The Climategate scandal pulled back the curtain on the upper echelon of UN IPCC scientists, who were caught artificially propping up the climate change narrative via a partisan campaign to boost only the science and scientists that support their cause and exclude science and scientists that didn't fit. Data manipula-tion, manipulation of the peer-review process, blacklisting, data destruction, and willful violation of Freedom of Information Act requests were some of the key revelations in the Climategate emails."[44]

According to a December, 2009 CBS News story on the Climategate scandal: "Those files show that prominent scientists were so wedded to theories of man-made global warming that they ridiculed dissenters who asked for copies of their data, plotted how to keep researchers who reached different conclusions from publishing, and discussed how to conceal apparently buggy computer code from being disclosed under the Freedom of Information Law."[45]

We know why some politicians and leftists promote man-caused climate change, but why do some scientists promote this hoax, especially with so much scientific evidence proving the fraudulence of man-caused climate change? Much of this hoax is perpetrated by the United Nation' intergovernmental Panel on Climate Change (IPCC). The United Nations is in fact an anti-American globalist organization which desires to end America's role as the world's superpower. Climate change treaties and other UN sanctioned international entanglements will cost America financially and allow authorities outside of the U.S. to dictate policy within our country which threatens our national sovereignty. The UN Intergovernmental Panel on Climate Change is one of many UN organizations that want to dictate policy to America. Unfortunately, many scientists have been taken in by the UN IPCC and its misinformation.

Mann's Hockey Stick

An entire book could be written on the Mann's Hockey Stick fraud, but in the interest of keeping this chapter shorter than a book, I noted only a couple of points.

The Hockey Stick theory shows a graph shaped like a

hockey stick which basically says that the 20th Century is the warmest in history and that everything else was relatively flat until the earth warmed in an unprecedented way, represented by the blade of the stick. Of course the flat part of the stick completely denies the Medieval Warming Period which was actually warmer than today. Atmospheric physicist Dr. Fred Singer, PhD, commented on many investigative studies debunking this theory noting that research: "'showed that even random data fed into the faulty Mann theory could always yield a record warmest 20th century.' Singer added, 'Medieval temperatures were substantially greater—and so were temperatures during the earlier Roman Warm Period.'" [46]

Geologist Robert Giegengack of the University of Pennsylvania gives a scathing rebuke of Mann's Hockey Stick theory: "'I didn't like it when I first saw it. And when I saw that occur, two things occurred to me. One—I missed the medieval warm phase, which was very, very well documented. And most people who look at the medieval warm phase think that the temperature was higher than it is now. And the second thing I saw was a kink in his curve, and the kink exactly coincided with the change in the way the measurements were made.' Giegengack's criticism of Mann's methodology was scathing. 'He's not combining apples and oranges, he is combining apples and elephants and joining them on the same plot,' Giegengack explained. 'Where is the medieval warm phase? It has been detected in glaciers now in New Zealand. The medieval warm phase was real.'"[47]

Consensus?

Barack Obama, Al Gore, John Kerry, and others have constantly made the claim that 97% of all scientists agree that climate change is human caused. But is that true? "The repeated claim of a 97 percent "consensus" in support of catastrophic man-made climate change? It's nothing more than a talking point designed to silence anyone who dares to question the very dubious "science" on global warming. UN IPCC lead author Richard Tol, a professor of the economics of climate change at Vrije University in Amsterdam, has examined the 97 per cent claim and found that it was simply "pulled from thin air."[48]

"American University climate statistics professor Caleb Rossiter talks about how he used to accept the alleged "consensus:" 'If we had this interview, ten years ago, I would have said I never thought about climate and I assumed all the scientists who are reporting and telling the president and the prime minister in England are right."[49] Unfortunately, the public is probably less skeptical.

"You take 400 economists and put them in the room and give them exactly the same data and you will get 400 different answers as to what is going to happen in the economic future. I find that refreshing because it tells me that these guys don't have an agenda. But if you take 400 climatologists and put them in the same room and give them some data about a system which they understand very imperfectly, you are going to get a lot of agreement and that disturbs me. I think that's arguing with an agenda."[50] Of course, that agenda usually depends on whether one is a leftist politician, a scientist needing grant money, a green energy corporation who can gain over a fossil fuels competitor, the carbon credit industry, or corrupt climate hustlers who can scam the world.

The left destroy everything they touch, including science. But the answer to the question concerning the motivation of climate scientists would be the following: First, follow the money. A lot of funding from the green movement and government grants has gone towards "climate research" in order to find a solution to the "crisis" of man-caused global warming. Second, with a financial incentive to come up with "evidence" of a problem, corruption inevitably occurs. Third, many scientists have been taken in by the propaganda, so peer group pressure kicks in where if enough colleagues repeat the same data, then everybody is supposed to believe it.

So certainly part of the "consensus" of some scientists is in keeping the grant money flowing for their "research" on climate change. "MIT climate scientist Richard Lindzen, now retired, ripped the consensus claims as being a "propaganda" tool to help fund scientists. 'It was the narrative from the beginning. In 1998, {NASA's James} Hansen made some vague remarks. *Newsweek* ran a cover that says all scientists agree. They never really tell you what they agree on. It is propaganda. All scientists agree it's probably warmer now than it was at the end of the Little Ice Age. Almost all scientists agree that if you add CO_2 you will have some warming. Maybe very little warming. But it is propaganda to translate that into it is dangerous and we must reduce CO_2,' Lindzen explained. 'If you can make an ambiguous remark and you have people who will amplify it 'they said it not me' and the response of the political system is to increase your funding, what's not to like?'"[51] Unfortunately, one can't be too cynical concerning the chicanery of the Left and its money grabbing global agenda.

Is there a human fingerprint? No, it's more like outright corruption! "What about the claims of the United Nations' intergovernmental Panel on Climate Change (IPCC); that they found a "human fingerprint" in the current global warming? That statement was inserted in the summary of the IPCC's *Climate Change 1995*, for political, not scientific, reasons. Then the "science volume" was edited to take out five different statements—all of which had been approved by the panel's scientific consultants—specifically saying no such "human fingerprint" had been found."[52]

Cancel Culture in Action

An important root of the problem of fraud in the scientific community regarding climate change is retaliation from peers: if an honest scientist goes against the false dogma of man-caused climate change, they are cancelled. One of many cases involved UN IPCC scientist Eduardo Zorita: "UN IPCC scientist Eduardo Zorita, for example, publically declared that his colleagues Michael Mann and Phil Jones, who had both been implicated in Climategate, 'should be barred from the IPCC process....They are not credible anymore.' Zorita also noted how petty and punitive the global warming science had become: 'By writing these lines I will just probably achieve that a few of my future studies will, again, not see the light of publication.' Zorita was making reference to Climategate emails in which IPCC scientists had discussed how to suppress data and scientific studies that did not agree with the UN IPCC line. He noted how scientists who deviated from the UN IPCC's position were 'bullied and subtly blackmailed.'"[53]

Zorita also noted how data is often corrupted to fit the desired narrative: "In this atmosphere, PhD students are often tempted to tweak their data so as to fit the "politically correct picture." Some or many issues about climate change are still not well known. Policy makers should be aware of the attempts to hide these uncertainties under a unified picture. I had the "pleasure" to experience all this in my area of research."[54]

A Covid-19 Type Crisis Model

Nobody can ever accuse the left of letting a crisis go to waste. We've had Covid-19 lockdowns, but I fear that we will now have climate lockdowns and even planned recessions. Remember, a prosperous, energy sufficient, and safe America is bad news for the left.

In the interest of keeping this chapter under book length, I left out so much more evidence debunking man-caused climate change. I also didn't mention very much about fraudulent computer models, especially Mann's "hockey Stick" fraud. But for more information on the fraud of man-caused climate change, please read the following books:

Unstoppable Climate Change: Every 1500 years: Dr. Fred Singer and Dennis Avery

The Politically Incorrect Guide to Climate Change: Marc Morano.

Endnotes

[1] Marc Morano, "The Politically Incorrect Guide to Climate Change," Regnery Publishing, A division of Salem Media Group, 300 New Jersey Ave. NW, Washington, D.C. 20001 (2018),166.

[2] Ibid. p. 168

[3] Jason Samenow, "Scientists React to Warmest Year: 2014 Underscores 'Undeniable Fact' of Human-Caused climate Change." Washington Post, January 16, 2015.Idem., Marc Morano, "The Politically Incorrect Guide to Climate Change," Regnery Publishing, A division of Salem Media Group, 300 New Jersey Ave. NW, Washington, D.C. 20001 (2018), 99.

[4] Unstoppable Global Warming-Every 1500 years by Dr. S Fred Singer, PhD and Dennis T. Avery, Rowman & Littlefield publishers,4501 Forbes Blvd. Suite 200, Lanham, Maryland 20706, (2007), p.xii

[5] Ibid. p.105

[6] Ibid.

[7] Ibid.

[8] Ibid. p.105-06.

[9] Ibid.p.106.

[19] Ibid. p.107

[11] Richard Lindzen, Ming-Dah-Chou, and Arthur Hou, "Does the Earth Have an Adaptive Infrared Iris?" *Bulletin of the American Meteorological Society* 82 (2001): 417-32., (Idem., Unstoppable Global Warming-Every 1500 years by Dr. S Fred Singer, PhD and Dennis T. Avery, Rowman & Littlefield publishers,4501 Forbes Blvd. Suite 200, Lanham, Maryland 20706, (2007), p.107

[12] Paul Homewood, "Arctic Ice growing Rapidly," Not a lot of People Know That, September 15, 2016, https://notalotofpeopleknowthat.Wordpress.com/2016/09/15/arctic-ice-growing-rapidly/.Idem., Marc Morano, "The Politically Incorrect Guide to Climate Change," Regnery Publishing, A division of Salem Media Group, 300 New Jersey Ave. NW, Washington, D.C. 20001 (2018), 68.

[13] David Whitehouse, "A Ten Year Hiatus in Arctic Ice Decline? Global Warming Policy Foundation, September 22, 2016, https//www.thegwpf.com/a-ten-year-hiatus-in-arctic-ice-decline/. Idem., Marc Morano, "The Politically Incorrect Guide to Climate Change," Regnery Publishing, A division of Salem Media Group, 300 New Jersey Ave. NW, Washington, D.C. 20001 (2018), 68.

[14] John Holdren, "Climate Wars," CBC, 2009, htpp://recluz.wordpress.com.blogspot.com/2009/02/complete-barking-mdness-from-ohm.html.Idem., Marc Morano, "The Politically Incorrect Guide to Climate Change," Regnery Publishing, A division of Salem Media Group, 300 New Jersey Ave. NW, Washington, D.C. 20001 (2018), 69.

[15] Marc Morano, "The Politically Incorrect Guide to Climate Change," Regnery Publishing, A division of Salem Media Group, 300 New Jersey Ave. NW, Washington, D.C. 20001 (2018), 69.

[16] Unstoppable Global Warming-Every 1500 years by Dr. S Fred Singer, PhD and Dennis T. Avery, Rowman & Littlefield publishers,4501 Forbes Blvd. Suite 200, Lanham, Maryland 20706, (2007), p.105.

[17] Justin Haskins, "New Report About Antarctica Is Horrible News for Global Warming Alarmists." The Blaze, April 30, 2017, htpp://www.the blaze.com,/news/2017/04/30. Idem., Marc Morano, "The Politically Incorrect Guide to Climate Change," Regnery Publishing, A division of Salem Media Group, 300 New Jersey Ave. NW, Washington, D.C. 20001 (2018), 65

[18] Media Hype on 'melting Antarctic ice Ignores Record Ice Growth,' U.S. Senate Environmental and Public Works Commission, March 27, 2008. https://www.epw.senate.gov;ublic/index.cfm/ Idem., Marc Morano, "The Politically Incorrect Guide to Climate Change," Regnery Publishing, A division of Salem Media Group, 300 New Jersey Ave. NW, Washington, D.C. 20001 (2018), 65.

[19] Unstoppable Global Warming-Every 1500 years by Dr. S Fred Singer, PhD and Dennis T. Avery, Rowman & Littlefield publishers,4501 Forbes Blvd. Suite 200, Lanham, Maryland 20706, (2007), p.109

[20] "Antarctic Sea Ice Reaches New Record Maximum," NASA, October7,2014,https://www.nasa.gov/constgant/goddard/antatctic-sea-ice-reaches-new-record-maximumfds. Idem., Marc Morano, "The Politically Incorrect Guide to Climate Change," Regnery Publishing, A division of Salem Media Group, 300 New Jersey Ave. NW, Washington, D.C. 20001 (2018), 62..

[21] Interview of Bob Carter, Marc Morano, "The Politically Incorrect Guide to Climate Change," Regnery Publishing, A division of Salem Media Group, 300 New Jersey Ave. NW, Washington, D.C. 20001 (2018), 78

[22] Ibid.

[23] Susan Crockford, "Polar Bears Have No Been Harmed by Sea Ice Declines in Summer—the Evidence." Polar Bear Science, August 18, 2013. Htts:// 27harmed-by sea-ice-declines in Summer-the evidence/., Idem., Marc Morano, "The Politically Incorrect Guide to Climate Change," Regnery Publishing, A division of Salem Media Group, 300 New Jersey Ave. NW, Washington, D.C. 20001 (2018), p. 78.

[24] Unstoppable Global Warming-Every 1500 years by Dr. S Fred Singer, PhD and Dennis T. Avery, Rowman & Littlefield publishers,4501 Forbes Blvd. Suite 200, Lanham, Maryland 20706, (2007), p.8,9.

[25] Ibid. p.9

[26] "Recent Regional Climate Cooling on the Antarctic peninsula and Associated Impacts on the Cryosphere," *Science of the Total environment, February 15, 2017, http//www.sciencedirect.com/ science/article/pil/S0048969716327152 Idem.,* Marc Morano, "The Politically Incorrect Guide to Climate Change," Regnery Publishing, A division of Salem Media Group, 300 New Jersey Ave. NW, Washington, D.C. 20001 (2018), 66.

[27] Marc Morano, "The Politically Incorrect Guide to Climate Change," Regnery Publishing, A division of Salem Media Group, 300 New Jersey Ave. NW, Washington, D.C. 20001 (2018), 97.

[28] David Whitehouse, "2016 Not Statistically Warmer than 1998, Satellite Data Shows," Global Warming Policy Foundation, January5,2017,http://us4campaignarchive2.com/?u=c920274f2 a364603849bbb505&id=dcd5a228f8&e=f4e33fd1e.Idem.Marc Morano, "The Politically Incorrect Guide to Climate Change," Regnery Publishing, A division of Salem Media Group, 300 New Jersey Ave. NW, Washington, D.C. 20001 (2018), 98.

[29] Varney, *scientists Criticize,* idem., Morano, "The Politically Incorrect Guide to Climate Change," Regnery Publishing, A division of Salem Media Group, 300 New Jersey Ave. NW, Washington, D.C. 20001 (2018), 98.

[30] Morano, "The Politically Incorrect Guide to Climate Change," Regnery Publishing, A division of Salem Media Group, 300 New Jersey Ave. NW, Washington, D.C. 20001 (2018), 98.

[31] James Hansen, Reto Ruedy, Jay Glascoe and Mkiko Sato, "Whither U.S. Climate?" NASA Science briefs, August 1999, https://www.glas.nasa.gov/research/briefs/hansen, 07/.Idem., Marc Morano, "The Politically Incorrect Guide to Climate Change," Regnery Publishing, A division of Salem Media Group, 300 New Jersey Ave. NW, Washington, D.C. 20001 (2018), 102.

[32] Sean Long, "Networks Blame Wildfires, Droughts on Climate Change, Despite Fact They've Declined," Newsbusters, June 5, 2014,https://www.newsbusters.org/blogs/nb/sean-long/2014/06/05/networks-blame-wildfires-drughts-climatechange-despite-fact they've. Idem., Marc Morano, "The Politically Incorrect Guide to Climate Change," Regnery Publishing, A division of Salem Media Group, 300 New Jersey Ave. NW, Washington, D.C. 20001 (2018), 210-11..

[33] Michael Bastasch, "Report" Global Warming Not Causing More Wildfires, "The Dailey Caller, June 3, 2014, http://dailycalle.com/2014/06/03/report-global-warming-not-causing-more-wildfires/. Idem., Marc Morano, "The Politically Incorrect Guide to Climate Change," Regnery Publishing, A division of Salem Media Group, 300 New Jersey Ave. NW, Washington, D.C. 20001 (2018), 212..

[34] Paige St. John, "Gov. Brown's link between Climate change and Wildfires is Unsupported, Fire Experts Say," *Los Angeles Times,* October 18, 2015, http://www.latimes.com/local/politics/la-me-pol-ca-brown-wildfires-20151019-story. Htnl. Idem., Marc Morano, "The Politically Incorrect Guide to Climate Change," Regnery Publishing, A division of Salem Media Group, 300 New Jersey Ave. NW, Washington, D.C. 20001 (2018), 212.

[35] Conservation International, "Lost There, Felt Here,: A Message From Tom Friedman—Conservation International [C1}. You Tube, December 8, 2008, Idem., Marc Morano, "The Politically Incorrect Guide to Climate Change," Regnery Publishing, A division of Salem Media Group, 300 New Jersey Ave. NW, Washington, D.C. 20001 (2018), 210-11.

[36] Unstoppable Global Warming-Every 1500 years by Dr. S Fred Singer, PhD and Dennis T. Avery, Rowman & Littlefield publishers,4501 Forbes Blvd. Suite 200, Lanham, Maryland 20706, (2007), p.10

[37] Interview of Roger Pielke Sr. , Morano and Curran, /Climate Hustle, Idem. Marc Morano, "The Politically Incorrect Guide to Climate Change," Regnery Publishing, A division of Salem Media Group, 300 New Jersey Ave. NW, Washington, D.C. 20001 (2018), 176.

[38] https://www.britannica.com/event/Tri-State-Tornado-of-1925

[39] Marc Morano, "The Politically Incorrect Guide to Climate Change," Regnery Publishing, A division of Salem Media Group, 300 New Jersey Ave. NW, Washington, D.C. 20001 (2018), 192

[40] National Hurricane Center, "U,S. Hurricane Strikes by Decade," National Oceanographic and Atmospheric Administration, http://www.nhc.n0aa.gov/pastdec.shyml.Idem., Marc Morano, "The Politically Incorrect Guide to Climate Change," Regnery Publishing, A division of Salem Media Group, 300 New Jersey Ave. NW, Washington, D.C. 20001 (2018), 193.

[41] Interview with Tom Wysmuller, Marc Morano and Mick Curran, Climate Hustle, 2016, www.ClimateHustle.com., Idem, Marc Morano, "The Politically Incorrect Guide to Climate Change," Regnery Publishing, A division of Salem Media Group, 300 New Jersey Ave. NW, Washington, D.C. 20001 (2018), 192.

[42] https://www.britannica.com/event/Tri-Galveston Hurricane-of-1900

[43] https://www.islamoradatimes.com/the-1935-labor-day-hurricane/

[44] Marc Morano, "The Politically Incorrect Guide to Climate Change," Regnery Publishing, A division of Salem Media Group, 300 New Jersey Ave. NW, Washington, D.C. 20001 (2018), 143

[45] Declan Mc Cullagh, "Physicists Stick to Warming Claim Post-Cl imategate,"CBSNews,December8,2009,https://www.cbsnews.com/neews/phycisit-stick-to-waringclaim-post-climategate/. Idem., Marc Morano, "The Politically Incorrect Guide to Climate Change," Regnery Publishing, A division of Salem Media Group, 300 New Jersey Ave. NW, Washington, D.C. 20001 (2018), p. 144

[46] "Gerald North Caught Fibbing about Hockey," Real Science, October 18, 2010, https://stevengoddard.wordpress,com/2010/10/18. Idem., Marc Morano, "The Politically Incorrect Guide to Climate Change," Regnery Publishing, A division of Salem Media Group, 300 New Jersey Ave. NW, Washington, D.C. 20001 (2018), 90..

[47] Interview of Robert Giegengack, Marc Morano and Mike Curran, *Climate Hustle*, 2016, www.ClimateHustle.com. Idem., Marc Morano, "The Politically Incorrect Guide to Climate Change," Regnery Publishing, A division of Salem Media Group, 300 New Jersey Ave. NW, Washington, D.C. 20001 (2018), p. 88.

[48] Dr. Richard Tol testimony, Full Committee Hearing—Examining the UN Intergovernmental Panel on Climate Change Process, U.S. House Committee on Science, Space, and Technology. May 29, 2014, htpp:// science-house-gov/hearing/full-committee-heringexamining-un-intergovernmentsaaclimatechangeprocess. Idem., Marc Morano, "The Politically Incorrect Guide to Climate Change," Regnery Publishing, A division of Salem Media Group, 300 New Jersey Ave. NW, Washington, D.C. 20001 (2018), 9-10.

[49] Interview with Caleb Rossiter, Morano and Curran, *Climate Hustle,* Marc Morano, "The Politically Incorrect Guide to Climate Change," Regnery Publishing, A division of Salem Media Group, 300 New Jersey Ave. NW, Washington, D.C. 20001 (2018), p. 28.

[50] Interview of Geologists Robert Giegangack of the University of Pennsylvania, Morano and Curan, Climate Hustle, Marc Morano, "The Politically Incorrect Guide to Climate Change," Regnery Publishing, A division of Salem Media Group, 300 New Jersey Ave. NW, Washington, D.C. 20001 (2018), p. 29.

[51] Marc Morano, "MIT Climate Scientist Dr. Richard Lindzen Mocks 97% Consensus: 'It Is Propaganda. "Climate Depot, February 15, 2016, htpp//www.climatedepot.com/2015/02/15/mitclimatescientist-dr.-richard-lindzenmocks-97consensus-it-is propaganda/. Idem. , "The Politically Incorrect Guide to Climate Change," Regnery Publishing, A division of Salem Media Group, 300 New Jersey Ave. NW, Washington, D.C. 20001 (2018), p. 29

[52] Unstoppable Global Warming-Every 1500 years by Dr. S Fred Singer, PhD and Dennis T. Avery, Rowman & Littlefield publishers,4501 Forbes Blvd. Suite 200, Lanham, Maryland 20706, (2007), p.9

[53] Marc Morano, UN Scientists Turn on Each their: UN Scientists Declares Climategate Colleagues Mann, Jones, and Rahmstorf "should be barred from the IPCC Process—They Are Not Credible Anymore," "Climate Depot, November 27, 2009, htpp:// www. climatedepot.com/2009/11/27..Idem. "The Politically Incorrect Guide to Climate Change," Regnery Publishing, A division of Salem Media Group, 300 New Jersey Ave. NW, Washington, D.C. 20001 (2018), p.148.

[54] Ibid.

Part Six:

The 2020 Election

Chapter 18

An Independent Voice

This next chapter is from my brother, David Frizzi, who is an independent thinker. This perfectly sums up the situation in our country and what is at stake for our future. The following, written before the 2020 election, expresses what is truly important. I have already commented on much of the content of this chapter with basic agreement, but it's always good to get another perspective.

To my friends and family,
and to anyone else who would listen:

These are indeed extraordinarily times we are experiencing in our nation, and I have many thoughts racing through my mind that I want to share with you. Whether you choose to read or delete my material, I hope you'll agree on one thing at the outset: Never at any time in history has there been more at stake for our country in the coming election! To begin with, I want you to know that politically I am an "independent." This political stance came about after my early upbringing in a staunch liberal/democrat family environment. As I aged, I moved my affiliation from democrat to republican, then to independent. The reasons for this progression will become apparent as I "present my case" to you. As I take you through a detailed discussion of our country's growing problems, I hope you'll clearly see some credibility in my perspectives. As an "independent," I have no allegiance to either the republican or democrat parties (which to me seem to be in sad disarray). In fact, my only allegiance is to the founding principles of our nation, as crafted by our forefathers; and, these I feel are under serious threat as you'll see. I hope you'll bear with me as I take you through a long dissertation relying heavily on history. As a confessed "history nut," I feel my historical approach provides me with the opportunity to lay out real facts before you—without the "clutter" of too much personal opinion. Granted, there will be some personal opinions coming from me—as I make "educated guesses" regarding where our country is headed, based on historical happenings. Yet, hopefully my mostly "factual approach" will keep you thinking and not yawning...!

Given all my school training in history, I have learned a lot that helps me understand the precarious position engaging our country today. Even more important, history provides me a "mirror" to the future, and I'm afraid things just don't look so "pretty" regarding our future direction. So, whether you ultimately agree or disagree with me, I respectfully hope my material will at least provide some "food for thought," along with opening a door to "robust dialogue" (which seems to be non-existent in today's toxic political environment)! Now, if along the way I strengthen your political resolve (or even affect a change in your thinking!), then my efforts will have been rewarded. Well, you can "quit yawning" 'cause I'm really now going to get into it! ...here goes:

Throughout history there have been notable examples of civilizations that have risen to power through what is known as "divide-and-conquer." One modern day world power that has perfected this "strategy" is China. After the violent mid-20th century upheavals of going from nationalism to communism, the China of today has quickly settled into a totalitarian- governed nation. The China we have come to know is strictly under the control of a very powerful, cen-tralized communist party. Almost overnight the Chinese leadership has morphed into a military and technological powerhouse that uses its perverted "strength-in-oneness" to bully others on the world stage; and, they have demon-strated all too often that they will do anything to dominate others. Given their totalitarian one-government system, China is presently in a unique position to do pretty much as they please—internally, and now externally on the world stage. As adversaries such as the USA (and possibly the Eu-ropean Union) undergo significant internal issues, the path is cleared for a patiently waiting China to engage in all sorts of suspect behaviors. The Chinese have become deeply im-bedded within the US In a multitude of ways: Our institu-tions of higher learning have been the home for many Chi-nese students; It is common knowledge that China makes a habit of pilfering our technologies; Significant ownership of major portions of our national debt is well documented; The influential partial ownership by Chinese interests of US-based companies exists throughout the nation; There is suspected undermining of our political landscape by Chinese operatives (...and the list goes on!). All of these are but the "tip of the iceberg," enabling the Chinese government to dig deeply into, and unethically "divide" from within, the very heart of our nation. To say the least, stopping this "bully-on-the-block" may prove nearly impossible as serious inter-nal issues continue to divide our nation. One can only hope that a strong, principled government may stem the tide....!

Continuing historically, if you look at the many exam-ples of "divide and conquer" that have occurred you will

see once great nations and empires who, through internal strife, have lost their leadership positions—often to merciless conquerors. Sadly for them, waiting to
pounce were highly organized "bad actors" who reveled
in the internal strife that occurred. It only takes a look
at the Biblical Jewish nation along with the once great
Greek and Roman empires to see how shockingly this fall
from grace happens: Each of these powerful civilizations
shared in common a progression of their citizenship down
a path of questionable social behavior, coupled with internal government erosion. Slowly but surely this betrayed
the promise of those founding ideals that once made them
strong; and, the inevitable result was their tragic demise at
the hands of others. Yes, almost always you'll find a "tiger in
the bushes", patiently waiting to pounce....!

So now let's take a look at the USA and our situation today. Hopefully, this will shed light on where we are now
and how we got here: From our founding fathers we were
given a solid base of principles by which to guide our lives
and grow our nation (Our Bill of Rights and our Constitution
stand out as sentinels here). These enabled our nation
to thrive internally and grow strong in becoming a world
leader. Granted, the players throughout our history didn't
always live up to the lofty ideals (such as "...all are created equal", etc., etc.) However, this was a problem with
the human players—NOT with the founding principles!

Yet, despite the many challenges associated with societal blending and rapid growth, our nation somehow
maintained an ethic of mutual hard work under a common
"umbrella" of shared principles and ideals. Sure, there were
opposing political parties for roughly the first 200+ years of
our "noble experiment." Yet amazingly the two main parties
always seemed capable of discussing and working through

their differences in a relatively civil manner. Most important of all, republicans and democrats alike always believed in and maintained the principals on which our country was founded—regardless of their political differences.

So, now we move into the upheavals of the 1960's and beyond, and things profoundly changed. Call it whatever you want: "...tune in-turn on-drop out" culture; the pervading influence of drugs; increasing racial turmoil; the ever tragic Vietnam war; rampant questioning of authority on our college campuses; the devaluation of human life and of our Supreme Being (...and the list goes on and on)! Whatever the causes, the results of these morphed into significant turmoil within our nation that has seemed to grow like a terrible cancer. Progressing down this path of profound change, we sadly find our founding principles under serious scrutiny—sometimes even under overt attack. In fact, growing numbers of emboldened citizens, along with some "bad actors," are increasingly seeking revolutionary change in virtually all aspects of society. Evolutionary change can be good, but revolutionary change rarely is: We are increasingly finding that the principals and governance formats established by our forefathers are no longer safe. Worst of all, in some influential quarters the founding principles are perceived in the undeserved role of "evil cuplrits," deserving major revision (or even cancellation!) What these social "bad actors" fail to realize is that it's never been the enlightened principles at fault for the ills and inequities within society...rather, it's how great principles have been misused or ignored by men of influence in our history....therein lies the problem!

Sadly, we've seen many of our present day "cherished institutions" take an ominously dark turn. For example, our education system (from colleges even down to the elementary school level) is teaching what can best be characterized as "real weird stuff"—we'll leave it at that. Then, there is our "once-great-but-less-than-stellar-now" media that seems to take devious joy in reporting "half-truths," or "no truths at all" (...oops, I'm getting opinionated now: "sorry"...). Finally, we have some very radical politicians in the halls of Congress that just can't seem to find anything good about our country (...oops again—more opinion...) It seems there's a constant "blame game" going on in society that's exacerbated a situation I'll call "mindless polarization". Now we find a toxic societal environment of irrational "competing camps". Unfortunately mutual free speech and respectful dialogue are conspicuously absent in such an environment! Now, think about this: If one cannot communicate, how can one ever hope to re-generate?!!

I firmly believe that the most frightening "institution" stemming from all these post 1960's changes is the emergence of a "cancerous growth" known as "leftist socialism." This "creeping tiger" has not only invaded the once great Democratic Party, but it has also invaded the very "ethos" of our nation—virtually overnight! Leftist socialism is nothing more than a boiling pot of radical ideas about the roles of societal governance. It typically starts as a seed (often planted in the younger generation), then quickly grows as a nation undergoes profound changes (like those of the post 1960's USA). Most dangerously for us is the position of socialism directly in opposition to our founding principles; and, it is seemingly staged to pose a very serious threat to our once healthy two party system of old.

The leftist agenda (let's call it "democratic socialism") has gained a frighteningly significant hold on many in our society. It already is a significant presence in today's Democratic Party, and it has gained alarming acceptance within the halls of our own congress. With its emergence we have seen a depressing number of behavioral fallouts, including the total inability of our congress to share and respectfully debate ideas or to reach agreement on anything! As earlier indicated, we are living in a "my-way-or-the-highway" bubble which is paralyzing our governance. And "who" do leftists blame? Why, of course, it's "those ancient founding principles"...go figure!!

Now let's shift gears away from history and the present day, and take a serious look at the future (...here comes a heavy dose of my opinion!) What might be in store for our country you ask? Sadly, I am convinced that over time we will see many "negatives" continue to play out nationally... there is just too much division existing between left and right. This will be magnified exponentially if we come under the rule of a leftist socialist government. You can be sure that societal moral decay and apathy typical of socialistic governance will drive a wedge into the heart of our nation from which we may possibly never recover! (...tough words, but don't think it can't happen here. Remember history: when societal apathy and decay take hold in an empire, "tigers" have always been waiting to pounce...!)

It's key to an understanding of where all this is headed as we look at the "motors" that drive a healthy society, and government's role therein. Up until recently US citizenship has been considered a cherished privilege to all who have it. With it, the right to "be-all-you-can-be" is guaranteed by law—no matter what your race or country of origin. And, these guarantees have always been a part of our country's founding principles—they have NEVER changed! Operating within this healthy environment has for years made us the greatest nation on earth—the envy of all before us!

However, with the ascendancy of leftist socialist ideas, we now see a severe test of wills going on: Whenever you have an increasing part of your citizens willing to abandon their healthy mindsets of "responsible initiative and enlightened independence" (which is endemic in socialistic environments), then societal collapse is a very real possibility. When citizens allow their government to assume ownership of these positive social "ethics," nothing short of disaster will be the result.

To support my position, look at history again: Massive central governments never have proven to be efficient, and in our history it's no different. (Granted, for short spurts of time there can be positive results from overriding government control, as in the case of our WWII centralized mobilization effort...but, that is the rare exception.). Inevitably, you'll find that large, bloated and centralized governance almost uniformly leads to rampant over-spending (look at our outrageous national debt!), self-serving/pointless growth, wasteful over-funded programs, and lots of corruption—all to the detriment of the citizenry supposedly being served. Should our country ever come under leftist socialism, rest assured our fate would be the «most tragic example" amongst a pantheon of past collapsed nations. All such nations fail, as can be readily seen in the case of Venezuela. This once great oil-rich nation was brought to its knees virtually overnight under the false promises of a new socialistic government. In a short span of time the people lost their wealth and suffered political repression, terror, and debilitating poverty. Simply put, leftist inspired governments do not make citizens' lives better... never have, and never will! The surest path to the destruction of independence, initiative, and patriotic pride within the hearts of citizens is a leftist socialistic governance, and such societies are usually bound for "divide and conquer"... ps: Oh how badly I wish there was a way to get through to the younger generation!! If only history and civics were still an educational requirement for study throughout all of our schools. If this was the case, students might become educated on good and bad forms of societal governance. They might learn how quickly a nation can go from principled government to tragic "leftist hell holes" in the blink of an eye!

I'd like to take a look now at some of the "gorilla" issues our nation faces. I personally feel that the significant issues I list can only be addressed successfully through the efforts of a responsible citizenry led by an enlightened government—one that is committed to the nation's founding principles. The list of issues is formidable indeed. Those most in need of national focus/resolution are: the national debt; our left-leaning education system; the polarization of our populace; our bloated central government (the "swamp"!); bad actors who would destroy our founding principles; .... amongst others almost too numerous to name here.

The question becomes now more than ever, "Which form of government do you believe gives our country the best chance to successfully confront "these gorillas"? I believe we are now at the proverbial "fork-in-the-road" regarding this question; and, which path we take after November's vote will determine which issues we do (or do not) work on. Most importantly, how successful we may be at resolving any issues we undertake will be highly dependent on which party assumes leadership in 2021. I feel certain of this!!

November then is sure to be a "watershed moment" in our history. The vote you cast will help determine which fork-in-the-road our nation takes—and the two diverging paths are vastly different. Again, you will be deciding which form of government gives our country the best chance to continue growing strong—both internally and on the world stage. Even more profound, you'll be deciding what form of government you want to leave behind for those you love. .... just a quick word on "personalities": As a political independent, I believe that the decisions we make in November need to go much deeper than individual personalities. History shows over and over that "defective" personalities disappear with the winds of time: After four to eight years it's likely that both of the current political "opportunists" (Trump and Biden) will be relegated to the seemingly endless "scrap heap" of self-serving politicians plaguing our nation for far too long.... strong words— yes; but, my feelings about politicians (including those in congress) aren't too positive, to put it mildly! ....just remember this: as you cast November's vote, it's not people that last—it's IDEALS that do! So now I rest my case (....and I›m sure you›re glad that I do!). HOWEVER, before I leave you in peace, I will conclude with some final thoughts that I call my "BAD - NO, GOOD YES" dissertation, as follows:

History is like time—you can never go back and change it.... What has happened has happened, be it GOOD or BAD; and, all the destruction of historic statues and monuments will not change one thing that happened. However, though you cannot change historical events, you most certainly can learn from them (and maybe cease the "blame game" in the process!). Remember this: only when we LEARN from past BAD things will we be able to move towards future GOOD things...

Our country's founders created lasting principles of GOOD governance enabling all citizens—no matter what their race or creed—to have GOOD things in their lives. Indeed, the "sky's the limit" provided one is willing to take personal responsibility in a GOOD free nation as a GOOD citizen living under GOOD founding principles.

In conclusion, try asking the following: "Have BAD citizens and leaders in history violated our GOOD founding principles in how they treated others? ....YES! Have we learned from these past BAD behaviors to assure a GOOD level playing field under law for all citizens today? ....YES! Will a small minority of BAD citizens (of all races and creeds!) still engage in socially BAD future behaviors even under our GOOD founding principles? ....YES! Should we then put the blame on our GOOD founding principles for current/future BAD behaviors, and abandon those GOOD principles accordingly? ....NO! Do all citizens need to take ownership for ceasing BAD behaviors, while maintaining allegiance to GOOD founding principles? ....YES! Should we erase BAD history—rather than learn from it—as the means to get "GOODER" in the future? ....NO! Do our government and citizens need to re-engage in civil constructively-motivated GOOD dialogue to resolve BAD problems? ....YES! Do all GOOD (and BAD) citizens need to believe that all lives matter and treat people GOOD accordingly? ....YES! Is it GOOD for you and I to accept blame for the transgressions of BAD actors and BAD leaders of the past? ....NO! Do all people within our GOOD free society need to demonstrate "the golden GOOD" of "do unto others as you would have them do unto you" ....YES! Will your vote this coming November determine whether the best country in the world takes a BAD path or a GOOD path? ....YES!

.............I think you get the point...........

THANKS FOR LISTENING AND STAY SAFE!

Chapter 19
The 2020 Elections

Despite President Trump's bombastic personality and, at times, questionable tweets, he did an excellent job with an America First agenda that greatly improved the economy and lowered unemployment thus creating millions of jobs (especially for minorities). His agenda also put an emphasis on the defending of our borders and tightening of illegal immigration—at the same time emphasizing nationalism as opposed to globalism; appointed three conservative Supreme Court Judges and many other federal judges; lessened Obama era economy-killing taxes and regulation; rebuilt our military and took a tough stance regarding China; led a massive government/private effort to quickly develop a vaccine (Operation Warp Speed) which was accomplished in an unprecedented period of time; and unapologetically emphasized the greatness of America (MAGA) and Western culture. He accomplished more in one term than other presidents had in two terms.

But the 2018 Midterm Election results indicated more power for the Democrat's leftist agenda in the House of Representatives which resulted in more obstruction for President Trump's agenda. In spite of that, in early 2020 the

U.S. had the greatest economy in its history. But sadly, that progress was halted by the Covid-19 pandemic and, despite the attempts by the left to play politics through keeping the economy down by shut-downs, the economy still came back. Trump has been great for America and that's a key reason why the Left hate him so much. Donald J. Trump was never the problem in destroying this country, the left are and have been throughout history.

The Left's Hatred of Donald Trump

So what was the agenda of the Democrats? Delegitimize Trump's election victory in 2016 and get rid of him! They wanted investigations of "Russian collusion," no doubt to detract attention away from Hillary Clinton's emails. The charge of Russian collusion in the 2016 election turned out to be a fabrication, but many people believed the lie. They then impeached Trump on a phony charge in trying to undermine his presidency. That's it—nothing constructive because the left have no agenda except hatred of Trump and conservatives, open borders, socialized medicine, more taxes and regulation, an authoritarian takeover of the country getting rid of all freedoms, destroying the middle class, and attaining power. That's what the left have done throughout history from Eastern Europe, Latin America, Asia, Africa, and everywhere they have taken control.

It's all about politics and the Democrats wanted to stop the Trump agenda because a successful Trump presidency meant less power and influence for them. It goes back to that truth about leftism: good news for America is always bad news for the left. Unfortunately, we have a dishonest media (except Fox news, conservative talk radio, and some websites) that don't report the news accurately which would uncover the true leftism of the Democrats. So the 2020 platform of Joe Biden and the Democrats was hatred of Donald Trump and hiding their true socialist agenda in platitudes. So they put up "moderate" Joe Biden who was the only obvious electable Democrat because all the other candidates were way too openly radical to be elected.

The radical left hate Trump because he stood up to those who want to destroy this country with a Socialist-Marxist agenda. The industrial complex hatred of Donald Trump, especially from Silicon Valley, stems from his nationalist vs. globalist stance and his toughness towards China. Their hatred also was simply because Trump was a threat to their power of controlling the country through their ability to determine truth. Too many people now are dependent on the internet for news and are influenced by quick headlines, rather than actual journalism—which is rare these days. Together with the media and others, big tech wants to control the narrative and ultimately control America. So many non-political or non-ideological people have been indoctrinated to hate Trump because of the media, which President Trump rightly calls "fake news;" but mainly on the national level more than on the local news.

The left also hate Trump because he is a true populist. The dictionary definition of a populist is the following: "a person, especially a politician, who strives to appeal to ordinary people who feel that their concerns are disregarded by established elite groups." Elites whether Democrat or Republican have contempt for the average citizen and feel they are superior to them. That's why they don't adhere to the restrictions regarding the pandemic that they impose on others.

The Washington establishment, or what Trump rightly calls "the swamp," hate him because he called them out for their corruption and threatened to dismantle their privileged positions in Washington. Who is the swamp? It consists of corrupt individuals in the intelligence agencies, the

DNC, some lobbyists, career politicians (especially Democrats), some in Wall Street and in the other financial institutions, and many corporation CEO's in the military-industrial-financial-media-high-tech complex.

Reasons Why Trump Lost

But despite the hatred of Donald Trump by many, one would still think that all his accomplishments would have easily won a second term. So why did he lose? The following are the reasons I believe that Trump lost and why our country is in serious trouble.

Reason One: Covid-19

Covid-19 is the biggest gift the Left could have hoped for and it's one of the biggest reasons why President Trump lost the election. Without Covid-19, he was practically a shoe-in for another term and would have won by a landslide in spite of almost four years of attacks on his presidency. But the media, high-tech, billionaire financiers, and others who wanted to see Trump defeated were able to convince enough people that the Covid-19 economic meltdown was Trump's fault. Of course, they gave China a free pass and to this day refuse to criticize China. Why is that? Maybe it's because high-tech, Wall Street, corrupt politicians, and others in the swamp are profiting from their alliances with China through business dealings and selling influence. One of the biggest unfolding scandals today is how much China has bought influence with people in power.

The election is over and Joe Biden is the 46th President of the United States. But even now, the left apparently are still using Covid-19 as an excuse to continue its war on the middle class. When all is said and done, Covid-19 greatly led to Trump's demise. Trump still should have won because, before the pandemic hit, things were great—especially the economy. The biggest winners of the 2020 election were China and the world wide America hating left!

Reason Two: The Media

In spite of all the reasons that are listed in this chapter, if we had an honest media without an agenda, Donald J. Trump would have won this election by a landslide. But, with a few exceptions, the media are largely corrupt. The media completely ignored Donald trump's first three years in office which included the greatest economy in American history; the lowest unemployment rate, especially among minorities; gaining a more equitable trade relationship with China; building up our military and dealing with world leaders from a position of strength and not weakness; his general "America First" policies with growth in wages; and more freedom and prosperity for most Americans.

After the Covid-19 pandemic hit, the media ignored the successful utilization of the war powers act, a private sector-government joint effort that developed ventilators and PPE's in truly unprecedented numbers. They further ignored "Operation Warp Speed" the medical miracle of a vaccine developed in under a year which all the naysayers said was impossible.

The media also used Covid-19 as an excuse to continue ignoring Trump's accomplishments, especially the great economic recovery news that, in spite of the pandemic, the third quarter was a comeback predicted by Trump as a V-shaped recovery. The October federal jobs report showed that 906,000 jobs were added in the private sector. Unemployment dropped for all demographic groups and wages were up 4.5%. The gross domestic product (GDP) grew at a record 7.4% in the third quarter (between July 1st and September 30th, 2020), and an annual rate of 33.1%. The pace of economic growth was unprecedented.

The news wasn't as good, however, for blue states like California and New York which continued shutdowns and overbearing control over small businesses, which are the heart of the middle class. California's unemployment in the fall of 2020 was approximately 11% and was well above the national rate of 6.9%.

But the media chose to not cover good third quarter economic news because that would have been good news for Trump and his chances of reelection. So because of politics and leftist inspired "journalists," the media have abdicated their responsibility of true journalism which is the reporting of facts without bias.

The media also suppressed bad news about Joe Biden; specifically, the Hunter Biden scandal concerning Russia and China. The Hunter Biden email scandal gives an indication that this alleged corruption goes back years. The New York Post ran a story in October, 2020 about the Biden family "business" and their questionable influence peddling dealings in China. A former business partner of Hunter Biden, Tony Bobulinski, testified in an interview with Fox News journalist/commentator Tucker Carlson concerning the Post article and the alleged but very plausible charges of influence peddling with China and money laundering. Bobulinski asserted that he personally talked with Joe Biden and that Joe Biden had knowledge and was involved. When Bobulinski asked Jimmy Biden, the president's brother, if they were worried about their questionable dealings being exposed, Jimmy Biden's response, according to Tony Bobulinski, was "plausible deniability."

"The meeting on May 2, 2017, would have taken place 11 days before a May 13, 2017, email obtained by Fox News, which included a discussion of "remuneration packages" for six people in a business deal with a Chinese energy firm. The email appeared to identify Hunter Biden as "Chair / Vice Chair depending on agreement with CEFC," in an apparent reference to now-bankrupt CEFC China Energy Co. The email includes a note that "Hunter [Biden] has some office expectations he will elaborate." A proposed equity split references "20" for "H" and "10 held by H for the big guy?" with no further details. Bobulinski has repeatedly said "the big guy" was Joe."[1]

Of course, Facebook, Google and other high-tech media practiced suppression of the news by censoring the New York Post story and the tucker Carlson interview as "Russian Disinformation." The other national TV media (except Fox News) totally ignored this story until weeks after the election when Hunter Biden admitted he was under criminal investigation. That practically forced the media to at least give the story some coverage.

The following are comments of Senator Chuck Grassley, Republican from Iowa, about the investigation of possible wrongdoing by the Biden family ignored by the media. He and Senator Ron Johnson, Republican from Wisconsin, conducted this investigation. I included the entire text because this, more than anything I could write, perfectly explains the corruption of the media, high tech, and some Democrats in congress to suppress the truth. The Hunter Biden cover up is one of many other hidden scandals. I also included the entire text because the time is fast approaching and, in some cases has already arrived, when any information critical of the "truth" as defined by the elites of high tech and others on the left will be censored.

"For over a year, Senator Johnson and I investigated the Biden family's financial dealings. For over a year, the liberal media and my colleagues on the other side of the aisle falsely said we were peddling Russian disinformation. They ginned up any story they could to falsely portray our investigation in an effort to delegitimize its findings. Even my colleague, Senator Wyden, whom I've worked with on many bipartisan investigations, said the following: "This disinformation also became the basis of the Johnson-Grassley investigation. The political nature of this investigation has been clear all along. Bottom line: the Johnson-Grassley investigation is baseless. It is laundering Russian propaganda for circulation in the U.S."

It seems the liberal media and the Democrats have a nervous tick. Any time a Republican gets close to the truth and is about to serve justice, the other side yells "Russian disinformation!" That's a load of garbage. As I've said on this floor several times before, our report was rooted in information from U.S. government agencies and a left-aligned U.S. lobby shop that represented a corrupt Ukrainian gas company.

And by now, the American people know that it's really the Democrats and liberal media that are connected to Russian disinformation. See the Steele Dossier. It was infected with Russian disinformation and paid for by the Democratic National Committee and Hillary Clinton campaign. The liberal media and those on the other side of the aisle were scared of the facts. They were scared that the American people would see the Biden family's deep and extensive links to foreign governments, including the communist Chinese government. And once we publicly issued our findings, those same liberal outlets said the report repackaged old material and that there was nothing new to it. They went into full Joe Biden protection mode. And they didn't even try to hide it. One Washington Post columnist said: 'Even after accepting disinformation from Russian agents, Johnson and Grassley couldn't come up with anything new or interesting on Hunter Biden.' Politico ran a story with this headline: 'GOP Senators' anti-Biden report repackages old claims.' And NPR said about the New York Post Hunter Biden stories: 'We don't want to waste our time on stories that are not really stories, and we don't want to waste the listeners' and readers' time on stories that are just pure distractions.'

Look at what Twitter and Facebook did to the Hunter Biden news. Simply said, they interfered in the election and gave the Biden campaign a multi-million dollar in-kind donation courtesy of their blatant and unforgiveable censorship. My fellow Americans, let us never forget what Twitter and Facebook did during the 2020 election.

Fast forward to today, now it's confirmed that Hunter Biden is under criminal investigation reportedly for his taxes and financial dealings – the very fact pattern that we described in our report. It shouldn't take Hunter Biden to confirm that he's under criminal investigation before the main stream press gets permission to report the news.

It's a complete outrage at the way the liberal media used its power to cover up facts relating to Hunter Biden and the Biden family yet ran story after

story with false information about the Russia inves-
tigation into Trump and the credibility of the Steele
Dossier.

The recent news also shows that our report
was not "baseless" and it didn't "repackage old
claims." Quite the opposite. It was well-founded,
ahead of the curve and right on the money – in
more ways than one. Our report teed up the facts,
but the mainstream press never stepped up to the
plate. Some of the nation's supposedly leading press
outlets with teams of investigative reporters were
scooped by Congress. Now they are scrambling to
chase the story they ignored. It didn't have to be this
way. We already did much of the heavy lifting before
issuing our report. The report made public informa-
tion that hadn't been known before. For example, it
showed the following:

Hunter Biden and his associates and family members
were connected to Chinese nationals and Chinese
companies linked with the communist party and
People's Liberation Army. This includes CEFC China
Energy Company Limited and its subsidiaries. Re-
cords show that a company linked to the communist
regime sent Hunter Biden's law firm millions of dol-
lars. Other records show that Hunter Biden opened
a line of credit with a Chinese national linked to the
communist regime and funded it with approximate-
ly $100,000. Then he, James Biden and Sara Biden
went on an extravagant global spending spree. Still
other records show that Hunter Biden, via his law
firm, also sent over a million dollars to James Biden's
consulting firm, the Lion Hall Group. These transfers
began less than one week after CEFC sent $5 mil-

lion to a company called Hudson West III, a company linked to CEFC and Chinese nationals associated with the communist regime, which then sent money to Hunter Biden's law firm. When the bank contacted Sara Biden, who was associated with the firm's bank account, she refused to answer their questions and provide additional documentation. According to records we have on file, the bank submitted the account for closure.

Senator Johnson and I recently issued a supplemental to our report that showed Hunter Biden's close business associate, Rob Walker, received $6 million from a Chinese company linked to the communist regime. There's yet another link in the chain from the Biden family and their associates to the Chinese government.

The report also showed that State Department officials believed that Hunter Biden's Burisma board membership created the perception of a conflict of interest and "was very awkward for all U.S. officials pushing an anticorruption agenda in Ukraine." Secretary of State Kerry publicly denied knowing of Hunter Biden's role on Burisma's board. We acquired evidence showing that he did, in fact, know about that role.

In December 2015, instead of following U.S. objectives of confronting oligarchs, Vice President Biden's staff advised him to avoid commenting on Burisma's oligarch and instead say, "I'm not going to get into naming names or accusing individuals." Joe Biden was running an anticorruption agenda in Ukraine and he pulled his punches while his son was on the board of Burisma. Based on witness testimony, Burisma's owner allegedly paid a $7 million bribe *to officials serving under Ukraine's prosecutor general to shut the case against him. When he allegedly paid that bribe, Hunter Biden was on the board.*

These examples are just a sampling from the report and the tip of the iceberg with respect to the Biden family's troubled ties to governments adverse to U.S. interests.

These associations, and the millions of dollars that passed between and among Hunter Biden, James Biden and others, create criminal financial, counterintelligence and extortion concerns. That's why I've since written to the Justice Department about the risk that Hunter and James Biden essentially served as agents of the communist Chinese government for purposes of the Foreign Agents Registration Act. After Hunter Biden publicly confirmed he was under criminal investigation, liberal news outlets reported on concerns that his financial associations could create criminal financial and counterintelligence problems. That's what we said in September 2020 and we were roundly criticized for it.

And just over the weekend, a new email was made public that reportedly says Joe Biden and his brother were "office mates" with the very same Chinese nationals we wrote about in our report. Those same individuals were the ones with links to the communist regime and it's military.

Based on all the facts known to date, Joe Biden has a lot of explaining to do. I've run many oversight operations and investigations during the course of my career. I'm interested in the facts, in the evidence, in the truth I learned a lesson long ago when I first started my oversight focus and that is: no matter how difficult the media or the other side of the aisle makes it to find the facts — never give up, keep working hard.

The American taxpayer deserves nothing less. That's the attitude and approach I've had my entire career and it's what I will take with me as I continue to look into the Biden family matters and as I move back to lead the Senate Judiciary Committee."[2]

Senator Chuck Grassley—R-Iowa

The real point of mentioning all of the accusations against Hunter Biden is to demonstrate the corrupt behavior by many members of the media in protecting their preferred candidate, Joe Biden, and willfully ignoring this story until after the election. Only Fox news, the New York Post, talk radio, Kimberly Strassel of the Wall Street Journal, and a few others, plus conservative web sites carried the late October story concerning the Hunter Biden emails and the damaging Tony Bobulinski accusations. Now the other media are finally covering the story, but well after the election. A few polls taken estimate close to 10% of Biden voters in the swing states would not have voted for him if they had seen this story.

While I do believe that voter fraud greatly influenced the 2020 election, equally to blame was the media and high-tech's willful suppression of important news stories damaging to their candidate of choice which are more and more turning out to be true.

Reason Three: Indoctrination in Education

Why have so many people in the media turned towards the left? We've already covered this point extensively, but to reiterate, most people in the media attended colleges and universities, which for the last fifty years have been insidiously corrupted by the left into political correctness, revisionist history, social and racial justice curriculum, and hatred of America.

When many news reporters reach the national network level, they eventually become commentators and cease being journalists. I'm sure pressure from some left-leaning network higher-ups and peers are involved, but the problem is that they don't admit any bias but insist they are objective "reporters."

But while more and more of the educational system in America is corrupt, I still believe that schoolteachers represent an honorable profession with the majority being mainstream people, but sadly, they are caught in an increasingly corrupt system.

Many CEO's, venture capitalists, intelligence community members, and politicians have been indoctrinated in the schools and universities as well. Corporate America largely abandoned Trump in favor of Biden. Many opposed Trump from the start because of their globalist policies and their desire for wealth and power. President Trump had to be destroyed because he was in the way of the media-corporate-Wall Street, intelligence complex (the swamp) and their agenda of wealth, power, privilege, and control.

Reason Four: Demographics

Many people from California, New York, or other blue states have moved to Arizona, Nevada, Colorado, Metro Atlanta, Virginia, and North Carolina and have turned them into purple states. America is a mobile population and many move because of job opportunities or being closer to family. Also, many people including a lot of businesses are moving from California because of its unfriendly business climate. Unfortunately, many of them also bring their left leaning politics with them and don't recognize that the reason they're leaving these blue states is because of leftist politics and the consequences.

Also, the Democrat's immigration policy is geared to deliberately flood the country, especially Texas and Arizona, with immigrants from south of the border in trying to change the demographics and turn these red states into blue.

Reason Five: Election Fraud

One telling statistic is that one third to almost half of the country (68% Republicans, 28% Independents, 17% Democrats) believe the election was stolen. The election was never going to be overturned, but this is no longer about who becomes president, but about something more important and vital to the country's survival: the reliability of future elections in America.

Reasons to Believe Election Fraud

- Winning Florida by 4 points and losing Georgia?
- Winning by 8 points in Ohio, yet narrowly losing Michigan and Pennsylvania with huge leads in both states going into the early morning hours of November 4 before huge numbers of "ballots" came in.
- Solid wins in Florida and Ohio almost assures victory.
- Republicans picking up 12 seats in the house, yet losing the white house.
- Changing of the rules before the election and allowing thousands of unsolicited mail in ballots to overwhelm the voting procedures, especially in some swing states that were not familiar with this new system.

Evidence: hundreds of sworn affidavits given under the penalty of perjury from whistleblower poll workers, poll watchers, postal employees, and in-person voters in Michigan, Nevada, Wisconsin, Pennsylvania, Georgia, and Arizona testifying to fraud from backdating ballots, not checking signatures, ballots being double counted, dead people voting, the intimidation of Republican poll watchers and whistleblowers, and other instances of fraud. Many voters also indicated that when they went to the polls to vote they were informed that a vote had already been cast in their name on a mail in ballot. Independent audits, testimonies, and security camera video showed voter irregularities in Fulton County Georgia. Illegal votes in PA were cast well past the required deadline, but the Pennsylvania Supreme Court illegally went over the Pennsylvania legislature in allowing the counting of ballots received after the Deadline violating the Pennsylvania state constitution.

Lower ballot rejection rate in key states, enough to affect election outcome:[3]

Georgia

2016 rejection rate 6.42%.....2020 rejection rate 0.60%

Nevada

2016 rejection rate 1.60%.....2020 rejection rate 0.58%

Pennsylvania

2016 rejection rate 0.95%...2020 rejection rate 0.28%

Michigan

2016 rejection rate 0.49%...2020 rejection rate 0.46%

Popular Vote: trump received twelve million more votes than in 2016; did better in every group where he needed to make gains, and yet lost? How did Biden get over eighty-one million votes? How were 128,000,000 votes cast in 2016 and over 155,000,000 in 2020?

2016 Clinton 65, 853, 514   Trump 62,984, 828

2020 Biden   81,283,098   Trump 74,222,957

In Wayne County Michigan (Detroit), voting percentage numbers of absentee ballots suspiciously weren't adding up with actual recorded votes causing Monica Palmer and William Hartmann, Republican Wayne County canvassers, to refuse to certify election results. They were then harassed and intimidated into reversing their stand and certifying the results. Initially, they wanted to certify Wayne county results outside of Detroit, which brought the predicted charges of racism and voter suppression of blacks. The real reason for doing this is because Detroit is one of the most corrupt cities in the country, especially regarding known voter fraud in the past, and has been run into the ground by Democrats for fifty years.

These and other suspicious occurrences are enough to at least have a day in court, but no judge was willing to hear the case. Why? Was it because no evidence existed, or something else? Is it possible that judges were intimidated into not taking the case, or else? Not too long ago, such an idea would be unthinkable, but in today's America greatly influenced by the left and their fascism through cancel culture retaliation, such a thing is entirely possible. Judges may have been afraid for their families. Also, they may have been afraid of the violence that would overtake the country if the election was overturned. But again, investigating fraud no longer involved overturning this election; it was all about future elections and public trust.

The "Cancel Culture" was being employed by anybody associated with Donald Trump, the Left's number one target. As a result, people were being intimidated and canceled by the media-corporate-high tech mob. Law firms representing the Trump campaign challenging the election results in court were being intimidated and threatened to never work again as a lawyer or have even experienced death threats. "This campaign to intimidate the lawyers who represent

Trump is not about vengeance but rather insurance. Even if the success of these cases is very small, his opponents do not want to risk the judicial scrutiny of the ballots. Posts on social media targeted clients of law firms such as Jones Day, and the Lincoln Project pledged $500,000 to make the lives of these lawyers a living hell. It is the kind of tactic which is used by Antifa and other activists to "de-platform" speakers or harass individuals at their homes."[4] It's the tactics of Nazi Germany, Russia, China, and Iran!

The Storming of the Capitol

With the Democratic takeover of the entire government as a result of the Georgia runoff election, our country will be irreparably changed for the worse. That was the unsettling news realized by Trump supporters and others who care about this country and its future. It also created an atmosphere of desperation and a sense that America is about to change forever. Yes, people were misled by some Republicans including the President about a last minute false hope of overturning the election. Right after the election though it would still have been possible but then the legal battles were lost and hundreds of eyewitnesses to voter fraud were not able to present their testimony. That alone built great frustration, especially when both Democrats and Republicans declared that there was no voter fraud and anybody who thought differently was a conspiracy nut.

On January 6, 2021 most of the protestors came to hear Donald Trump speak and support him voicing their protest against a fraudulent election and most of them remained peaceful. Of course, the left and their media sycophants lied about the "violent" Trump crowd in Washington; actually a small percent stormed the Capitol. Yes it was terrible and they should be criminally prosecuted, but what about the BLM and Antifa riots? They were basically condoned by the media as fighting for racial justice. But once again, a double standard exists of Trump supporters as criminals, and BLM protestors as "peaceful protestors."

The riots were wrong and Trump appearing before the crowd with this false last minute hope of overturning the election was a mistake. He called for peace and for people to go home, but that would never stop some of the more violent people in the crowd. There's even evidence that at least one leftist revolutionary (probably more) was posing as a Trump supporter and egging on the crowd. Even so, the violence was still wrong. The riot also made us look bad to the world; caused the loss of five lives and caused Donald Trump to end his presidency ingloriously during a tragic situation.

Democrats are now pushing the false narrative that Trump organized the whole storming of the Capitol as an insurrection and figuratively led the charge. This is way over the top but is a perfect excuse for impeachment. Some Republicans shamefully supported the Democrat's phony impeachment effort. This impeachment, especially the removal of Trump, would further exacerbate the division and tension breeding violence in the country. But that's exactly what leftist Democrats want.

The left are also using the riot as a pretext to further crack down on civil liberties. Free speech is now under further attack as a result of the riot. Emboldened by election victories, they are pushing for Trump supporters to be punished. Senator Josh Hawley, a Republican from Missouri and Trump supporter who objected to the certifying of the electors in the Senate, is now in the process of being cancelled by Simon & Shuster publishers who cancelled the publishing of his book "The Tyranny of Big Tech." Some are calling for his being disbarred. Fortunately, Regnery publishing will publish his book.

Big tech is further cracking down on free speech by cancelling Parler, an alternative to Twitter, and President Trump's Twitter account in the name of preventing "speech that will incite riots." Any speech that disagrees with the agenda of the left will now be referred as inciting violence. Even more dangerous, many are labeling Trump supporters, Republicans in general, and others who disagree with the Democrat's agenda as seditionists and domestic terrorists. They are placed in the same category as far-right militia groups, neo-Nazis, white supremacists, the KKK, and other fringe groups. So the American public is now being indoctrinated to believe that the real threat against the overthrow of the country is coming from conservative "domestic terrorists" and cite the Capitol riot as evidence. Of course the real domestic terrorists, Antifa and BLM, are not even considered a threat.

We are witnessing the "Pravdazation" of news and free speech where big government and the elites will now decide what is truth and what constitutes misinformation. A new position in the Biden administration, "truth Czar," is being considered which should scare every freedom loving individual. This is one of the evidences that America has slipped from a Judeo-Christian nation into a postmodern society. When you add authoritarianism to such a society, the result is totalitarianism and loss of all freedoms.

So the days of objective truth are quickly coming to an end and suppression of free speech by the tyrants of high tech and others will continue affecting the media, especially conservative, outlets. One of the ways this will be done is that, either the billionaire oligarchs will purchase media outlets like Fox News and also buy radio networks of conservative talk radio stations (or individual stations), threaten sponsors of these media outlets, or the federal government through the FCC will target these conservative outlets to further stifle free speech. Fewer to no media outlets would then be available to give a rebuttal to the false government/ media leftist dogma. A large part of the country won't have opportunities to vent their justifiable outrage. This is never good, because when no outlets exist, then what?

Shameful Republicans

Ted Cruz and others who had the courage to object to the senate's certification of the electoral vote are being attacked by fellow Republicans who are also turning on Trump. Under Donald Trump, the Republican Party became the party of the people, but now they will revert back to the establishment party of Mitt Romney, Jeb Bush, and the special interests. It will no longer be the party of Donald Trump, but the Democrat party will continue to be the party of Barack Obama and the far left.

The Republicans are playing right into the hands of the left. Never Trumper Republicans like John Kasich, Mitt Romney, Arnold Schwarzenegger, Liz Cheney, Bill Krystol, Jonah Goldberg, and others should know better. They may not like Trump, but they certainly should know better than the ignorant people who believe everything they hear on CNN or MSNBC. But apparently not! If they thought about the country's future for one minute, they would realize that Donald Trump's agenda was the only thing stopping the left's takeover of America. That's why he has been under severe attack since he first announced his candidacy in 2015; the left knew he was beholding to nobody and was a true populist and threat to their power

In the tradition of "never let a crisis go to waste," Chuck Schumer, Nancy Pelosi, and others were playing politics when they called for removal of Trump possibly under the 25th Amendment—when a president is no longer fit to serve, but finally settled on impeachment. If Trump were removed, he would supposedly be ineligible to run for president in 2024—that was their motivation. Arnold Schwarzenegger, one of the worst governors in California's history, ridiculously compared the riot to the November, 1938 Nazi rampage of Kristallnacht. Where was he when the real Nazis were rioting, looting, and destroying businesses this past summer?

Our Leaders Should Take Heed

Rioting and violence should never be condoned, but it had a definite cause and to dismiss it without looking at why many thousands of Trump supporters were gathered in Washington would be a great mistake. So why did Trump supporters show up? The answer is because Democrats and the rest of the left have demonized and lied about supporters of Donald Trump and conservatives in general. They have deemed them as worthy of being canceled and now they have the power to do so like never before. For four years, their president was subjected to a fraudulent vicious campaign to unseat his presidency. Then they watched their country ravaged by a virus from China which was blamed on Trump and enabled Democrat politicians to shut parts of the country and ruin their lives in many ways. Under the lie that maintaining the shutdowns indefinitely was necessary to defeat the virus, small businesses were crushed while real science was ignored. Churches and many mom and pop small businesses were declared unessential while liquor stores and many big box stores were allowed to stay open. People were told to stay home while many hypocritical politicians in predominantly blue cities and states were caught at restaurants and beauty parlors without masks or social distancing. Then they saw their country being torn apart by the murderous and ungrateful thugs of BLM and

Antifa, the worst of America! Then they saw the media take the side of these thugs as "peaceful," "justified" violence against an "unfair" country. Apparently these thugs have never lived in or been taught about third world authoritarian countries. Then they saw their vote nullified by a stolen election, yet the media and even Republicans continued to self-righteously tell them to move on. The final straw was not being to have their day in court, or at least at a Senate or full congressional hearing to present the affidavit evidence from witnesses testifying that they observed voter fraud. This evidence needed to be on the record, not to overturn an election, but to prevent further voter fraud. They saw congress as sweeping any investigation of voter fraud under the rug.

Mitch McConnell sanctimoniously droned on about how these thugs failed to stop the business of the Senate in certifying the election. Maybe if he had done his job earlier and called for a senate or full congressional hearing for people to air their grievances and present evidence, none of this would have happened. The Republicans didn't care enough to fight for truth or fair elections and now we will all reap the consequences.

What is Next?

The left have sent a message to Donald Trump and all his supporters: "we will punish you." The cancel culture is full speed ahead. But the first and most important item on their ruling agenda will be the cessation of fair elections. It will be done in a covert manner, but make no mistake, that's their number one immediate goal. Yes, the Green New Deal, packing the Supreme Court, Medicare, Social Security and college for all regardless of legality of citizenship, open borders, statehood for D.C. and Puerto Rico, getting rid of guns in private hands, suppression of free speech and dissent, joining climate treaties, lifting sanctions on our enemies, letting more criminals out of jail, and other leftist agenda items are important goals of the Democrats. But, unless they get rid of fair elections or elections period, they can't freely do many of those things for fear of being voted out of office in a fair election.

They'll push for a national system of running elections overriding individual states. The national standard will resemble the highly questionable or the outright corrupt voting procedures of states like Pennsylvania, Georgia, or Michigan. If they can't constitutionally accomplish that, they will push for the abolishing of the Electoral College. If the Democrats are successful, then we'll lose the right to vote in an honest election and all of our freedoms will vanish!

The left also hate elections because they hate the idea of being answerable to regular non-elitist people whom they basically hold in contempt. This explains a lot about their effort to destroy the middle class. If the election of 2022 is a fair one, the Democrats will suffer an even greater midterm loss than in 1994, and 2010.

The Biden Presidency

When you look at the early indications of what a Biden administration's policies would be, one thing is clear: these policies will be destructive to America. Of all the executive orders Biden signed, not one of them is good for Americans. From the cancellation of the Keystone XL pipeline and stopping oil exploration on federal lands and his war on fracking; unlimited abortion; rejoining WHO, the Paris climate treaty and trying to get back into the Iran nuclear deal; reintroduction of politically correct racial sensitivity training in government institutions; encouraging Critical Race Theory and the 1619 Project to be taught in schools; cancelling of as much of the Trump America First agenda as possible, and other harmful leftist policies. An example would be immigration policy such as getting rid of Trump's border security enforcement along with the wall and allowing thousands more poor people from Central America to cross the border. This is especially at a time when we are in a pandemic and yet now want to allow many possibly infected people into our country when some of our hospitals are already stressed. Add to that our economy which is damaged with fewer jobs available for American workers and now allowing even more workers to compete for fewer jobs. To a rational person, this is a no brainer and a policy that doesn't make sense. This begs the question: why would the Biden administration pursue such policies so obviously harmful to America? If one believes the premise that the left truly care about the country, then their policies make no sense and are downright irrational.

But the real answer is something I have stated before in this writing and is the most controversial aspect of this book which many would consider conspiracy theory: First, harming America is intentional because the left want to destroy the country in order to create and control their own socialist state, and second, the Democrat party has turned to the far-left. If you approach irrational policies from that premise, then such policies make perfect sense.

In the next chapter, there is a chilling section concerning the Inquisition and how today's left are embarking on a similar strategy to the historic Inquisition begun in the 12th Century and lasting into the 15th Century. The purpose of the Inquisition was the war against heresy according to the Catholic Church. Muslims and Jews were the main victims and had to be converted, or else. The strident rhetoric today by Maxine Waters, Kamala Harris, and many others from the radical left calling for the punishment of Trump supporters is to-day's Inquisition.

As a born-again Christian, the good news is that God determines who becomes president, even by fraud. So no matter what has happened, it's not beyond God's control. Since God's will is always perfect, as a believer, I have nothing to worry about. But why did God allow Joe Biden to become president? In the next chapter, I hope to shed some light on this and other questions.

Endnotes

[1] Adam Shaw and Brooke Singman, www.Fox News.com 10-27-20

[2] https://www.grassley.senate.gov/news/news-releases/grass-ley-explains-democratic-cover-hunter-biden-investigation, Dec. 14, 2020.

[3] Balloteria

[4] BY JONATHAN TURLEY, OPINION CONTRIBUTOR — 11/14/20 10:00 AM EST 1,075 THE VIEWS EXPRESSED BY CONTRIBUTORS ARE THEIR OWN AND NOT THE VIEW OF THE HILL

Chapter 20

What About God?

Not everyone reading this book will agree with me about matters of faith, but I hope that you will realize that I am not a self-righteous hypocrite. I'm a Born-Again Christian because I have received Jesus Christ as my Savior and Lord, but I'm still not perfect, so even though saved, I'm still a sinner! But I have a different attitude towards sin and I'm growing spiritually. The fact that Christians still sin does not make us hypocrites; it reflects the reality that we still have a sinful nature (the flesh—Rom. 7:13-25; Gal. 5:16-26); along with our divine nature (1 Cor. 12:13; Eph. 1:13-14); but not a license to sin (Rom. Ch. 6). Someone who claims to be a born-again Christian and believes that he or she can now return to their old life of willful sin has never truly been born again (Jas. Ch.2), although only God knows the heart. I'm now forgiven of my sins because of Jesus Christ's shed blood on the cross paying the penalty of my sin and receiving God's forgiveness based on that sacrifice.

Born-Again Christians view the world with a biblical perspective in terms of what the Bible says concerning mankind, the corrupt satanic world system, sin, salvation, and prophecy. I guess it would be fair to say that I possess an apocalyptic view of the world, but having said that, I don't live in a constant state of negativity and dread. On the contrary, I enjoy the many wonderful things that the world has to offer. If one stops to really notice, so much God created beauty exists in the world with so many things to enjoy. I also appreciate family and friends whom I love and care about and the blessing they truly are in my life.

Apocalyptic can mean the ultimate destruction of the earth which I believe will eventually happen, but not by so called man-caused climate change. My view of the end of earth's history concerns mankind's final destiny: what will happen to the world and what happens after one dies. I believe that we are now in the end times and the world is heading for the final series of events before the return of Jesus Christ. Many false teachers have tried to set a date when Jesus Christ will return to this earth, but the Bible says that only the Father knows (Matthew 24:36).

The end times is the subject in a series of sixteen books by Tim LaHaye and Jerry B. Jenkins called "Left Behind" published in the years 1995 through 2007. This series gives a fictional dramatic account based on what the Bible says about future events leading up to and coming to pass at Jesus Christ's return: the rapture of the church; the seven-year tribulation period under the totalitarian one world government rule of antichrist leading up to Armageddon; and the return of Jesus Christ to earth with His literal one-thousand year Millennial Kingdom rule on earth. Another apocalyptic book with a similar theme that gained some fame was the "Late Great Planet Earth" (1970) by Hal Lindsey.

The last book of the Bible, which deals with all of these end time events, is called Revelation, or in the Catholic Bible, it is called The Apocalypse. I have been discussing the upheaval in America, but the future apocalyptic end time events described in Revelation will dwarf what is happening today and the seeds are now being sown. The main world events to watch indicating that we are getting closer to Jesus Christ's return are the political changes in Europe and the events happening in the Middle East; especially Israel's hostile neighbors and Russia's influence there. Another indication is the current rise of world-wide anti-Semitism demonstrated by the notable increase of anti-Semitic hate crimes and an increasing hatred of Israel; even opposition to its very existence.

It's also quite notable that the United States is not even mentioned in Biblical prophecy. Those on the radical left who hate flags, nations, borders, and desire globalism should be careful what they wish for because they will someday get their wish of a one-world government under antichrist. It will not be the utopia they imagine!

Prior to becoming a Christian, I thought such prophecies were nonsense and believed the world would certainly last forever. I imagined the afterlife, if it truly existed, as some sort of peaceful floating around in space of the spirits of "good people," while all the evil ones ceased to exist. I couldn't imagine the good people I knew in life as possibly going to hell, it was simply unthinkable. I believed that the notion of heaven and hell was ridiculous and a way for churches to justify their existence and scare members into giving more money and trying to be "good." I reasoned that certainly a loving God, if he existed at all, would not send anyone to hell. Of course, at that time I didn't really believe in hell and also wasn't sure about the existence of God either.

To me, those who claimed to be Born-Again Christians were hypocritical members of some kind of weird religious cult. At that time, I definitely had a leftist-leaning view of God. But late in the evening of March 20, 1991, God opened my heart to the truth of the Gospel, saved me, and changed my whole life. The fact that it happened on the first day of spring is only fitting. It was my Saul of Tarsus moment while on the Damascus Road (Acts 9:1-6). My question to any skeptic is: "what happened to change me?"

Unbiblical Imposters

Leftism destroys everything it touches, and unfortunately, theological leftism has corrupted Christianity. Many movements in theological leftism such as Jehovah's Witnesses, Mormonism, Christian Science, the Emergent Church, Liberation Theology, Social Gospel, Jesus Seminar, Gospel of Thomas, Christian Palestinianism, Word of Faith Theology, Gender Neutral Bibles, and many others deny some or all of the five fundamentals of the faith: the triune God and deity of Jesus Christ; the virgin birth of Christ; the substitutionary atonement for sin on the cross; the bodily and physical resurrection of Christ from the dead; and the physical second coming of Christ to this earth. In addition, much of theological leftism also denies the depravity of man, inerrancy and sufficiency of the Bible, and salvation by faith alone apart from good works.

The cornerstone of the Protestant Reformation is:

Sola scriptura (by Scripture alone)

Sola fide (by faith alone)

Sola gratia (by grace alone)

Solus Christus or Solo Christo (Christ alone or through Christ alone)

Soli Deo gloria (glory to God alone)

What is God's View of Today's Events Based on Scripture?

So what is God's perspective on Covid-19, the 2020 election, and everything currently happening and all that has happened all throughout history?

I've talked about some events which signify America's upheaval: the attack on school prayer, Vietnam War, rise of the radical left, protests on our college campuses and in the streets, and riots in the ghettos during the long hot summers. I believe that the movement away from God into an increasingly secular society is the root cause of America's upheaval demonstrated by these and other events and the tumult we see all too often today. America was once a Judeo-Christian nation, but has now largely turned away from that heritage. America is still largely "Christian," but increasingly in name only. If the basic fundamentals of the founding of America based on the Bible and the God-given rights we enjoy are done away with, then essentially we'll be no different from the many third world authoritarian countries today and cease to exist as God's greatest and blessed country.

Throughout history, Christians have been the enemy of the authoritarian left, from Nero, Hitler, Lenin, Stalin, Castro, Chairman Mao, and today's worldwide secular left. In the later 1920's and 1930's, most Germans supported Hitler, but the church was the main opposition to the Nazis. "The great scientist Einstein pointed out the origins of the most effective resistance: 'Only the church stood squarely across the path of Hitler's campaign to suppress truth... it had the courage to stand for intellectual truth and moral freedom.'"[1] That Nazi-like suppression of the truth is happening today through the government-media-high tech propaganda and their declaration of what is true and what is "Russian Disinformation."

God's Love

The Biblical verse most describing God's love for mankind is John 3:16:

For God so loved the world that He gave His only begotten Son, that whoever believes in Him should not perish but have everlasting life.

God's eternal plan and greatest act of love was to send His Son Jesus Christ to the cross as payment for sin. Sinful man is not able to have a relationship with God in his present state and has no hope of heaven unless his sins are forgiven by God. The only way that can happen is to accept the sacrifice at the cross, which was the payment for the sins of the world, and receive Jesus Christ as Savior and Lord.

The heart of Jesus Christ can best be described in Matthew 11:28-30:

28 Come to Me, all of you who labor and are heavy laden, and I will give you rest.

29 Take My yoke upon you and learn from Me, for I am gentle and lowly in heart, and you will find rest for your souls.

30 For My yoke is easy and My burden is light.

Jesus is gentle and humble and loves mankind. Most religions reach up to a god, but in Christianity, God reaches out to us with His declaring "come to Me" in verse 28.

So how can a loving God also be capable of executing judgment for unbelief? It's because God is love but He is also holy and cannot be in the presence of sin. But again, God's love is perfectly demonstrated in His holiness because of His eternal plan to sacrifice His Son at the cross (Romans 3:20-26) as the only way to satisfy His wrath against sin and reconcile a person to Him. In John 15:13, Jesus said:

Greater love has no one than this, than to lay down one's life for his friends.

That's what God did for us so sin could be forgiven.

God's Judgment?

One Bible passage that is hotly discussed in the Christian community is Romans 1:18-32 which describes God's judgment of sin, and how that would possibly relate to America historically and today. This was written in the first century by the Apostle Paul and describes God's judgment against unrighteousness and illustrates man's total depravity, his enmity against God, and the resulting judgement in rejecting God. It uses terminology of the ancient world such as worshipping idols and false gods, but the Bible is a book applicable to all ages and men still worship their idols and have their false gods.

Regarding the state of America, many Christians believe that Covid-19 and all the other terrible things happening in our country represent God's judgment today; specifically the removal of God's blessing and protection of America. Three times in this passage in Romans One you see the words "God gave them up" or "God gave them over" to their own sin. To paraphrase it would be like God saying: "If you don't want to worship me and be thankful for my blessing and love in receiving my free offer of salvation, I'm removing my blessing and giving you what you want—your sin and the resulting consequences."

The main questions are the following: are the events of 2020 a warning from God to return to Him as a nation and reject the secular immorality destroying our country?—or is this the final straw and God allowing America to destroy itself?

Christians also speculate on when Jesus Christ will return for His church which is referred to as the "rapture of the church." America is the stabilizing force in the world. If America becomes a socialist authoritarian ruled country, it will eventually become another weak third world dictatorship and will no longer be that stabilizing force. A power vacuum will then exist which will be filled by China, Russia, and other bad actors vying for world power. Israel will be under the threat of annihilation from worldwide leftist anti-Semitism and hatred of Israel. World War III will be imminent and then a man of "peace," the antichrist, will appear on the scene and offer a false "peace." The world will hail him as the great peacemaker and worship him.

The rapture of the church will take place before the appearance of antichrist along with the beginning of the tribulation. The tribulation period, described in the Book of Revelation, will be a seven year time of war, pestilence, famine, and death. After seven years, Jesus Christ will return to the earth in His second advent, save Israel, who will be facing annihilation, by destroying the armies of the world at Armageddon and rule on a renewed earth for a one-thousand year millennial period. Again, nobody knows the beginning of these events, although false teachers have tried to set dates for the rapture and Christ's return. Here is the chilling text in Romans:

Romans 1:18-32 NKJV

18 For the wrath of God is revealed from heaven against all ungodliness and unrighteousness of men, who suppress the truth in unrighteousness,

19 because what may be known of God is manifest in them, for God has shown it to them.

20 For since the creation of the world His invisible attributes are clearly seen, being understood by the things that are made, even His eternal power and Godhead, so that they are without excuse,

21 because, although they knew God, they did not glorify Him as God, nor were thankful, but became futile in their thoughts, and their foolish hearts were darkened.

22 Professing to be wise, they became fools,

23 and changed the glory of the incorruptible God into an image made like corruptible man—and birds and four-footed beasts and creeping things.

24 Therefore God also gave them up to uncleanness, in the lusts of their hearts, to dishonor their bodies among themselves,

25 who exchanged the truth of God for the lie, and worshiped and served the creature rather than the Creator, who is blessed forever. Amen.

26 For this reason God gave them up to vile passions. For even their women exchanged the natural use for what is against nature.

27 Likewise also the men, leaving the natural use of the woman, burned in their lust for one another, men with men committing what is shameful, and receiving in themselves the penalty of their error which was due.

28 And even as they did not like to retain God in their knowledge, God gave them over to a debased mind, to do those things which are not fitting;

29 being filled with all unrighteousness, sexual immorality, wickedness, covetousness, maliciousness, full of envy, murder, strife, deceit, evil-mindedness; they are whisperers,

30 backbiters, haters of God, violent, proud, boasters, inventors of evil things, disobedient to parents,

31 undiscerning, untrustworthy, unloving, unforgiving, unmerciful;

32 who, knowing the righteous judgment of God, that those who practice such things are worthy of death, not only do the same but also approve of those who practice them.

A simplified analysis of this passage is the following:

This passage illustrates God's wrath against man's sin, especially denying God's existence and not glorifying Him; sexual sin, creating and worshipping his own reality and morality, and suppression of the truth and replacing it with lies. Some of many examples of man's sin against God are atheism and/or the rejection of the Gospel of Salvation, the embracing of Evolution, Modernism, Postmodernism, Communism, abortion, Feminism, LGBTQ, denial of biological defined gender, man-caused climate change, denial of intelligent design as indication of the existence of the God of the Bible, and worship of idols. Idols include anything that man considers more important than God. All of this sounds a lot like America today. In fact, many of the previous sins mentioned are now sacred cows to the left.

Verses 24, 26-32 describe the various sins characteristic of fallen mankind and sinful societies. It is notable that the internal decay of ancient empires has been associated with the embracing of homosexuality.

The part of this passage that is most debated among Christians concerns the beginning of verses 24 (Therefore, God also gave them up to uncleanness...); 26 (For this reason, God gave them up to vile passions...); 28 (God gave them over to a debased mind). Though written in the first century, this passage in Romans is applicable to us today. As we saw earlier, does this mean that God has finally removed His blessing from America? It's interesting to know that God even judged His beloved nation Israel when they fell into idolatry. He used such things as droughts, violent weather, earthquakes, defeat at the hands of surrounding enemies, internal strife, and plagues. But when Israel had a righteous king, repented and removed idols turning back toward God, He restored them. Will that happen to America? That's my prayer!

But many believe that the Covid-19 virus could be the beginning of God's final judgment on America. When you consider all the negative effects of the virus; the deaths, economic and social destruction; the weakening and further division of America; the rise of China; the influence that internal and external enemies had on the 2020 election victory for the left; suppression of truth in the media, it's very plausible that the virus could be the tipping point in the beginning of America's downfall.

How Did We Get to This Point?

While America's slide away from God started ramping up in the 1960's, in reality its root cause goes further back into history. Some extremely destructive ideas, many since 1850, have resulted in consequences being felt today. The one consistent thing all of these ideas have in common is that they are anti-God, anti-Bible, and based on lies. These destructive ideas and their consequences are being felt today and have contributed to America (and the world) moving further away from biblical truth. But bad ideas of man have always existed throughout history. Unredeemed mankind has devised all of these evil ideas because he or she is a lost sinner separated from God. The phrase: "Man is not a sinner because he sins, he sins because he is a sinner" describes fallen humanity.

The Original Bad Idea

The original bad idea of man was the denial of God's truth and rebellion against God, which began in the Garden of Eden.

Genesis chapter 3 gives the account of Satan's deception.

At the end of Chapter 3 verse 1, Satan asks Eve a question:

"Indeed, has God said, 'You shall not eat from any tree of the Garden'?"

Of course, God didn't say any tree, only from the tree of the knowledge of good and evil (Genesis 2: 16-17). Satan is a liar and was trying to cast doubt on what God said. When Satan said *"Has God really said that?"* he is actually saying what many would say today: "aw come on man, God didn't really say that, did He? How could anybody believe the existence of the Garden of Eden, or that man was made from the dust of the earth, or anything else the Bible says?"

In verses 2 and 3, the woman answers the serpent:

2 The woman said to the serpent, "From the fruit of the trees of the garden we may eat;

3 but from the fruit of the tree which is in the middle of the garden, God has said, 'You shall not eat from it or touch it, or you will die.'"

The woman answered Satan and said it was forbidden to eat the fruit of only the tree in the middle of the garden, but she inaccurately added that it couldn't be touched as well. Then the serpent (Satan) calls God a liar and lies about God's motives:

4 the serpent said to the woman, "You surely will not die!

5 "For God knows that in the day you eat from it your eyes will be opened, and you will be like God, knowing good and evil."

Satan is contradicting what God had told the woman and

he is tempting the woman by appealing to her pride; the same selfish motive and pride that he had in wanting to be like God. Satan rebelled against God and wanted to make himself God, so he was cast out of heaven as judgment. This pride is the same sin common today because man wants to be God and in control of the world. The pride of man is the biggest barrier to the worship of God. The Self-absorption and narcissism common in today's society result from mankind's pride in replacing God. When a society moves away from God into secularism, then humanism and narcissism take over and we worship ourselves rather than God.

So Adam and Eve bought Satan's lie and sinned against God:

6 *So when the woman saw that the tree was good for food, that it was pleasant to the eyes, and a tree desirable to make one wise, she took of its fruit and ate. She also gave to her husband with her, and he ate*

So because Adam and Eve both doubted God's word; they disobeyed God and ate of the forbidden fruit thereby, because of their sin, became separated from God and cast out of the Garden of Eden. Their disobedience caused sin to enter the world and put all men and God's perfect creation under the curse of sin. War, pride, lies, theft, murder, hate crimes, rebellion, vandalism, rioting, gossip, prejudice, selfishness, bitterness, idolatry, sickness, decay, and physical death are all results of this curse. Man became spiritually dead and separated from fellowship with God. We see the tragic results of man choosing to go his own way contrary to God's Word—simply watch the news. Man is still rejecting God and His Word thereby serving Satan's desires and goal to destroy the biblical Christian faith and God's plan for the redemption of the world. God had to send His Son into the world in order to restore man's relationship with Him—paying the penalty of man's sin on the cross so repentant sinners could be forgiven and reconciled with God.

The Inquisition

Leftism is dangerously close to taking absolute power in America and one of the results will be a new inquisition. Although it is Godless and secular, leftism is a religion and violating its dogma will have serious consequences.

The historical Inquisition was a system set up within the Roman Catholic Church to root out and punish heresy throughout Europe and beyond and was similar to the Crusades. It was infamous for the severity of its tortures and its persecution of Jews, other Christians, and Muslims. The purpose of the Inquisition was not only to combat heresy, but to also convert those "heretics" to the Catholic faith. The inquisition resulted more in the punishment of driving out and killing the non-believers than converting them.

The Inquisition began in 12th-century France in order to combat religious dissent: in Catholicism the dissent was with the Spiritual Franciscans, who regarded the wealth of the Church and individual church members as scandalous. They openly revolted against the authority of the Church and were declared heretical in 1296 by Pope Boniface VIII. Christians who rejected Catholicism and held to the first century biblical Apostles' Doctrine were also persecuted and killed.

The Protestant Reformation caused the Inquisition to significantly expand in order to counter the "heretical teaching" of salvation by faith alone and Scripture as the only authority for truth and practice. The Inquisition also expanded to other European countries which resulted in the Spanish Inquisition. The Spanish and Portuguese operated inquisitorial courts throughout their empires. The Spanish inquisition focused mainly on King Ferdinand and

Queen Isabella's concern over the issue of Jewish wealth and economic power and their growing numbers in Spain. They believed this posed a threat to the power of their Roman Catholic Monarchy. Ferdinand and Isabella had chosen Roman Catholicism to unite Spain; in 1478 they asked Pope Sixtus IV for permission to begin the Spanish Inquisition to "purify" the people of Spain. Of course purification meant driving out Jews, Protestants (mainly Lutherans), and other "non-believers."

Today's inquisition will be the purifying of dissidents through re-education camps and gulags. This is what's done in repressive regimes like China. The heretics will be those who disagree with leftism's version of the truth in their progressive policies and refuse to kneel down and admit their guilt of being white and racist, especially conservatives and Trump supporters. We are already experiencing the early manifestation of today's inquisition through the cancel culture and the persecution of anybody with a conservative point of view. We are living in the beginning of the 21st Century version of the Inquisition.

The Renaissance

Many bad ideas from secular humanistic philosophers occurred after the Inquisition and they lead up to the next key godless movement—the Renaissance, which occurred during the 14th and 15th centuries. The Renaissance was a secular humanistic anti-Christian movement and was the early predecessor to the modernist movement, especially regarding the emphasis of science, reason, and skepticism over faith and doctrine. By elevating science and reason over God, the Renaissance reduced Christianity to one of several man-created religions with no special significance.

The Renaissance also greatly affected the world of religious scholarship. One of the consequences may be seen in the eventual rise of the school of comparative religion. Again, it quickly became popular to assume that religion is man's invention and that differing forms are equally valid, so no religion is unique and forever binding. But in John 14:6, Jesus said that He is the only way to the Kingdom of God. But contradicting what Jesus declared, this kind of reasoning during the Renaissance was the beginning of what eventually led to Ecumenicalism—the belief that all religions are equally valid and should cooperate in order to make the world a better place. The Renaissance, and later Modernism, was the origin of the secular humanist world's and even the "church's" attack on the absolute truth of scripture; its inerrancy and sufficiency. Secular devaluing of scripture led to regarding the Bible as an error-filled human book.

Darwinism

A truly horrible idea preceding the late 19th and early 20th century Modernist movement was Darwinism. Charles Darwin, an English naturalist, in 1859 published a book entitled "Origin of the Species." The basic idea was that the origin, changes, and perpetuation of new species of animals and plants are caused by natural selection in the offspring of a given organism which varies. The natural selection favors the survival of some of these variations over others; that the strongest or fittest of these survive while the weaker ones perish.

Part of Darwinism is the theory that widely divergent groups of plants and animals have arisen from the same ancestors. So in the case of man, a subhuman creature crawling out of the sea could have eventually evolved over millions of years into a human being. But the "missing link," which would connect man from this lower separate species has never been found, although many examples of fake "evidence' have been proclaimed. Evolving from one distinct species to another is macro-evolution which most scientists have long considered a fraud. Micro-evolution, however, is very real and consists of a species changing according to its environment, but still remaining the same species.

So Darwinism not only denied the biblical account of the creation of man, but demoted man into another soulless animal. If man has no soul, then what was the need of the Cross of Christ in saving souls? But having a soul is part of man being created in the image of God. The term in Genesis 1:27, *wherein "God created man in his own image"* does not mean that God is in a human form so we look like God, but rather that humans are in the image of God with a soul and a moral, spiritual, and intellectual nature that's absent in animals. So, through the godless comparison of humans to other soulless animals and even possibly descending from monkeys, it's easier to consider abortion as the destruction of an unviable tissue mass and not a real human being and unique creation of God.

The Scopes Monkey trial in 1925 pitted ailing and out-matched creationist William Jennings Bryan against famed attorney Clarence Darrow and further illustrated the perceived division between science and God and also between Secularism and Christianity. It reinforced the early 20th century secular progressive world's painting of Bible believing Christians as unsophisticated, backwoodsy, and ignorant.

Darwinism not only led to this division, but also led to the dangerous concept of superior and inferior races thru natural selection and the survival of the fittest. This led to the disastrous idea of Eugenics, the racist concept of selective breeding to make an improved human free of diseases. The "inferior" races were primarily considered to be blacks and other people of color. Margaret Sanger, founder of Planned Parenthood, is considered a pioneer in Eugenics.

The Oxford dictionary defines Eugenics as the following:

The study of how to arrange reproduction within a human population to increase the occurrence of heritable characteristics regarded as desirable. Developed largely by Sir Francis Galton as a method of improving the human race, eugenics was increasingly discredited as unscientific and racially biased during the 20th century, especially after the adoption of its doctrines by the Nazis in order to justify their treatment of Jews, disabled people, and other minority groups.

Darwinism and Eugenics very much influenced a rising German politician in the 1920's & 1930's, Adolph Hitler, and led to the concept of the Aryan Master Race and getting rid of "inferior people". The Chinese today are experimenting on how to make their soldiers stronger through gene altering and possibly experimenting on minority groups housed in Chinese gulags. Does all this sound familiar? The Communist Chinese leadership represent the godless Nazi's of today.

The following gives a historical view into the Eugenics movement and the racism involved. It also shows the double standard regarding who is worshipped today and who is demonized:

"All across America, video of activists attacking statues plays on a loop while some political leaders voice their support for removing all reminders of people whose personal histories put them in a negative light. In asking for the U.S. Capitol to be cleansed of Confederate statues, House Speaker Nancy Pelosi said they must go because their efforts were "to

achieve such a *plainly racist end." New York Gov. Andrew Cuomo said on NBC›s 'Today' show that removing statues is a* "healthy expression" *of priorities and values.*

For those identifying historical figures with racist roots that should be removed from public view because of their evil histories, Planned Parenthood's founder, Margaret Sanger, must join that list. In promoting birth control, she advanced a controversial "Negro Project," *wrote in her autobiography about speaking to a Ku Klux Klan group and advocated for a eugenics approach to* breeding for "the gradual suppression, elimination and eventual extinction, of defective stocks — those human weeds which threaten the blooming of the finest flowers of American civilization."[2]

"The Negro Project, instigated in 1939 by Margaret Sanger, was one of the first major undertakings of the new Birth Control Federation of America (BCFA), the product of a merger between the American Birth Control League and Sanger's Birth Control Clinical Research Bureau, and one of the more controversial campaigns of the birth control movement. Developed by white birth control reformers, who consulted with African-Americans for help in promoting the project only well after its inception, the Negro Project and associated campaigns were, nevertheless, widely supported by such black leaders as Mary McLeod Bethune, W. E. B. DuBois, and Rev. Adam Clayton Powell, Jr. Influenced strongly by both the eugenics movement and the progressive welfare programs of the New Deal era, the Negro Project was, from the start, largely indifferent to the needs of the black community and constructed in terms and with perceptions that today smack of racism.[3]

Defenders of Margaret Sanger argue that the goal of Eugenics was the breeding out and elimination of diseases, mental retardation, and other biological problems. They also claim that, regarding the Negro Project, Sanger and others were concerned about a growing population of poor blacks and how to control that growth through birth control. This coincided with a racist attitude existing in America that worried about the population explosion of too many poor black people causing an emerging social "problem." So the racism is clear in Eugenics in defining the identity of the "inferior" people. This took place during the depression and many poor white people, especially in the rural south, also had a growing population. Birth control was also discussed regarding poor whites, but it's clear that the attitude was different towards them, as opposed to blacks.

Modernism

Modernism was a late 19th and early 20th Century secular humanistic movement which continued the emphasis of science over the Bible. With regard to modernism creeping into biblical Christianity, it continued the attack on the absolute truth of scripture into a movement toward modifying traditional beliefs in accordance with modern ideas, especially regarding science and the effort to reconcile unchristian pagan ideas into the faith. It was a misguided effort by some in "Christianity" to stem the criticism of Fundamentalism by making the church more inclusive and less "judgmental." What it essentially accomplished was to make Christianity more compatible to worldly ideas. This same error occurred in the New Evangelical movement and continues today. The Bible specifically warns against loving the satanic world system (Jas. 4:4; 1 John 2:15-17).

Regarding Christian doctrine itself, because of the 19th Century skeptics' criticism of the Bible, many religious modernists also assumed that the Bible was simply a human book and that Jesus was a great moral teacher, but only a man and not God. They were also much more willing to accept evolutionary theories in order to reconcile Christianity with Darwinism. For example, one such rationalization of Darwinism was Theistic Evolution which declared that God created man through evolution. The problem is that it contradicts the biblical account of creation. This is why Creationism is under such attack by the religious and secular left: because the left deny the supernatural but can't scientifically explain how God made Adam from dust, so they declare that the Bible is not true and instead assert that science and human reasoning are the key to truth. So again, left leaning "Christianity" display the effects of Modernism concerning the denial of the truth of scripture and define Jesus, not as God who came to this earth to die on the cross, but as a good man and teacher.

Modernist theology also believes people are basically good and not sinners who need salvation, therefore, the modernist adheres to the leftist idea that poverty and racism are the cause of why so much trouble exists in the world, rather than man's depravity and the absence of God in his or her life. The question would be: What are the basic causes of poverty and racism? The answer is Sin!

Communism

Communism is the most destructive idea ever devised by man and has killed more people than any other ism in history. A dictionary definition of Communism would be the following: *"a political theory derived from Karl Marx, advocating class war and leading to a society in which all property is publicly owned and each person works paid according to*

368

their abilities and needs." That's a recipe for overthrowing a government, wealth redistribution, and mediocrity. Today, many people work hard, but a larger part of their taxes go to support those who don't work. The basic difference between Communism and Socialism, besides some ownership of assets by the people, is best described by the saying: "Communism is Socialism with a gun pointed at your head." The Russians refer to it as "ruling with an iron fist."

Class warfare fermented by the left can be seen today, but it's not about rich vs. poor; it's now portrayed as whites against people of color, but it's actually about the elites vs. the middle class. Destruction of the middle class is a goal of Communism and the left are using Covid-19 and its lockdowns plus so called "racism" to destroy the middle class in America.

Basic Characteristics of Communism

The state owns all capital in a communist system including all land, machines, buildings and infrastructure so private property is non-existent. Under Socialism however, all citizens share in a nation's resources, but pretty much in theory only depending on what type of Socialism. Some "socialist" countries like Sweden are not really socialist in the textbook sense. In Communism, all administration and planning is done through a strong central government—the opposite of Jeffersonian federalism and state's rights.

The bureaucratic elite exist with either no elections, or sham rigged elections and the people are under repression with no basic rights. The elite live well, but most of the people live in what would be considered poverty here in America, or worse. The people are under a system of austerity and told it is for the "common good," which really means the continuance of the state and the privilege of the elite class. The state is a substitute for God and religious faith is heavily persecuted. Individualism is suppressed in favor of the common good.

Two Important Truths about Humanity Relating to Communism

Other than forcing people to conform or else, which is the left's definition of unity, what other reason causes people to conform to Communism or any other totalitarian system? The answer lies in two basic truths about humanity: (1) Man's natural desire for freedom is a myth; man's natural desire is to be taken care of by someone else. (2) People want to be a part of a group who think alike. The leftist media today perfectly illustrate this. Then how does one explain Americans and their desire for freedom? The truth is many Americans today, unlike the founders of this nation, also want to be taken care of by somebody else. Look at the massive and unearned entitlements; all of the free stuff given out by the government. Democrats use this to win votes because it works. But America began as the greatest experiment in freedom because this trend of being taken care of was going to be challenged. From the beginning of this country, individualism and freedom were ingrained in the American psyche. During the depression, people had to either make it on their own, or starve. The only safety nets were family, churches, and charity. After massive welfare became institutionalized in the 1960's, receiving it was still considered shameful until the entitlement culture eventually took hold. Many people now believe they are owed free stuff.

Postmodernism

One can see that the attacks on Christianity and the Bible by the previously mentioned bad ideas have taken a toll and have led to the next bad idea: Postmodernism. Although Postmodernism broke with Modernism, they both remained anti-God and anti-Bible. It is a complicated movement, but for the purposes of keeping this an understandable book, the most notable damaging effect of Postmodernism seen today is its denial of objective and absolute truth. So denial of this truth, especially denying the Bible as the absolute standard of truth and morality, has fueled the existing view that no absolute truth or morality exist; only different people and societies with their own version of the truth and morality. So according to Postmodernism, truth and morality can only be defined by man, and is relative to each society and their own moral values and no one have the right to judge any "truth" and "morality" which differs from their own. Therefore, no absolute system of truth and morality from God can apply to all people.

Apolitical people often say: "I look at both sides of the issues and find a lot of gray areas." That illustrates the effect Postmodernism has on many people. The idea of gray areas opens up a dangerous idea that, according to one's human reasoning and version of science and truth, any behavior and lie can now possibly be justified since no absolute standard of truth and morality exist. So a godless mindset such as Postmodernism in rejecting objective and absolute truth can easily justify going from a fetus, a human being created by God, to the abortion of an unviable tissue mass; from feminism, to sex with anybody, and eventually the denial of biological defined sexual identity leading to questioning one's gender.

Feminism/Abortion/Sexual Revolution

Feminism ceased to be a valid movement fighting for women's suffrage and other equal rights for women, and instead, the left turned it into a war against God, the Bible, and Conservatism--especially regarding abortion, which is not a constitutional right regardless of Roe vs. Wade, one of the worst decisions in Supreme Court history.

God said that He knew us while we were still in our mother's womb. Jeremiah 1:5 and other verses declare that God knew us before the beginning of time and He formed us in the womb. Abortion is the most destructive and anti-God idea of radical Feminism and is the murder of a human being, period. The idea that a woman's body belongs to her alone and God has no right to tell her what she can do with an unborn child perfectly defines the rebellious anti-God attitude of Feminism. But radical Feminism, like all of the other leftist movements, doesn't consider the existence of God. Now with modern medical technology, abortion is harder to defend when the form and heartbeat of a fetus can now be observed.

The Women›s Liberation Movement of the 1960s, along with the Sexual Liberation Movement, are products of radical feminist ideologues and their goal of challenging conservative biblical ideas regarding female sexuality. This also morphed into the challenge against tradition through homosexuality and gender re-identification. The sexual liberation of women involved a woman's right to choose her sexual partners free of outside interference or judgment. The result of all of this "liberation" was acceptance of LGBT people now being able to be open with their sexuality, thus helping to end "sexual oppression." But they aren't free because, in the end, godless behavior leads to judgment because of the natural consequences of sin, which are always bad; AIDS and other STD's are examples.

It's taboo these days to criticize LGBTQ, but the fact is this is a big part of the fascism of the left through political correctness; so do not criticize LGBTQ because they're a sacred victim group of the left. Since God is the main subject of this chapter, it's important to realize what God says about

LGBTQ. God's word says that it is perverted, an abomination, and sin in the following scriptures:

We've already seen the verses in Romans One which are pretty clear, especially versus 26 & 27:

26 For this reason God gave them up to vile passions. For even their women exchanged the natural use for what is against nature.

27 Likewise also the men, leaving the natural use of the woman, burned in their lust for one another, men with men committing what is shameful, and receiving in themselves the penalty of their error which was due.

So these verses specifically refer to Gays and Lesbians. Genesis Chapter 19 tells of God's destruction of Sodom because of their wickedness, specifically homosexuality involving males which the Bible refers to as sodomy.

In the Book of Leviticus, God's moral law is given to the Jews and chapter 18, verse 22 declares:

22 You shall not lie with a male as with a woman. It is an abomination.

1 Corinthians 6:9-10 declares:

9 Do you not know that the unrighteous will not inherit the kingdom of God? Do not be deceived. Neither fornicators, nor idolaters, nor adulterers, nor homosexuals, nor sodomites,

10 nor thieves, nor covetous, nor drunkards, nor re-vilers, nor extortioners will inherit the kingdom of God.

Some translations refer to "homosexual" as "effeminate."

Dr. John MacArthur gives an explanation concerning the biblical position on homosexuality:

Homosexuals...sodomites. These terms refer to those who exchange and corrupt normal male-fe-male sexual roles and relations. Transvestism, sex changes, and other gender perversions are included (cf. Gen. 1:27; Deut. 22:5). Sodomites are so-called because the sin of male-male sex dominated the city of Sodom (Gen. 18:20; 19:4-5). This sinful perversion is condemned always, in any forms by Scripture (cf. Lev. 18:22; 20:13; Rom 1:26-27; 1 Tim. 1:10).[4]

Homosexuality is just one of many sins that, if unforgiven, will deny entrance into heaven. But those of you who are straight are not off the hook because all sin is condemned by God. God loves the sinner, but hates the sin. By the way, any faith that advocates the killing of homosexuals is a false faith.

Gender Re-identification

The Bible says that God made humans male and female, pe-riod (Genesis 5:2) and quoted by Jesus in Mark 10:6 and Matthew 19:4, but the left pervert God's truth into re-iden-tifying humans as consisting of many possible sexes. Like ev-erything else coming from the left, this causes division and confusion. Imagine poor young children growing up in such a school or home that teaches this garbage. Only ungodly perverted minds can conceive of the possibility of 58 different sexes according to some. A gender studies degree is a degree in perversion. When objective truth now becomes "one's own version of the truth" such as in Postmodernism, then biological definition of the sexes is no longer necessarily valid and the definition of the sexes can be made to mean anything according to what an individual believes is truth.

Gender Neutrality

Some Democrats in the new congress want gender neutral language. The following is a perfect example of what is destroying our country:

"House Democratic Caucus Chairman Rep. Hakeem Jeffries, D-N.Y., defended his party's proposed new House rules for the 117th Congress, specifically addressing new language that would replace gendered terms with more general ones. For example, if passed the rules would replace terms such as "mother," "father," "daughter," "son," "sister" and "brother" with "parent," "child" and "sibling," respectively. Examples of other terms include the replacement of "chairman" with "chair" and "seaman" with "seafarer."

> 'From my standpoint, the gender-neutral language is just consistent with an effort for the House, in the best tradition of the House, to reflect the gorgeous mosaic of the American people in the most sensitive fashion possible,' Jeffries told reporters when asked about the language. 'And the House, of course, is designed to be the institution closest to the American people to reflect the hopes, the dreams, the aspirations, the fears, concerns, anxieties, in the words of the framers the passions of the American people.' The congressman went on to note that the closeness to the people is why members of the

House serve two-year terms instead of four years like presidents, six years like senators or lifetimes like Supreme Court justices."⁵

The man is an absolute fool and would fit in perfectly as a commentator for MSNBC!

Once again, God created mankind and made them male and female, period. Using a gender based noun simply declares that reality. To substitute anything else reflects the narcissistic and easily offended "snowflake" culture of today. The mosaic of the American people consists of men and women first; thank God!

Radical Environmentalism and Climate Change

The anti-God aspect of so called man-caused climate change is simply that man is in control of the earth and can control climate. But the Bible says that the heavens and the earth were created by God and He sustains them.
Nehemiah 9:6 declares:

You alone are the LORD;
You have made heaven,
The heaven of heavens,
with all their host,
The earth and all things on it,
The seas and all that is in them,
And You preserve them all.
 The host of heaven worships You.

The fact that so many people in America believe the fraud of man-caused climate change (see chapters 16 & 17) is one of many testimonies to how far our nation has strayed from God, the sovereign ruler of all creation.

The Good News of the Gospel

As you've read this sobering book, keep in mind that, according to God, sin is the natural state of man and the world is slowly passing away. Yes, there are many nice and good people in this world, but all are sinners (Romans 3:23) and fall short of God's standard of righteousness which is moral perfection. Therefore, since nobody is perfect, everybody is a sinner, not basically good. No amount of righteous living or good deeds can ever earn salvation. Mankind's biggest need is forgiveness of his or her sins and, as a result, becoming righteous in Gods eyes.

But, in order for that to happen, sin has to be paid for to satisfy God's wrath against sin. God's wrath against sin has to be directed somewhere and that somewhere is either the unrepentant sinner—a person who is not born again through saving faith in Christ, or that wrath has already been suffered by Jesus Christ as a substitute on behalf of born again Christians who have escaped the wrath they deserve. So if one is a true born-again Christian, the wrath they were under as a sinner was put on Jesus Christ at the cross.

What Is Meant By "Born Again?"

The Bible clearly states that in order to go to heaven, one must be Born Again. Jesus said it in John 3:3:

> *³Most assuredly, I say to you, unless one is born again, he cannot see the kingdom of God.*

Nicodemus misunderstood what Jesus meant by being born again and thought that somehow Jesus was referring to being born again from the womb. But when one is born again, he or she undergoes a true spiritual transformation by the cleansing of sin and regeneration through the Holy Spirit.

John 3:5 states:

> [5]*Most assuredly, I say to you, unless one is born of water and the Spirit, he cannot enter the kingdom of God.*

The act of being born again is clearly illustrated in Ephesians 1:13-14:

> [13] *In Him you also trusted, after you heard the word of truth, the gospel of your salvation; in whom also, having believed, you were sealed with the Holy Spirit of promise,*

> [14]*who is the guarantee of our inheritance until the redemption of the purchased possession to the praise of His glory.*

This scripture in Ephesians chapter one really describes what it is to be born again. Trusting Christ's work at the cross after hearing the gospel is saving faith, in fact, true saving faith has the idea of relying upon and adhering to God. That can only happen as the Holy Spirit opens up a person's understanding so he or she can receive the truth of the gospel in their heart and not simply in their head through intellectual assent. Upon faith, a person receives the baptism of the Holy Spirit and he or she is washed of sin (Ephesians 6:11); is sanctified (Set apart from the world); sealed and indwelled by the Holy Spirit, and placed into the body of Christ, which is the Church (1 Corinthians 12:12-13).
Being sealed by the Holy Spirit in Ephesians 1:13 means that one who is truly saved cannot lose their salvation be-

cause they are sealed until the day of redemption (Eph. 4:30) so they can never finally turn away from God or become lost again.

Romans 10:17 declares:

So then faith comes by hearing, and hearing by the word of God,

Again, hearing has the idea of understanding the gospel, not only intellectually, but receiving it in the heart, or what is called heart faith. This heart faith causes one to repent or turn away from their old lifestyle of sin and turn to God with a desire to no longer willfully sin, but to follow God. A common expression exists concerning head vs. heart faith: "missing heaven by 18 inches." In other words, an average distance between the head and the heart is about 18 inches and simple head faith isn't true faith. A wonderful scripture demonstrating true faith is Romans 10:9 stating:

That if you confess with your mouth the Lord Jesus and   believe in your heart that God has raised Him from the dead, you will be saved.

So a person is born again who believes in his or her heart and trusts that Jesus is God who came to this earth to die and pay the penalty of their sins and believe that Jesus rose from the dead. This person would realize that he or she is a sinner and is willing to repent of that sinful life and turn to Jesus Christ trusting and following Him as Savior and Lord.

Whatever happens, the hope (sure thing) of born-again Christians is that they belong to Jesus Christ and are secure in their relationship with God which can never be broken. Those who are not born again are lost and one heartbeat away from eternal hell with its unimaginable torment. I hope that America will turn back to God and realize that this godless earth is broken and that it will hopefully cause a spiritual revival away from secularism. Whether America turns back to God or soon perishes, God's will accomplish His plan for the world.

Don't get sidetracked by UFO's and aliens, angels, or dinosaurs, which are the most common topics that secular people speculate on. They are irrelevant to the Gospel of salvation on which everybody should be focused.

I've purposely cut down on news watching because I wanted to end this book, but if I continued to watch the news, I would be tempted to add the latest news since many changes are happening so fast. When would it end? Therefore, as of today, February 6, 2021 (Ronald Reagan's 110th Birthday) this book is finally finished!!!

Endnotes

[1] D. Mac G. Jackson, *Moral Responsibility and Clinical Research,* Tyndale Press, 1958, p.17, Idem., Don Stephens, "War and Grace," EP Books, 6 Silver Court, Watchmead, Welwyn, UK, AL71TS, p. 46

[2] *Kristan Hawkins Opinion contributor July 23, 2020 USA Today*

[3] Newsletter #28 (Fall 2001)"Birth Control or Race Control? Sanger and the Negro Project "The Margaret sanger papers project.

[4] The John MacArthur Study Bible, Word Publishing, a Division of Thomas Nelson Bibles, P.O. Box 141000, Nashville, TN37214-1000, (1997), p. 1736.
[5] Ronn Blitzer fox news Jan 4, 2021

JDF

Made in the USA
Middletown, DE
18 May 2021

39509285R00215